**WITHDRAWN
UTSA Libraries**

PALGRAVE STUDIES IN CULTURAL AND INTELLECTUAL HISTORY

Series Editors

Anthony J. La Vopa, North Carolina State University.
Suzanne Marchand, Louisiana State University.
Javed Majeed, Queen Mary, University of London.

The Palgrave Studies in Cultural and Intellectual History series has three primary aims: to close divides between intellectual and cultural approaches, thus bringing them into mutually enriching interactions; to encourage interdisciplinarity in intellectual and cultural history; and to globalize the field, both in geographical scope and in subjects and methods. This series is open to work on a range of modes of intellectual inquiry, including social theory and the social sciences; the natural sciences; economic thought; literature; religion; gender and sexuality; philosophy; political and legal thought; psychology; and music and the arts. It encompasses not just North America but Africa, Asia, Eurasia, Europe, Latin America, and the Middle East. It includes both nationally focused studies and studies of intellectual and cultural exchanges between different nations and regions of the world, and encompasses research monographs, synthetic studies, edited collections, and broad works of reinterpretation. Regardless of methodology or geography, all books in the series are historical in the fundamental sense of undertaking rigorous contextual analysis.

PUBLISHED BY PALGRAVE MACMILLAN:

Indian Mobilities in the West, 1900–1947: Gender, Performance, Embodiment
    By Shompa Lahiri

The Shelley–Byron Circle and the Idea of Europe
    By Paul Stock

Culture and Hegemony in the Colonial Middle East
    By Yaseen Noorani

Recovering Bishop Berkeley: Virtue and Society in the Anglo-Irish Context
    By Scott Breuninger

The Reading of Russian Literature in China: A Moral and Manual of Practice
    By Mark Gamsa

Rammohun Roy and the Making of Victorian Britain (forthcoming)
    By Lynn Zastoupil

The American Bourgeoisie: Distinction and Identity in the Nineteenth Century
(forthcoming)
    By Julia Rosenbaum and Sven Beckert, eds.

Science in Practice: Law, Practices, and Institutions from the Renaissance to the Present
(forthcoming)
    By Jessica Riskin and Mario Biagioli, eds.

Carl Gustav Jung: Avant-Garde Conservative (forthcoming)
    By Jay Sherry

Character, Self, and Sociability in the Scottish Enlightenment (forthcoming)
    By Thomas Ahnert and Susan Manning, eds.

Culture and Hegemony in the Colonial Middle East

Yaseen Noorani

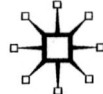

CULTURE AND HEGEMONY IN THE COLONIAL MIDDLE EAST
Copyright © Yaseen Noorani, 2010.

All rights reserved.

First published in 2010 by
PALGRAVE MACMILLAN®
in the United States—a division of St. Martin's Press LLC,
175 Fifth Avenue, New York, NY 10010.

Where this book is distributed in the UK, Europe and the rest of the world, this is by Palgrave Macmillan, a division of Macmillan Publishers Limited, registered in England, company number 785998, of Houndmills, Basingstoke, Hampshire RG21 6XS.

Palgrave Macmillan is the global academic imprint of the above companies and has companies and representatives throughout the world.

Palgrave® and Macmillan® are registered trademarks in the United States, the United Kingdom, Europe and other countries.

ISBN: 978–0–230–62319–4

Library of Congress Cataloging-in-Publication Data

Noorani, Yaseen, 1966–
   Culture and hegemony in the colonial Middle East / Yaseen Noorani.
     p. cm.
   Includes bibliographical references and index.
   ISBN 978–0–230–62319–4 (alk. paper)
    1. Egypt—Politics and government—1882–1952.
2. Political culture—Egypt—History. 3. Hegemony—Egypt—History. 4. Nationalism—Egypt—History. 5. Ideals (Philosophy)—Social aspects—Egypt—History. 6. Egyptian literature, Modern—History and criticism. 7. Middle East—Politics and government. 8. Political culture—Middle East—History. 9. Hegemony—Middle East—History. 10. Middle East—Colonial influence. I. Title.

DT107.N66 2010
962'.04—dc22
                                                2009039958

A catalogue record of the book is available from the British Library.

Design by Newgen Imaging Systems (P) Ltd., Chennai, India.

First edition: April 2010

10 9 8 7 6 5 4 3 2 1

Printed in the United States of America.

Library
University of Texas
at San Antonio

For my parents, Ahmed and Zakia Noorani

Contents

Acknowledgments	ix
Introduction	1
1 Sovereign Virtue and the Emergence of Nationality	23
2 The Death of the Hero and the Birth of Bourgeois Class Status	49
3 Order, Agency, and the Economy of Desire: Islamic Reformism and Arab Nationalism	71
4 The Moral Transformation of Femininity and the Rise of the Public–Private Distinction in Colonial Egypt	107
5 Fiction, Hegemony, and Aesthetic Citizenship	149
6 Excess, Rebellion, and Revolution: Egyptian Modernity in the *Trilogy*	171
Epilogue	209
Notes	213
Bibliography	235
Index	243

Acknowledgments

I am grateful to everyone who helped me to write and publish this book. It is not possible to name all those to whom I owe gratitude, but I can name some of them. My colleagues in the Department of Islamic and Middle East Studies at the University of Edinburgh, and my current colleagues in the Department of Near Eastern Studies at the University of Arizona, have provided me over the years with a supportive professional and collegial environment and plenty of intellectual engagement. I am honored to have worked with them. A number of these colleagues—Carole Hillenbrand, Leila Hudson, Elisabeth Kendall, Yasir Suleiman, and Kamran Talattof—have discussed ideas in this book with me at great length, enabling me to articulate them more fully. Laleh Khalili and Brian Silverstein read parts of the manuscript at different stages and provided me with substantial feedback. In developing the ideas and arguments that have gone into this book, I have benefited a great deal from the presentations I have made in various venues. I am grateful to the people who made these presentations possible, to the audiences who attended them, and thankful especially to those who engaged with my work at a deeper level and provided me with comments and criticisms. I have also incorporated a number of central ideas in this book into graduate courses that I have taught at the University of Arizona. My thanks to the graduate students for the valuable discussions that we have had, and especially to those who have read parts of the manuscript. I am also grateful for the extremely useful comments and suggestions provided by other readers of the manuscript.

Over the past few years, I have had the pleasure and good fortune to receive intellectual and moral support from a number of people. I owe a special debt of gratitude to Jaroslav Stetkevych, who taught me how to read Arabic poetry and showed me what it means to be a scholar, and who continues to support my intellectual work. I have benefited tremendously from Suzanne Stetkevych's writings as well as her support of my work. Anton Shammas has given me his time and encouragement. Salah Hassan has read substantial parts of the manuscript and provided me with extensive commentary. His intellectual input has been invaluable to me. John Chalcraft was present to critique many of the ideas in this book as they took shape and has read substantial portions of the manuscript. It was a privilege to have him as a colleague at the University of Edinburgh. Rachana Kamtekar's contribution to this book is inestimable. Aside from the spiritual sustenance of her intense and fervent engagement with ideas, her rigor as a philosopher has made me aim for a higher standard. I am thankful to her.

I would also like to acknowledge Koninklijke Brill N.V. for permission to include material in Chapter 2 of this book from my previously published article, "A Nation Born in Mourning: The Neoclassical Funeral Elegy in Egypt" in *The Journal of Arabic Literature*, 28:1 (1997) 38–67.

Introduction

New notions of political authority, social order, publicity and privacy, gender relations, and individual subjectivity became increasingly prominent in the Arabic public sphere as it emerged during the late nineteenth and early twentieth centuries. These notions were overwhelmingly promoted, contested, and justified through appeal to nationality—not nationalism, in the sense of a political ideology or doctrine, but the more general and fundamental idea of attachment, belonging, and moral allegiance to a nation. Intellectuals, reformers, and political leaders urged their compatriots to struggle for the sake of social and political transformation, invoking a disposition to national duty and devotion regarded as innate in all individuals. The emergence of this legitimizing ideal of nationality along with a new framework of normative notions raises two central problems that have not been adequately explained either in existing studies of the period or in general theoretical works. The first is the nature of nationality as a moral ideal—how it demands the allegiance of individuals, what it promises them, and on this basis, how it gives authority to political and reformist ideologies, programs of social ordering, and literary representations of society. The second problem is the linkage between the emerging moral ideal of nationality and the moral ideals already present in literate Arabic culture. That is to say, on what basis were people able to make sense of nationality and find it appealing on their own terms? The aim here is to address these questions by investigating how nationality works as a new kind of communal ideal that is based on a new understanding of individual and social moral order. This account focuses on the promotion by Middle Eastern reformers and intellectuals of values like patriotism, popular sovereignty, citizenship, and the bourgeois family. It shows that what took place in the rise of these values was not a clash of two irreconcilable cultures—the onslaught of secular Western modernity against an Islamic patriarchal premodernity—but the transformation of traditional cultural ideals from within, a process whose central dynamic lay in the transformation of virtue into nationality.

This book examines a body of literary, reformist, and political writings extending from the late nineteenth to the mid-twentieth century, mainly by Egyptian authors. These writings range from the women's liberation of Qasim Amin to the Arab nationalism of Sati' al-Husri, and from the classicizing poetry of al-Barudi to the realist fiction of Nagib Mahfuz. I have chosen these works because they elaborate the logic of nationality in ways that allow insight into its nature and development; in most cases, these works were widely influential. The works are primarily Egyptian because Egypt was the earliest Arabic-speaking land to harbor a centralizing political authority, reform-minded bureaucratic and professional classes, and a cohesive and expanding public sphere. Analysis of these works shows that despite their wide divergences in genre, ethos, and political orientation, their appeal to nationality is rooted in an underlying model of the self. Through their manipulation of this model and investment of it with their own ideological content and historical specificity, these works set up different depictions of the nature of social order. In doing so, they progressively transform the traditional model of the self and its relation to collective order. For they depict collective order as arising from innate human dispositions rather than from the sovereign authority of virtuous figures. The resulting democratization of virtue provides the moral basis for numerous modern norms—the autonomous citizen, the bourgeois family, the public sphere, the institutions of the administered society. Understanding the relationship between virtue and nationality provides fundamental insight into the nature of these norms and their operation in conflicting modern ideologies.

The focus in this study on nationality as a moral ideal results in a different emphasis and approach from the current approaches that deal with the nation as a social form or with nationalism as a political ideology. I am not concerned here with the question of whether or not nations *actually exist*—that is, whether or not there are some objective realities of nationhood that necessarily bind people together and induce the formation of collective units. Whether or not this is the case, we are confronted with a separate issue that is equally critical in understanding the formation and persistence of nations. How are people persuaded that they belong to a nation and that they are obliged to perform self-sacrifice for it? What is the nation, or how is the nation represented to people, such that it bears this absolute moral right over its members? Included in this moral status of the nation are notions of its collective unity, will and agency, which justify its right to exist, to determine itself, to exercise sovereignty over its land and members. Whether or not nations have an "objective" existence, the nature and origin of the moral status claimed for the nation requires its own analysis.

Nationality in its moral dimension is the idea of an individual's innate identity with a collective unit that provides its members with fulfillment and for whose sake they must be willing to perform self-sacrifice. The nation, in this sense, is a normative entity—it is held to be always present as a moral ideal even when existing reality does not conform to it, even when it has no corporate or political existence, and even when its own members are not aware of their national identity. Consider, for example, the Pledge of Allegiance to the American flag, which describes the United States as "one nation, under God, indivisible, with liberty and justice for all." These descriptions may be all empirically false at any given moment in American history. They are not, however, meant to describe the actually existing reality of America, but the true America that its citizens must continually strive to realize. America is indivisible in a moral, not an empirical sense, and it is this moral truth of America to which allegiance is pledged and which makes serving America obligatory whatever may be the actual state of affairs at a given moment. A similarly instructive example is the call to serve the Arab nation despite its lack of any corporate or political existence. One may maintain, as did the Arab nationalist Sati' al-Husri, that so long as there are speakers of Arabic who share a common history, these individuals are bound together as an Arab nation. But what this further means for al-Husri and others is that Arabs are morally bound to love and serve the Arab nation even against the demands of the polities they actually live in.

The problem then is to understand what new conception of community arose that not only claimed this kind of allegiance, but did so in a way that made it seem necessary and legitimate to transform society in comprehensive ways and to demand of individuals an unprecedented level of incorporation into the social order. This is an issue of nationality rather than of nationalism. Liberal and leftist reformers, who have frequently been inimical to nationalists, have nevertheless appealed to the needs and values of the nation and our duties toward it in promoting their programs just as much as have nationalists. Such appeals can only have force if the nation is seen as requiring and demanding a specific kind of order that is universal in nature, and if the nation's attainment of this order is somehow critical to the nation's members. For this reason, nationality is more fundamental and pervasive than nationalism, which is merely one kind of political ideology that draws upon nationality.

The new form of communal order implied by the nation and the new kind of integration it demands of individuals cannot be explained by recourse to preexisting types of social feeling thought to be innate or inveterate, like ethnicity. It cannot be doubted that in some times and places, people have been conscious of ties that we would call ethnic and accorded those ties importance. But such ties did not habitually, if ever, cause people to call for and attempt to establish the kind of autonomous, self-ordering community that we identify as the modern nation. This changed only when a new conception of community emerged in the eighteenth and nineteenth centuries that was capable of transforming the meaning and value of ethnic ties. The same holds true for language or folk culture or shared history. This new conception of community, which was capable of endowing these elements with a moral force that they did not previously possess, is what calls for explanation. Nationality and its distinctive moral logic is located in this new communal ideal, because it is this ideal that links historical specificities like ethnicity to communal agency and self-determination, as well as to the rights and duties of citizens, in a manner that they had not been linked before. Preexisting social ties, though they were touted by the promoters of nationality, cannot account for the moral authority that nationality claims over individuals.

Current theories of nationalism and the rise of nations fail to show how nationality works as a communal ideal because they do not show where the moral authority of the nation comes from, nor how this moral authority is related to modern social, political, and human ideals. These theories regard the nation as the necessary social form of modernity, which they connect with rationalism and universalism, yet they regard the nation's hold over its citizens to lie in innate, exclusivist, and nonrational sentiments. Many theorists see an outright opposition between national attachment and liberal or universalist political values. This makes it impossible to understand how there can be any connection between nationality and modernity. Ernest Gellner, for example, argues that nations and nationalism come into being because modern industrial social organization requires a political unit in which a uniform literate linguistic culture has been instilled in all citizens.[1] Rationality, as expounded most clearly by Hume and Kant, is "the secret of the modern spirit" that engenders and animates industrial society.[2] Yet nationalism, which for Gellner is a form of social self-worship that takes the place of religion, is inimical to modern rationality and individualism.[3] Nationalists are "repudiators of the abstract rationalism of the Enlightenment" and "delight in feelings of submission or incorporation in a continuous entity greater, more persistent and more legitimate than the isolated self."[4] Gellner does not explain how the nation can be based on these two antithetical orientations.

Anthony Smith's more nuanced account finds the raison d'etre of the nation to lie in the aims of the bureaucratic state and of modern intellectual and professional classes, but attributes national attachment and solidarity to a preexisting "ethnic core," enhanced and elaborated for the purpose.[5] This creates a disjuncture between the nation's civic, legal framework and its ethnic substrate. For Smith, this disjuncture is the basis for his two antagonistic models of the modern nation: the civic nation, in which ethnicity is a submerged yet necessary element, and the ethnic nation, in which rights and legal institutions are outweighed by cultural uniformity and presumed kinship. The former national type is connected with Enlightenment ideas of rationalist republicanism and "national character." The latter comes from the Romantic glorification of folk culture, historicism, and "national genius."[6] The moral hold of these ideas seems to come solely from ethnicity. "*Ethnie* and nation are seen simply as families writ large," he argues.[7] Essentially, Smith is accounting for the nation's moral claim by attributing it to some kind of innate propensity of human beings to bond with family units.

Family feeling, however, cannot be the origin of the nation's claim to moral authority, nor of the transformations authorized by it. If it is not believed that families have an intrinsic right to self-determination or cultural autonomy, how does the nation acquire this moral status as a family writ large? Families are not usually regarded as sovereign, self-ordering communities, but rather as building blocks of the nation and therefore subject to public authority. The national will is empowered to regulate the family, but no external force may impose itself on the national will. Moreover, it would not have made sense in the time of patriarchal familial norms to argue that women should be given new roles and rights because the nation is our extended family. On the contrary—what we see in the modern period is the argument that the patriarchal family and the social status of women must be transformed because the realization of the nation depends on it. The real questions then are why anyone should care about this nation and why it should determine things like the status of women or the political rights of individuals. This cannot be explained by those who deny that there is any connection between universalist political ideals and the cultural distinctness claimed for the nation, like John Breuilly and Elie Kedourie. For Breuilly, "[n]ationalist ideology never makes a rational connection between the cultural and the political concept of the nation because no such connection is possible."[8] Nationalism is merely a program for taking over the state, which it can somehow accomplish without any substantive moral appeal. For Kedourie, nationalism, a totalitarian doctrine dreamed up by disgruntled German metaphysicians, holds that linguistic communities must be sovereign, self-determining entities in which "the will of the individual should merge in the will of the nation."[9] So when English or American liberals employ the term "nation," it is merely a short-hand for a political community based on rights and representation that is antithetical to the "nation" of nationalists.[10] With Breuilly and Kedourie, we are required to believe that the ubiquitous association of political universalism with the idea of distinct nations is nothing more than a conceptual confusion. I will argue that to understand nationality, it is necessary to understand its immanent logic of individual and communal agency that makes cultural and historical specificity the necessary means for attaining human universality.

Nationality as a moral ideal is not addressed by Benedict Anderson's notion of the "imagined community." Anderson proposes sociological preconditions necessary for the emergence of the nation-state as a communal form, which include the rise of print-capitalism, vernacular languages, and the idea of "homogeneous, empty time," among others. One of the key preconditions, according to Anderson, was the development of the cognitive capacity to imagine a community whose population is too large and too dispersed to be perceived directly. The community that the mind learned to imagine, however, is not in itself imaginary but is the real, actually existing nation. Whether or not Anderson is correct in correlating the supposed emergence of this cognitive capacity with the rise of nations is a question I will not address. But it is clear that the capacity to imagine membership in a community that exceeds direct perception tells us nothing about why this community should exist, why anyone should want to belong to it, or why it should gain the authority to demand self-sacrifice. What is it about the nation that gives it this absolute degree of moral obligation?

Anderson attempts to account for this with his own humanistic ideal of nationality. He attributes national feeling to the pregiven, nonchosen nature of national ties—"precisely because such ties are not chosen, they have about them a halo of disinterestedness."[11] On this basis, he assimilates the moral claim of the nation to that of the family, asserting that "the family has been traditionally conceived as the domain of disinterested love and solidarity. So too...for most ordinary people of whatever class the whole point of the nation is that it is interestless. Just for that reason, it can ask for sacrifices."[12] Anderson believes that disinterested, selfless love is a natural human impulse. The family and the nation naturally realize this love because the members of each are bound together accidentally and inseparably, rather than by choice based on self-interest. Love of these entities, therefore, is purely love of humanity, and the nation is the largest scale on which love of humanity can take communal form.[13] On this view, a nation is an objective entity and each individual knows her nation and feels a natural, spontaneous love for it. Yet what we find in any public sphere is that there are competing versions of the nation and its values making opposing demands upon individuals. Anderson's view does not allow us to understand the nature of this competition or why it exists, much less the strategies by which these competing versions stake their claim to authenticity. Anderson's account does show, however, what is common to all representations of nationality as a moral ideal: the derivation of the nation from an inner necessity within the human self.

The aim here is not to offer speculations on human nature or the workings of the psyche, but to show how nationality is represented as that which people truly desire, and that for which they are internally obligated to perform self-sacrifice. Certainly, such representations are influential in shaping people's actual emotional and moral attachments, as well as their notions of the self, but I will not attempt to investigate in what way this may actually occur or to what degree. Nor do I take up the economic, political, organizational and technological developments that enabled the rise of modern nations. These elements make nations possible, but they cannot coalesce into the social form of the nation unless the concept of national belonging, with its internal moral structure, is present and effectively normalized within society, and invested in a specific national content.[14] Nationality, or any moral ideal, cannot be regarded as the spontaneous outcome of a particular social configuration. Social transformations do not directly generate their own meaning out of themselves but are always understood and shaped within an existing normative context. The premise I adopt here is that the mutual interaction between increasing productive capacities and economic integration on the one hand and state expansion and centralization on the other fostered the growth of bureaucratic and professional classes. The increasing social importance of these classes encouraged the progressive modification, within the public sphere, of existing notions of social order and collective integration. This modification eventually resulted in the transformation of the traditional conception of order.

National Selfhood

During the colonial period in the Middle East, public discourses insistently connected new social and political ideals with the moral condition of individuals. Reformist intellectuals condemned the moral degradation and social practices of their compatriots and equated the deficit of individual virtue with an absence of collective agency and progress. They held up in contrast the ideal of an integrated, powerful nation constituted through the self-sacrifice of morally ordered citizens. Whether we consider the rhetoric of those who envisaged a territorial nation such as Egypt, an ethnic or linguistic or racially defined nation such as the Arab nation, or even the religiously defined nation of a number of Islamists, we find that the ideal of a collective agent that is a morally integrated body of citizens retains its fundamental legitimizing role. To understand the nature and emergence of this ideal, it is necessary to investigate the underlying assumptions about what the individual self is and what it means for the self to be ordered.

The writings examined in this book depict the nation as the higher self of the individuals that make up the nation. These writings represent national order and agency as the outcome of the order and agency that individuals must attain with themselves. As long as individuals are disordered, the nation has only a potential existence. The unification and integration of individuals in a collective body that is itself an individual is only possible through a state of order that is the same for all individuals. Through the nation individuals attain fulfillment—not only because they have achieved internal order, but because they cannot maintain or exercise this order unless society as a whole is ordered. The nation therefore always exists within individuals as their internal condition of order toward which they naturally aspire whether or not they have yet succeeded in bringing the nation actually into being. Herein lies the universality of the nation—its internal integration is the order common to all human beings. Yet at the same time, there is some factor that makes the individual nation the necessary stage for the realization of this universal human order. At the extreme of national autarky, this is some objective factor, like language or ethnicity, that is depicted as the necessary means of the full expression of human order, but which requires that each nation remain a distinct, fixed entity. At the opposing extreme, this factor is merely a historical deficit that has to be rectified at the level of the society that suffers it for human order to come about. In this latter case, the nation is the necessary platform for an eventual total human integration.

The key element in this national model of the self, and the element that links it to the preexisting communal ideal of virtue, is the process by which the self attains the state of order, which can be understood as a process of self-negation. This process accounts for how it is possible for human beings, seen as inherently inclined to act only on the basis of their own immediate desires and lusts, to attain a state of control over their desires to the extent that they adhere to moral principles—that is, sacrifice their own desires for the sake of others. In this model, the self in its primordial state consists of disordered desire, yet contains within itself the possibility of order and perfection. Desire must turn against itself as the impulse to disorder so as to realize its internal possibility of order and attain fulfillment. Otherwise, it is dissipated in futile attachments to objects that offer ephemeral and illusory gratification. Order, in other words, is depicted as desire that has negated itself by going against itself as the immediate surge to gratification. This way of depicting the relation between desire and moral order is critical to the ideals of nationality and virtue because it makes the generation of order a perpetual and inexhaustible process. It makes the community and its moral order, which result from the negation of desire, the true object of desire. And it makes self-sacrifice for the sake of the community definitive of morality, agency, and fulfillment.

The transformation of virtue into nationality is the transition from an *externalizing* to an *immanent* conception of how this internal moral process takes place. What I am calling the ideal of virtue is the depiction of moral and communal order present in the premodern Arabic intellectual tradition. In central discourses of this tradition, self-governance and political governance are conceived to be an external imposition of restraint upon chaotic desire. Justice, or order within the self, is depicted as the rule of reason over the self, which results in virtuous actions in accord with divine commandments. This state of justice, however, a continual confrontation with and mastery over desire, is by its nature attainable by very few people. For this reason, society is prone to disorder and requires a just ruler whose function is to restrain and control the desires of individuals. Justice on the social level is thus the outcome of the self-mastery attained by a small minority of human beings, who thereby command social and political authority. In this conception of virtue as self-rule, order within the self as well as within society is externalized. It issues from an ordering element—reason or sovereignty—that is differentiated from yet definitive of the self or community it rules. This results in a hierarchical conception of the self as well as of society.

The representation of nationality, however, alters the relationship between desire and order by transferring the locus of communal order from virtuous figures of authority to the national body as a whole. The idea of a community that is a corporate body that orders itself of its own accord is not possible unless it is believed that individuals themselves are naturally self-ordering. In other words, order must be understood as arising *immanently* within the individual self, without the need of an externalized, differentiated element that imposes restraint. Public order and national agency can only exist if individuals are reliably ordered from the outset, rather than subject to a ceaseless struggle with desire that can only be mastered by the heroic. In this context, an aesthetic conception of individuality develops in which innate desires and emotions are not irremediably chaotic but are the origin of the moral order of the productive citizen. But this requires at the same time the positing of social mechanisms and institutions that enable the proper development of innate human nature to take place.

The transformation of virtue into nationality projects a social body in which individuals are integrated laterally through their common internal order rather than in a hierarchical sequence. As a result, defining the process that engenders this common internal order comes to be central to competing social visions. The economy of desire within the self, that is, the internal configuration of the self such that its desire automatically turns into order without any dissipation, becomes definitive of social order. The burden of ensuring this ideal configuration of the self falls upon the private sphere and the processes that take place therein, and on the institutions of public order, which replicate the internal order of the self and thereby generate collective agency. The private sphere is the domain in which morally ordered individuals—citizens—are formed. The private sphere may be distinguished from the public, but its function is conceived as public in nature. Any attempt to define the nature of the moral order created in the private sphere and particularly the role of women in this process is at bottom an attempt to define the constitution of the social body. At the public level, processes of social ordering are justified on the basis that they enable the development of ordered individuals and thereby give rise to a social order that replicates the internal order of the self. Societies are condemned on the charge that they repress and misdirect the proper development of innate humanity through their tyranny and disorder. It can be seen then that the ideal of nationality is intrinsically tied to modern norms of private and public, whose fusion on the basis of the internal order of the self constitutes its normative framework.

The immanent conception of moral order alters the manner in which order itself is understood, giving rise to aesthetic and psychological conceptions of the self as well as a modern cultural dynamic of ever-changing representations of innate humanity. Innate feelings and impulses, no longer imagined as externally restrained, must be shown to turn somehow into order of their own accord. Moral, aesthetic, and psychological theories arise to explain how this comes about. Art, particularly literary art, takes up the task of representing an innate human nature that is initially, and thus inherently, outside of moral order yet gives rise to it. Since this innate human nature is outside of order, it is unbounded and inexhaustible. The release of this nature therefore does not result in a fixed order, but in a human emancipation that is simultaneously unbounded and morally directed. Representing an innate humanity of this nature requires the representation of a form of desire that appears to be outside of order in its danger and transgression, but turns out to be the origin of freedom and authentic morality. It turns out that this desire, which is innate humanity, only seems transgressive because it has been repressed by social injustice. It can be seen then that any form of desire that can be successfully represented in this manner eventually becomes socially acceptable and loses its transgressive and dangerous associations. This results in a cultural dynamic in which innate humanity is continually represented anew in the form of desires at the threshold of social acceptability.

In all of these respects, the movement from virtue to nationality entails the emergence of a new notion of humanity. This notion did not arise on the basis of a reevaluation of human beings in themselves, but from a new conception of human integration into a communal order. It cannot be thought that simply adopting a more positive outlook on human capacities at a certain point in history led to a new framework for conceptualizing the moral status held to be definitive of humanity. The new notion of humanity emerged rather through the increasing emphasis on the collective body in itself as the source of its own order. The central dimension of this new notion of humanity, the immanence of moral order, is therefore intrinsically communal and national in nature. This can be seen in the fact that the agency of individuals is conceived as political in nature. The morally ordered individual, the citizen, expresses his order as participation in the public sphere, that is, participation in the agency of the nation. The new moral status of femininity shows this character as well, in that this new status was justified on the basis of the role attributed to women in the formation of moral order within individuals, which is to say, the formation of citizens. The communal nature of humanity is seen above all in its world-historical character. The immanence of order means that ordering is a process that will not reach completion until collective human agency has made the world perfectly correspond to the innate desire of humanity.

Hegemony and the National Self

The fusion of self and society, public and private, is an ideal that grounds the moral authority claimed by discourses of social order, and is in this sense hegemonic. The political and reformist ideologies examined in this book in each case posit a principle of order identified as the means by which individuals realize their authentic humanity and societies achieve collective integration and agency. This principle of order, be it Qasim Amin's liberal autonomy, al-Kawakibi's "communality" (*ishtirak*), or Sati' al-Husri's linguistic "sociality" (*ijtima'iya*), is put forward as the key to freedom and civilization. The principle of order acquires the moral authority of nationality because it is cast as the means by which self-negation—the capacity for self-sacrifice—comes about within the self, thus bringing the nation into being. In this way other ideologies, reforms, and social values can be depicted as only partially universal or as antiuniversal. They are either comprised within and subordinate to the principle of order of the universal ideology, or are inimical to it in being impulses of egoism, enslavement, and tyranny. The central element of discursive hegemony—the claim to moral authority in ordering the national body—is thus the positing of a principle of social order that brings about self-negation within individuals.

The operation of discursive hegemony requires that the nation be conceived as an autonomous collective agent, a "collective will," whose order replicates the selves of its individual members. This is seen especially clearly in the formulations of Antonio Gramsci, who pioneered the notion of hegemony as the "intellectual and moral leadership" of a national class and its political apparatus. Gramsci believed that hegemony had been won by the revolutionary bourgeoisie of Europe but must now transfer to the proletariat.[15] For Gramsci, such hegemony is attained only when a "social group is really progressive—i.e. really causes the whole society to move forward, not merely satisfying its own existential requirements..."[16] Hegemony is established by the political party of this universal class, designated the "modern prince" (after Machiavelli's "prince"), which Gramsci describes as "the first cell in which there come together germs of a collective will tending to become universal and total."[17] The task of the modern prince is "awakening and developing a national-popular collective will"—and this is the fundamental nature of hegemony as Gramsci sees it.[18] "The modern Prince must be and cannot but be the proclaimer and organiser of an intellectual and moral reform, which also means creating the terrain for a subsequent development of the national-popular collective will towards the realisation of a superior, total form of modern civilisation."[19] In other words, hegemony is the process in which a social group that embodies the universality implicit in the national body orders this body so as to actualize its universality and bring it into being as an autonomous agent. This ordering is not coercive because the universality of the hegemonic group fulfills the authentic aspirations of the entire social body.

> The modern Prince, as it develops, revolutionises the whole system of intellectual and moral relations, in that its development means precisely that any given act is seen as useful or harmful, as virtuous or wicked, only in so far as it has as its point of reference the modern Prince itself, and helps to strengthen or to oppose it. In men's consciences, the Prince takes the place of the divinity or the categorical imperative, and becomes the basis for a modern laicism and for a complete laicisation of all aspects of life and of all customary relationships.[20]

In this striking statement, Gramsci makes the political party the origin of moral order within the individual conscience as well as society as a whole.

The party takes this role because it embodies the principle of authentic social order. Until the collective will has been fully realized, the hegemonic agent is the only embodiment of the universal principle and must therefore exercise total leadership.

The idea of the nation as a collective self is no extraneous element in Gramsci's thinking, but is constitutive of the hegemony, the framework of order and leadership, that he envisions. This is seen further in his conception of how the strata of the nation are to be "psychologically" organized into collective agency. Gramsci makes a characteristic division of the nation into mutually dependent rational and emotional segments. "The popular element 'feels' but does not always know or understand; the intellectual element 'knows' but does not always understand and in particular does not always feel." The intellectual stratum must connect with and harness the "elementary passions of the people" for the nation's collective agency to come into being. "One cannot make politics-history without this passion, without this sentimental connection between intellectuals and people-nation." Intellectuals, in other words, are responsible for the transformation of raw popular emotion into order on the collective level.

> If the relationship between intellectuals and people-nation, between the leaders and the led, the rulers and the ruled, is provided by an organic cohesion in which feeling-passion becomes understanding and thence knowledge (not mechanically but in a way that is alive), then and only then is the relationship one of representation. Only then can there take place an exchange of individual elements between the rulers and the ruled, leaders and led, and can the shared life be realised which alone is a social force—with the creation of the "historical bloc".[21]

This "historical bloc" is precisely an individual unit, whether a collectivity or a person, that has attained order and agency. Describing the nature of the human individual, Gramsci says: "Man is to be conceived as an historical bloc of purely individual and subjective elements and of mass and objective or material elements with which the individual is in an active relationship. To transform the external world, the general system of relations, is to potentiate oneself and to develop oneself."[22] The process that takes place within an individual, resulting in the capacity "to transform the external world" is here seen as equivalent to the hegemonic process that takes place on the collective level where it results in the making of "politics-history." Gramsci conceives of the "people" as the emotional substrate and motor-force of the realized nation. The people can only accede to this role, however, when the intellectuals liberate them from their elemental, irrational, precapitalist condition through "a catharsis of modern civilisation."[23] Otherwise, their primal emotional energies will remain invested in religious superstition and other dissipations under the tyranny of reactionary classes and the nation will persist in a state of non-being. Modernity is here conceived as a process of ordering, of national self-discipline, and hegemony is the political form that this process takes.

Gramsci's belief in the universality of the working class and Communist Party for the Italian nation has by now lost its appeal. The value of Gramsci's political analysis, however, lies in that it names and reveals the nature of the normatively binding political authority claimed by reformist ideologies and aspirants to power. It will be seen that across a wide spectrum of political and social discourses the hegemonic claim to national representation enables the assertion of social differentiation and hierarchy within a national body in which all citizens are in principle equal. Gramsci's derivation of the concept of hegemony itself from a traditional norm of political primacy based on personal status indicates its hierarchical lineage, now reformulated on an altered basis. "Hegemony," or "leadership," originally belonged to the ancient Greek *hegemon*, or political leader, who is the same sort of figure as Machiavelli's *principe*. National hegemony transfers the political primacy of such a figure from a notion of intrinsic personal status to a notion of the embodiment by a particular group of the order and universality implicit within the social body as a whole. As we will see in the Middle Eastern context, this kind of transfer becomes the basis, most fundamentally, of bourgeois class status and class publicity. And conversely, it establishes the pervasive notion of "the people" as the unconscious, premodern, not-yet-ordered desiring element of the national self. More recently, in Subaltern Studies scholarship, this premodern and irrational character of the "national-popular" becomes the basis of a historical metaphysics centered on an irreducible division of West and non-West.

It is necessary, in the context of the argument I am advancing here, to extricate the concept of hegemony, which enables the identification and analysis of hegemonic claims, from notions of world-historical development that posit radical divisions between the modern and premodern and between the West and the non-West. Such notions distinguish a modern, bourgeois, hegemonic politics based on mobilization of the people through moral and rational persuasion, from a premodern, closed political order based on faith and domination. In this way, the concept of hegemony is deployed to promote an emancipatory or politically oppositional view of human history. This can be seen, for instance, in the attempt by the political philosophers Ernesto Laclau and Chantal Mouffe to liberate the concept of hegemony from Gramsci's notion of the universal role of the working class and its political party in their work, *Hegemony and Socialist Strategy*. Laclau and Mouffe do away with the class-based narrative of world history and ultimate human emancipation that anchors Gramsci's understanding of hegemony. They argue that the actual terrain of hegemonic struggle consists of discursively formed, contingent, nonexclusive social identities that form political blocks on the basis of the discursive articulation of political interests. These interests revolve around the continual spread of demands for equality, of "democratic discourse," into new domains and types of social relations. This "equality," however, has no inherent content or defining *telos*; it is continually defined through the struggle of competing groups. Above all, Laclau and Mouffe seek to bar hegemonic claim-making from identification with any moral process definitive of humanity within the self that would give such claims the authority to demand self-sacrifice.

Yet to envision even this attenuated, ambiguous, and nearly empty form of emancipatory politics, Laclau and Mouffe find it necessary to posit a radical and foundational divide between the "sutured" political orders of the pre-1789 world and the liberal democracies in which political struggle for equality takes place. Predemocratic societies are governed by a singular and transcendent principle of order, resulting in fixed hierarchy and subordination. The emancipatory nature of democratic societies comes from the presence of democratic discourse, which allows those who are subordinate to see themselves as oppressed, thereby setting political contestation in motion.[24] This way of setting up politics means that the initial eruption of democratic discourse into a world of self-contained hierarchy in the eighteenth century founded politics and initiated the spread of equality, but is in itself inexplicable, since "sutured" societies do not generate democratic discourse. It must supervene on their "discourses of subordination" from the outside.[25] Where then could its origin lie, other than in an innate human desire for emancipation that stands outside of any social order? Laclau and Mouffe have emptied this putative human moral impulse of any predefined political content, other than the "elimination of... inequalities," but they have by no means done away with it. In this case, then, the cost of instating a progressive vision of political struggle is the exclusion of the origin and possibility of politics from most of human history.

Modernity and Premodernity, West and Non-West

The positing of modernity as something absolutely outside of premodernity in this manner is a feature of many theories of modernity. Such theories not only make it impossible to fathom any process of transition from a normatively closed premodernity to a fluid and dynamic modernity, but also obscure the nature of modern norms by finding their origin in an autonomous force that lies outside of history rather than in their relation to the preexisting norms from which they necessarily emerged.

The externality of the modern to the premodern is frequently taken for granted in reference to the non-West. This is the assumption that modernity, originating in the West, supervenes on and displaces premodern cultures, marking non-Western societies with radical historical discontinuity. Modernization must be imposed, either by colonialism or by Westernized elites and reformers. Since the Western and premodern sets of norms are regarded as fundamentally incompatible, any perceived persistence of the premodern is seen as resulting in social, moral, and cognitive disjuncture. For social critics, the false, illegitimate fusion of the premodern with the modern creates dysfunctional imitations of modern social order, like the "neo-patriarchy" described by Hisham Sharabi.[26] At the heart of such social deformity lies the inauthentic, psychically incoherent individual who outwardly displays modern norms but is at bottom premodern, irrational, and authoritarian.[27] Among the victims is the modern intellectual who is unable to commune with his tradition-bound compatriots, or is riven by persisting premodern attachments. The assumption that Western modernity is intrinsically exterior to non-Western cultures appears to have a geographical and historical plausibility. Yet it cannot explain how non-Westerners, from within their premodern modes of thought, were able to comprehend, embrace, and adopt a wide range of modern norms. And the tendency of this assumption is to create a metahistorical opposition between the West and the non-West.

Critiques of colonial modernity developing out of twentieth-century German philosophy and French poststructuralism tend to preserve the absolute divide between the premodern and the modern, but invert the relationship between the two by making premodernity and the non-West exterior to Western modernity. This is seen in the development that Gramsci's concept of hegemony finds in Subaltern Studies scholarship. Gramsci forged his political analysis of hegemony in the context of explaining the "backwardness" of Italian politics. Gramsci argued that the Italian bourgeoisie failed to replicate the development of the French bourgeoisie. It did not modernize Italian society by eliminating feudalism and religious dogma because it was too weak to be revolutionary. It grasped power, instead, by means of compromise and alliance with feudal elements, a "passive revolution," a counterfeit social leadership. The founder of Subaltern Studies, Ranajit Guha, takes this as the point of departure for a similar analysis of Indian history, arguing that the Indian bourgeoisie never achieved the universality and hegemony enjoyed in Europe by the "Western bourgeoisie."[28] Instead, the Congress Party, the face of bourgeois ascendance, attained "dominance without hegemony." Colonial rule, based on force and manipulation, stimulated neither authentic economic development nor the emergence of universalist norms of political persuasion like those of bourgeois liberalism. This left the Indian order with two incompatible yet paradoxically fused sets of political values: those of the foreign colonizer and, those of indigenous medieval social orders.

> Whatever is indigenous in that culture is mostly borrowed from the past, whatever is foreign is mostly contemporary. The element of the past, though moribund, is not defunct; the contemporary element, so vigorous in its native metropolitan soil, finds it difficult to strike roots as a graft and remains shallow and restricted in its penetration of the new site. The originality of Indian politics of the period lies precisely in such paradoxes, which pervade the entire spectrum of power relations.[29]

Because the native bourgeoisie was not the product of a real basis of social power but rather of its collaboration with the colonial rule of force, it could in no way transcend the prevailing norms of political subjugation, whether those of the colonial power or those of Indian feudal relations. As a result, the liberalism taken on by the Indian bourgeoisie was nothing more than a shallow façade.

In *Nationalism and the Colonial World*, Partha Chatterjee works this Gramscian analysis into a critique of modernity. According to Chatterjee, third-world bourgeois nationalism could not be an autonomous discourse because it reinstated Enlightenment rationality, the framework of knowledge that ensures Western domination, thus neutralizing its own assertion of national independence. This paradoxical situation arose because, as seen previously, the colonized bourgeoisie was not a "a fundamental social class infused by a revolutionary urge to transform society and to stamp it with the imprint of its own unquestioned hegemony," but an artificially cultivated colonial protégé.[30] It "had no historical links with the revolutionary mission of a progressive bourgeoisie seeking to create a nation in its own image" and is therefore "selective about what it takes from Western rational thought"—that is, it never authentically became rational and liberal.[31] The colonial bourgeoisie came to power through "passive revolution," preserving colonial structures of rule and alliances with feudal classes,[32] and was thus incapable of modernizing "[p]opular consciousness, steeped in centuries of superstition and irrational folk religion," which it instead manipulated through the use of premodern values and symbols.[33] For Chatterjee, bourgeois third-world nationalism takes little more from Enlightenment than what he regards to be its inherently orientalist perspective: "nationalist thought accepts and adopts the same essentialist conception based on the distinction between 'the East' and 'the West'."[34] Yet so also does Chatterjee's own argument. For as long as the third-world bourgeoisie fails to be properly capitalist—and it must always fail—it cannot achieve enlightened liberal rationality, and thus will remain, along with "popular consciousness," on the premodern, nonuniversal side of the opposition with Enlightenment, the side of irrationality, superstition, and coercion. Adorno and Horkheimer argued that Enlightenment reason could never achieve a total conquest of nature without destroying itself because this would require the elimination of the nature within human beings.[35] Chatterjee extends this critique to the colonial situation only by identifying the colonized world—its culture as well as its social relations—with nature.[36] "If nationalism expresses itself in a frenzy of irrational passion, it does so *because* it seeks to represent itself in the image of the Enlightenment and *fails* to do so. For Enlightenment itself, to assert its sovereignty as the universal ideal, needs its Other; if it could ever actualize itself in the real world as the truly universal, it would in fact destroy itself."[37]

Asserting the externality of the premodern non-West to Western modernity as a strategy for undermining the normative claims of the latter thus reinstates a metaphysics of East and West. The Subaltern Studies historian Dipesh Chakrabarty turns the dictum that Enlightenment "needs its other" into a Derridean theory of history.[38] For Chakrabarty, non-Western premodernity, with its "times of gods" as opposed to the secular temporality of bourgeois rationalism, is the logical "outside" that defines and constitutes capitalist modernity. "This 'outside'...is something attached to the category *capital* itself...something we are able to see only because we can think/theorize capital, but something that also reminds us that other temporalities...coexist and are possible."[39] This means that from a modern, rationalist perspective, premodern non-Western cultures cannot be grasped as a positivity, but only negatively as the "unassimilable," unfathomable outside of capitalist modernity; "they cannot therefore be defined except with reference to the category *capital*." The persistence of these "times of gods" shows on the cultural level that capitalist modernity can never be total and universal because it requires its natural, prerational, premodern other. This logic arises from capitalism's necessary but unrealizable conversion of "real" labor into "abstract" labor.[40] In the Indian context, bourgeois hegemony, based on this unattainable universality, is incapable of completing itself by subsuming the "peasant," that is, the nonsecular, mythical, and hierarchical indigenous Indian culture.[41] Again, premodernity is the "real" or the "nature" that must always exceed modern processes of ordering because it is always required by them.

A comparable effect can be seen in the modern/premodern divide instituted in critiques of colonial modernity outside of the Subaltern Studies approach. Timothy Mitchell's analysis of the modernization of Egypt does not rely on a Gramscian notion of hegemony, invoking instead impersonal processes of ordering that are independent of class interests. Moreover, there is no distinction in Mitchell's scheme between the modernizing native bourgeoisie and modernizing Western colonialists. Both are exponents of the definitively modern cognitive orientation of "enframing," in which the world is "divided in two, into the material realm of things in themselves, as could now be said, and an abstract realm of their order or structure."[42] Yet Mitchell endows this purely epistemic framework with a normative aim whose origin is left unexplained. For he treats it not simply as a postulate that the world has an intelligible order, but as a drive to impose a specific kind of order on the world. Modernization, or to call it as Mitchell does, colonization, "would try and re-order Egypt to appear as a world enframed...In other words it was to be made picture-like and legible, rendered available to political and economic calculation."[43] This process can never be realized, however, because "modernity is something contingent upon the exclusion of its own opposite."[44] What it excludes is precisely the premodern—the spontaneously generated "order without frameworks" of Mediterranean lived spaces, or the Derridean "play of difference that produces meaning" to which "Arabic is much closer than European languages."[45] To make this argument, Mitchell, like the Subalterns, excludes from premodernity that which he regards as definitive of modernity: the capacity to generate ideals, whether cognitive or normative, of universality and order.

These critiques of colonial modernity are actually critiques of the discursive logic of liberal rationalism, taken to be the logic of modernity. History, however is not a discourse, and there is no reason to believe that it operates as one. Moreover, it is arbitrary to regard modern history and social relations as constituted by a single discursive logic and the "outside" it generates when there are many competing modernizing discourses, including those which subordinate reason to a superrational force. To privilege a single discursive logic as the universality that comprises all others, including that which has no identity except as its "outside," is to accept its claim to hegemony. In any case, there is no reason to accept the radical exclusion of premodernity that is a feature of liberalism and other modernizing discourses. For there can be no historical origin of modernity other than some so-called "premodernity." There was no point at which Western societies annihilated their cultures and spontaneously generated bourgeois rationalism or "enframing" without any dependence upon and articulation with previously existing norms. Nor is it conceivable that non-Western reformers had first to efface their cognitive and moral consciousness in order to be receptive to Western modes of thought. Conversely, there is no way to imagine a society, a culture, or an individual consciousness that simultaneously consists of two mutually impenetrable modes of thought and sets of norms. If we do so by grasping premodernity as the logically necessary exterior of modern consciousness, the inaccessible "unconscious" or "id" that makes modernity possible, we have reduced the history, values, and practices of other people to a dimension of our own putative collective psyche—even if this dimension is privileged as the foundation of capitalist rationality in the "Real" or in "nature."

Let us assume that we put aside the idea that hegemony in Western politics is or at some time was achieved through a pure, universalizing, liberal rationalism, whereas the political discourses of the non-West, or of nations that are not liberal democracies, are inherently coercive and manipulative. This would require us to grasp the universal claims put forward in a variety of discourses, whether Western or non-Western, and understand how they are related to each other in the context of nationality and citizenship. Let us assume, moreover, that we put aside the axiom that "premodern culture" and "modern culture" are radically other and mutually impenetrable to each other. This would require us to understand how norms that we regard as premodern could turn into norms that we regard as modern. It would also require us to understand this process in terms of hegemony. If modern norms are not spontaneously generated out of a new economic base, or imposed preconstituted from an external source, but emerge in the context of already existing norms, then the claim to universality of these norms can only be conceived and formulated in relation to existing moral ideals. This process takes place in the dialogue, debate, and contention of public discourses, which, in seeking to draw to themselves the authority of nationality, build up its moral framework. What I propose, then, is to understand the emergence of modern norms like citizenship, popular sovereignty, and the public–private division, not in terms of a cognitive or epistemic break, but in terms of a transformation within the structure of moral ideals.

Since the aim of this book is the investigation of the structure and logic of the normative dimension of nationality, which belongs to the realm of ideas and representations, the chapters of the book focus on the analysis of influential writings that are shaped by and manipulate this normative dimension in revealing manners. Chapter 1, "Sovereign Virtue and the Emergence of Nationality," suggests that the initial representation of the nation as a collective agent was made possible through the transference of the model of the virtuous individual to the collective body as a whole. The first part of the chapter lays out central features of premodern Islamic models of individual and social order as seen particularly in al-Ghazali (1058–1111) and Ibn Khaldun (1332–1406). The second part focuses on the deployment of this kind of model in the poetry of political rebellion composed by the Egyptian general, statesman, and Urabist leader Mahmud Sami al-Barudi (1839–1904) and the Levantine intellectual Ibrahim al-Yaziji (1847–1906). Chapter 2, "The Death of the Hero and the Birth of Bourgeois Class Status," investigates how it was initially possible for the professional and bureaucratic classes in early twentieth-century Egypt, the *efendiya*, to represent themselves as the class that embodies national agency. The focus here is on funeral elegies composed for heroic figures of this class, which dramatize the birth of the nation as the mourning for these figures and in this way identify bourgeois class attributes with moral order.

Whereas the corporate nature of nationality and national hegemony becomes more prominent in the funeral elegies discussed in Chapter 2, it was outside of classically derived poetry that the immanent depiction of national order found fuller development. This new conception of the nature of individual and collective order has been central to state and ideological programs of social transformation and provides their moral imperative. Chapter 3, "Order, Agency, and the Economy of Desire: Islamic Reformism and Arab Nationalism," analyzes two opposing strategies by which political ideologies anchor the ordering of society that they call for in their depiction of an economy of desire within the self. In the republican, antidespotic appeal for an Islamic political and economic order made by the anti-Ottoman Syrian dissident Abd al-Rahman al-Kawakibi (d. 1902), universalist political reform is the means of realizing the national community. On the other hand, the linguistic Arab nationalism of the Syrian/Iraqi governmental figure Sati' al-Husri (d. 1968) makes Arab identity the key to the creation of a collective body of unlimited order and power. Chapter 4, "The Moral Transformation of Femininity and the Rise of the Public–Private Division," argues that in the new moral framework of nationality, femininity came to be cast as the primary catalyst by which citizens attain the state of order within their private selves that they are to enact collectively in public. Defining the nature of this state of order and how femininity brings it about therefore became one of the main battle grounds in defining the nature of national order. The chapter shows how the relationship between femininity and moral order was recast by contrasting a classically derived representation of femininity, that of the poet al-Barudi, with early-twentieth-century programs of female emancipation in Egypt—liberal and rationalist in the case of Qasim Amin (d. 1908), and Arab-Islamic in the case of Malak Hifni Nasif (d. 1918).

The two final chapters consider the role of realist fiction as a counterpart to social and political ideologies in its exploitation of the moral framework of nationality. Chapter 5, "Fiction, Hegemony and the Aesthetic Dimension of Citizenship," argues that an immanent conception of moral order, in which aesthetic processes are necessary for the moral formation of citizens, is intrinsic to nationality as well as realist fiction, and underlies the particular kind of hegemonic authority claimed by realist novels. The chapter examines the nature of the aesthetic dimension of citizenship, its appearance in Egyptian political discourse from the 1920s through the 1950s, and its role in the seminal Egyptian novel *Return of the Spirit* (1933). Chapter 6, "Excess, Rebellion, and Revolution: Egyptian Modernity in the *Trilogy*," examines the immanent conception of moral order as elaborated in a celebrated novel by the Egyptian author Nagib Mahfuz, published in 1957. The chapter argues that the aesthetic dimension of citizenship as it is exploited in a novel like the *Trilogy* reveals the underlying logic of a wide range of theories of modernity. The manner in which the novel sets up the relationship between Egyptian modernity and the traditional social order from which it emerges as rooted in the human psyche shows that progressive, emancipatory theories of modernity rely on the same underlying logic as their political adversaries.

Chapter 1

Sovereign Virtue and the Emergence of Nationality

The rise of nationality in the Middle East in the late nineteenth century entailed a new way of conceiving the relationship between the individual self and social order, a new way of understanding the integration of individuals into a community that is an autonomous moral unit. This new understanding of social integration served as a primary means for imagining and legitimizing social and political ideals that we regard as characteristic of modern societies. Nationality, however, in this moral sense, did not appear ex nihilo, as a moral framework alien and inimical to existing ways of understanding the self and social order, but was necessarily launched out of existing moral ideals in a manner that made it both intelligible and persuasive. Investigating the relationship between nationality and the ideals of virtue that it drew upon and superseded not only enables us to understand the basis on which nationality emerged in the Arabic public sphere, but the moral logic of nationality as a distinctive ideal of social integration.

I propose therefore to investigate nationality in terms of its linkage with preexisting ideals of virtue and on this basis to discern the transformation that took place. I argue that discourses grounded in nationality are linked with premodern Arabic–Islamic discourses of virtue in that both posit self-sacrifice, the negation of desire, as the means of moral order and social integration. They differ, however, in their conceptions of the self and the nature of its moral order, and thus in their conceptions of the nature of social order. The key difference here hinges on the capacity of individuals to integrate into society in an ordered manner of their own accord. Premodern discourses of virtue tend to view this capacity as the by-product of an internal state of self-rule, the control and containment of one's desire, that can be attained only by very few. Therefore, social order requires a sovereign authority that controls and restrains people's desires externally. Social integration is conceived as occurring in a hierarchical order that attains fulfillment in a static equilibrium. Modern discourses of nationality, however, center on the immanence of moral order within individuals. The innate capacity of individuals for ordered social integration expresses itself spontaneously and naturally so long as it is nurtured by social institutions and not repressed or corrupted by social disorder or domination. Social integration is envisioned not hierarchically but as the inner unification of all individuals as an autonomous collective body whose agency grows without limit.

In the present chapter, I will focus on the first part of this overarching argument in order to show how the ideal of the virtuous individual could serve as the initial basis for representing an entity like Egypt or the Arabs as a self-standing collective agent for which self-sacrifice is obligatory. In subsequent chapters, I will show that the positing of the nation as an autonomous moral unit in this manner required and legitimized new ways of understanding the individuals who make up the nation. The argument here will therefore have a double-edged character. On the one hand, I will suggest that the conception of virtuous agency as self-rule made it possible to represent the nation as a collective individual. On the other hand, I outline this conception of virtue as self-rule here so as to show later how nationality entailed its transformation into a new framework of moral order. In the first part of the chapter, I argue that the classical conception of virtue as self-rule serves to justify a sovereign authority external to the ruled society. I focus particularly on the moral theory of al-Ghazali (1058–1111) and the political theory of Ibn Khaldun (1332–1406) because these theories bring out clearly and extensively the underlying logic of the concepts and doctrines of order that are pervasive in Arabic premodern discourses. In the second part of the chapter, I examine a key instance of the early representation of nationality in the political poetry of the Egyptian general, statesman and Urabist prime minister, Mahmud Sami al-Barudi (1839–1904), and more briefly, a celebrated poem by the Levantine intellectual Ibrahim al-Yaziji (1847–1906) addressed to the Arabs.

Part One: Classical Virtue and Sovereign Authority

Premodern Arabic–Islamic thought on the nature of political and social order and its relation to the self found expression in a number of discursive frameworks that were increasingly synthesized by major scholars, as we see in figures like al-Ghazali and Ibn Khaldun. These frameworks can be characterized as Islamic jurisprudence, Arabic poetry, Persianate kingship, and Greco-Islamic philosophy. I will argue that a key element in all of these is the posing of an externalized relationship between order and desire, both within the self and within the polity, such that self-rule, in both cases, is conceived as a relation between two opposing yet mutually constitutive elements. This means that sovereignty or legitimate authority is always depicted as external and hierarchically superior to that which it orders. This relation stands in contrast to typically modern representations of psychic and social order, in which order emanates directly and spontaneously from within, without any kind of externality. The classical conception of virtue has the far-reaching effect of separating reason (*'aql*), the ruling agent in the self, from the desires and impulses of empirical existence, conceived as the worldly and bodily dimension of the self (*nafs*). Reason, associated with the immutable divine realm, successfully orders the worldly self only when it is freed from the influence of this self and occupies a position external to it. This again stands in contrast to modern trends of thought in which order is expressed precisely from within and through empirical, particular features of the personality and the collective body. This contrast between externalized and immanent order, however, only leads to momentous divergences when the two orientations are drawn out in their opposing directions.

We may begin by considering how a specific ideal of political authority and governance was justified through its relation to a specific notion of the self. The overwhelming trend among premodern Islamicate writers was to attribute the necessity of political authority to the chaotic nature of individuals' errant desires (*ahwa'*) that bring about violence and disorder. The restraint imposed by the ruler, so long as it is in accordance with reason and law, orders and unifies the community.[1] We may consider a typical explanation provided by the literary figure and theologian al-Jahiz (d. 868): "Had God not established for the people restraining rulers in authority, and protecting kings and political leaders, they would have become dispersed with no order (*nizam*), and frenzied with no restrainer. The strongest would dominate, hardship would prevail, disorder, deception and barrenness predominate, to the extent that every trace of them would disappear..." It can be only under autocratic rule, al-Jahiz asserts, that "interests come together, mutual affection comes about, and the state of the community is sound. With community enmities come to an end, and errant desires abate."[2] The renowned jurist al-Mawardi (d. 1058), identifies a "dominating ruler" as the second foundation of worldly order, after religion. To illustrate his point, he cites the following verse from the poet al-Mutanabbi: "Injustice is an inborn trait of the self so that if you find one who holds back, it is from some cause that he refrains." Al-Mawardi explains, "this cause preventing injustice can only be one of four things: reason that restrains, religion that blocks, a ruler that repulses, or weakness that hinders. On reflection, you see that there is no fifth and that awe of the ruler is the most effective because reason and religion may be weakened or overcome by impulses of desire (*hawa*)..."[3] The ruler, in this outlook, is not simply external to the individuals that he governs, but to the community itself, even though rule is for the sake of this community and ultimately belongs to it. Consider the gloss given by the jurist Ibn Taymiya (1263–1328) on the nature of sovereign authority (*wilaya*): "The people are the servants of God, and rulers are the deputies of God over his servants and the trustees of his servants over themselves in the position of one partner in respect to the other. Thus [rulers] are characterized by both sovereignty (*wilaya*) and trusteeship (*wakala*)."[4] Here, the community's ordering of itself is something that it must entrust to the ruler. But this puts the ruler in the position of the deputy of God from which he exercises sovereign authority over the community, which is in turn bound to obedience.

A particularly full statement of the nature of governance is provided by the seminal scholar al-Ghazali in the context of his argument that jurisprudence (*fiqh*) is a worldly science of governance rather than a religious science per se.

> God created the world as sustenance for the journey so that what would be appropriate for sustainment could be taken from it. Had [human beings] taken of it by way of justice disputes had ceased and jurists had been idle, but they have taken it by way of lust (*shahwa*), giving rise to disputes, creating the need for a ruler (*sultan*) to govern them. The ruler requires a law (*qanun*) by which to govern them. The jurist is the one learned in the law of governance (*qanun al-siyasa*) and the manner of mediation between the people when they dispute due to lusts. The jurist is the teacher of the ruler and his guide to the means of governance of the people and containment (*dabt*) of them so that in their rectitude their worldly affairs come to order. Religion reaches completion only in worldly life. Sovereignty (*mulk*) and religion are twins. Religion is the root, and the ruler is the guardian. That which has no root is destroyed, and that which has no guardian is lost. Sovereignty and containment are attained only through the ruler and the means of containment lie in the articulation of ordinances in jurisprudence.[5]

Whether or not Islamic jurisprudence can be coherently understood in this manner, the concept of political governance (*siyasa*) as the restraint and containment of individuals' chaotic desires is clear. Governance is seen as necessary because the internal restraining powers of reason and religion fail to fulfill this task in most individuals. Without social order, religion, which is the path to salvation and happiness, cannot be fulfilled. Thus, political rule, by securing religion, ensures the possibility of the internal rule of the self.

This view of the nature of political governance should not be understood simply as the outcome of a pessimistic or severe assessment of human nature that has improved in modern times. It is connected rather with a distinct conception of what moral order within the self consists in and how this order comes about. Order, in this conception, requires the rule of one element of the ordered entity over the others.[6] The capacity of individuals to achieve virtue, or self-rule, and thereby play a role in creating social order is not spontaneous, but requires a substantial progression in knowledge and a difficult practice of self-discipline. The degree of virtue that one has attained corresponds to the degree of social authority for which one is worthy. This conception, therefore, is hierarchical in nature and is conducive to justifying a hierarchical understanding of social order and the moral status of individuals, although it does not necessarily require such an understanding. We can see the political dimension of this conception of self-rule by considering al-Ghazali's programmatic account of virtue in his work *Mizan al-'Amal*, which reproduces and expands discussions included in his celebrated *Ihya' 'Ulum al-Din*. Al-Ghazali's account is valuable in that it synthesizes the Greco-Islamic philosophical theory of the self with notions popular in juristic and literary writings.[7]

In al-Ghazali's account, justice (*'adala*) within the self, the proper order of its elements, gives rise to and corresponds with social justice. "Justice in the character of the self is necessarily attended by justice in transactions and in politics, which are branches of it."[8] When the elements of the self "come into balance, their justice issues forth to even far-removed relatives and children, and to the general inhabitants of the land" (232). The order of justice within the self corresponds to that of the polity, which becomes "like a single person," and to that of creation as a whole. "By this arrangement and justice stand the heavens and the earth so that the universe is as one individual in whom powers and parts are mutually dependent" (273). To understand social justice, therefore, it is necessary to understand the nature of psychic justice. Al-Ghazali adopts the philosophical model of the self, which derives ultimately from Plato and especially Aristotle, dividing the self into vegetative, animal, and human powers, which are further subdivided into constituent powers. The animal power of the self is responsible for bodily movement and impulses, and sensory capacities, and is defined primarily by the irascible (*ghadabiya*) and appetitive (*shahwaniya*) powers, while the human power, reason, is divided into its theoretical ('*alima*) and practical ('*amila*) powers (201–204). Order within the self leads to happiness, the state "whose pleasure is permanent, whose ease does not vanish for all eternity, which is joy in the perfection of the self with the self's virtues, particularly dominion over all through knowledge and reason" (310). Order arises through the rule of the rational power of the self over the irascible and appetitive powers. This rule is effected by the practical power of reason, which requires that it be free of the influence of the two lower powers. "When these three powers are rectified, and controlled in the proper manner and to the proper degree, and the two powers are made subservient to the third, the rational, then justice comes about. With this kind of justice the heavens and earth stand" (234). Virtues are dispositions of practical rationality to control the lusts, accompanied by dispositions of the lusts to be led by reason, while vices are dispositions of practical reason to succumb to the lusts (204). The function of practical reason is governance of the lower powers of the self as well as governance of households and polities (232, 265). Practical reason serves theoretical reason by freeing the latter to "face the angels" and acquire divine knowledge, the ultimate purpose of human life (205).

The state of virtue, therefore, is understood as freedom from the empirical, worldly dimensions of the self. This means freedom not only from bodily desires, but from all investments in one's personal, social, and historical existence. To be rational, to exercise agency, is to seek happiness, which "has no meaning but the self's achievement of the perfection possible for it" (196). This perfection lies in the liberation of the self's rational power, which binds it to what is universal, eternal, and unchanging, from enslavement to objects that provide only ephemeral and insubstantial gratifications. These objects attract and hold the self through its lower powers. Thus, "he who conquers his lusts is the one who is truly free; indeed, he is the king" (192). Happiness can only be attained "by freeing oneself from worldly attachments" ('*ala'iq al-dunya*) that include love of persons, wealth, property, power, or status (196, 391–392). This does not mean the elimination of the lower powers, because rational order consists precisely in the subordination of these powers and their objects. "The ascetic is not the one who has no wealth, but the one who is indifferent to wealth, though he may have the wealth of both worlds" (386). The lower powers and their objects may be cultivated only in so far as is necessary to preserve the rational power and no further; they are not valuable in themselves and their pleasures constitute enslavement if enjoyed for their own sake (246). Order, in other words, cannot be an intrinsic property of worldly desires and objects, but must be imposed on them externally. This view of rational agency as consisting in liberation from that which is not reason and is to be ruled by reason, creates an absolute externalization of reason from the self and empirical existence, even though reason belongs to the self as its chief power.

The externalizing conception of order is inherently hierarchical and correlates with al-Ghazali's account of social hierarchy. The virtuous self is seen as a hierarchical series of powers in which each power serves the one above it and is served by the ones below it (211). The social body is understood in the same manner. "Justice in politics is that the parts of the city be arranged in the manner corresponding to the parts of the self... The residents of the city consist of the served, those who serve, and a class which serves in one aspect and is served in another, as we mentioned regarding the powers of the self" (273). When justice obtains in the polity, "the king is perspicacious and dominating, the army is powerful and obedient, and the subjects are weak and submissive" (272). Justice within the self creates the capacity to rule over one's household and in society (265). The common people ('amma), however, are motivated by their lusts and worship their desire (hawa); very few people attain any degree of self-governance (240). Of the fundamental trades of social life, three of them—agriculture, textiles, and building—are subordinate to the fourth, political governance, which includes the externally imposed rule of Caliphs and kings as well as the internally imposed rule of scholars, sages, jurists, and preachers (329). The desire of most people for lower vocations and forms of knowledge is a necessary false consciousness, for if everyone pursued only the highest and most valuable knowledge, this pursuit would become impossible (359–360). Al-Ghazali's correlation of individual justice to social justice thus contains two fundamental dimensions. One dimension is based in the idea that order requires a ruling element, capable of realizing the end and perfection of the whole, and ruled elements, which are incapable of realizing this end but are necessary for it. The other dimension is the idea that justice is fundamentally internal order within an individual. Only when this order is attained does it contribute to effecting social justice. This stands in contrast to prevalent modern views in which innate impulses engendering social order are effective in normal individuals from the outset.

The externalizing conception of order emerges from the fundamental problem in conceiving of order and agency as a condition to which the self must bring itself. If the self begins in a state of disorder, without agency, how does it bring itself to order? If order requires the curbing of the unruly desires that constitute the self before it is an ordered agent, how are these desires curbed so that the self can come into being? The positing of reason as the definitive power of the self, distinct from the rest of the self in its immutable nature and controlling capacity, endows the self with the capacity for self-ordering. This raises the problem, however, of how reason and desire, if they are distinct and opposed in tendency and nature, are both properties of a single, noncompound entity. Al-Ghazali sees "the struggle against desire" (*mujahadat al-hawa*) as constitutive of order within the self (240). In his earlier work, *Ihya' 'Ulum al-Din*, he defines the self or soul (*nafs*) as "a divine, spiritual, subtle substance," which is "the truth of the human being and its cognitive agent."[9] The terms "heart," "spirit," and "reason," he tells us, can also be used in this sense. The term *nafs*, however, is also used in another sense, that of "the irascible and appetitive powers together," indicating "the comprehensive root of the human being's reprehensible characteristics." This is the self that must be "broken" or contained. The lower powers, however, are only regarded as a separate self in this manner from the perspective of their danger to seduce or overcome reason. Under proper control, they are necessary properties of the true self. "The virtue of reason does not appear in one who has no vehement feeling (*hamiya*)," which is the essence of the irascible power (237). Moreover, love and pleasure, defining conditions of the lower powers, are also the ultimate conditions of the true self in their proper forms. Passionate love (*'ishq*) for an individual is "folly in itself," a condition that goes beyond animality through its enslavement of reason to desire (317–318). Yet love of God, in whom lie absolute beauty and perfection, is the aim of all love, the highest pleasure, and the ultimate perfection of the self (401–402).[10] The control of reason, indeed, means the proper balancing of the two lower powers against each other, which is in itself the state of virtue. Reason rules by inducing the two powers to curb each other, "because it can do nothing more than indicate what is right" (237). The virtues themselves are nothing more than desires and impulses that are restrained to the proper extent.[11] It is therefore fundamentally the power of desire to negate itself in the proper manner that enables desire to achieve its true nature as virtue and its ultimate pleasure and fulfillment. From this perspective, reason is merely the externalization of this potentiality within desire of negating itself, the potentiality underlying human agency and selfhood.

The conception of the self outlined here, in which the self is thought to be realized through the constraining action of a rational power that rules over the self as a whole, had a substantial political dimension as has been indicated.[12] This political dimension can be understood more deeply by considering the political theory that the historian Ibn Khaldun developed from it. Ibn Khaldun held the same assumptions about the self and its relation to political order that were widespread among premodern Islamicate thinkers.[13] His distinctive contribution, however, was to propose the specifically political forms taken by chaotic desire and virtue, and to show how the former turns into the latter, thus resulting in legitimate political rule. Ibn Khaldun thereby created a premodern theory of sovereignty, that is, a theory of how morally legitimate sovereign authority comes into being.

His account demonstrates how the logic of virtue as self-governance gave rise to notions of political legitimacy differing from those arising from the logic of national representation at work in characteristically modern conceptions of political hegemony.

Ibn Khaldun, in his celebrated *Muqaddima*, develops the notion of *'asabiya*, or group feeling, as the chaotic desire whose constraint gives rise to the monarchical rule that is necessary for human civil existence. As he puts it, "human beings require in all social life a restrainer (*wazi'*) and ruler to restrain them from each other, and this can only be one who dominates them through group feeling...This domination is sovereignty."[14] For Ibn Khaldun, human beings have inherent tendencies toward injustice and disorder. Yet human social life (*'umran*), in order to reach its realized form as urban life (*hadara*) with its division of labor and institutions, requires cooperation and docility. This form of life cannot exist in his view without "some kind of autocratic rule" (2.29). The theory of group feeling explains how a social element that is restrained in itself comes into being and imposes restraint on a wider body of people, thus initiating civilization. The principle at work within group feeling, Ibn Khaldun tells us, is a general principle of nature. "The inner consistency of an entity cannot come about if its elements are equally balanced. One must be dominant, or else constitution [of the entity] cannot take place. This is the secret of the necessity of dominance within group feeling" (2.11). Such dominance is at work as well within the polity as a whole under the rule of group feeling (3.10).[15]

Sovereignty arises from the rational and virtuous capacities of human beings, which distinguish them from animals. Sovereignty is indeed the final cause or ultimate goal of human virtue (2.20). Group feeling, the basis of sovereignty, likewise comes from innate human nature (*fitra*), before this nature has attained order. The inhabitants of cities cannot produce group feeling or sovereignty because they are removed from innate human nature. Their innate nature is corrupted by the material needs and luxuries of civilization, which cultivate their lusts and desires for worldly gratification, thereby dissipating their internal forces (2.18). Moreover, the external and coercive imposition upon them of laws required for civilized life deadens their innate courage (*ba's*), which is central to group feeling (2.6). Without the internal violent forces that refuse and resist any kind of external coercion, settled peoples are incapable of generating the violent power and ambition required by sovereignty (2.19).

Savage peoples, however, those who do not live in settled urban communities, and particularly nomads, are closest to innate human nature and most characterized by group feeling (2.4, 2.7). Nomadic peoples are free from the coercive rule of a sovereign and resist such rule. They have no luxuries to corrupt their innate nature. They rely on blind group feeling within their tribes to secure their lives and livelihood. They are courageous and fierce and willing to perform self-sacrifice. For Ibn Khaldun, the more savage a people are, the greater is their capacity to dominate others (2.16). Group feeling is therefore the social correlate of innate human nature, but in this unrestrained, chaotic form it cannot give rise to sovereignty. Savage peoples, such as the nomadic Arabs, are inimical to the order and institutions of civilized life. They seek plunder above all else, and destroy civilization wherever they find it. They create "chaos without rule" (2.26). The reason is that their innate violent forces, expressed in group solidarity, have free reign, and resist externally imposed order. Such resistance is indeed, in Ibn Khaldun's account, the definitive feature of group solidarity in its natural form. Yet it is precisely the feature that makes sovereignty possible.

For Ibn Khaldun, the *telos* (*ghaya*) of group feeling is sovereignty. This inherent purpose of group feeling comes about when an internal restraining force harnesses the group feeling of a nomadic people, thus turning this group feeling into the restraining force of civilized human society. Raw group feeling, the absence of restraint in its pure form, does not spontaneously generate virtue, but is in prime condition to be captured by virtue. Raw group feeling is captured by the form of restraint that perfectly harnesses it, converting it thereby into order. This perfect restraint is religion, whose authority savage peoples readily internalize. Whereas the nomadic Arabs in their natural state are "the farthest of peoples from the governance of sovereignty" (2.28), they become, under the influence of religion, the founders of a civil polity. In their natural condition, they submit to no dominating leader and "rarely do their errant desires come together" (2.27). They seek material benefit through plunder and nothing more. "But when religion through prophecy or authority restrains them from themselves, and the traits of pride and competition leave them, they become amenable to being led and to social unity" (2.27). In other words, "religion gives them a restrainer from within themselves and causes them to protect people from one another" (2.28). It is thus innate human resistance to constraint, harnessed by the emergence of internal restraint, that makes virtue, sovereign authority, and social order possible. Virtue and sovereignty are synonymous in that sovereignty is the outward expression of the internal order that is virtue. Thus, "men of group feeling," that is, political rulers, are characterized by virtue which enables them to exercise "the deputyship of God among humanity" (2.20). The decay of virtue in a line of rulers signals the dissolution of their sovereignty (2.15).[16]

The principle of externalized order is the basis of Ibn Khaldun's theory of sovereign authority, as he himself indicates, and of the relationship between virtue and social hierarchy. The order of the civilized polity as a whole comes from the group feeling of the ruling group. The order within this group comes from a sub-group, a clan or "house" whose internal group feeling enables it to exercise leadership over the group as a whole. Without this dominance of one sub-group over the rest, group feeling among the group as a whole cannot come about (2.11). The leader of this sub-group, to whom the others defer, is the sovereign. The internal order of the sovereign, as well as of the ruling group as a whole, comes either from reason alone, or from religion. At every stage, order is externalized as a distinct element linked to a higher power. Yet this higher power must at the same time be located within. Rule that is purely external and coercive is inimical to virtue and to courage, which enables the expression of virtue.

The central, highly original feature of Ibn Khaldun's theory is the way in which primordial human nature, in the form of group feeling, is made the origin of virtue and sovereignty on a political level, such that when the original connection to innate nature that founded the polity has withered (by a dynasty's fourth generation), the polity must reach its demise. In al-Ghazali's account of virtue, the active power of virtue comes from its nature as desire that has been ordered but not extinguished. The power to act virtuously arises from the appetitive and irascible powers, but these powers continually threaten to exceed the order of reason. Their power when constrained is the result of the harnessing of their inherent disorder. Ibn Khaldun moves this relationship to the social level by deriving sovereign order from the innate human nature exhibited by savage peoples. As soon as the chaotic violence of savage individuals is provided with "an internal restrainer," they impose order on themselves and on other peoples and create a polity. The civilized life of the polity, however, removes the rulers from the primordial condition and progressively weakens their courage as well as their virtue. By the fourth generation, the contact with innate human nature that characterized the founders is fully lost, and sovereign power is lost alongside it. Ibn Khaldun identifies the courage of group feeling with the lower powers of the soul (3.25). In citied life, however, the lower powers are not in their primal condition, from which group feeling arises, but in a corrupt and blunted condition. For this reason, "urban life is the limit of human social life and its decline into corruption" (2.4). The externalizing conception of order necessarily envisions a static, hierarchical ordered state. When the proper hierarchy of powers or elements has come about, equilibrium and perfection are reached and no higher state of order is possible. In al-Ghazali's account of virtue, no human being aside from a prophet or saint can fully reach this state in this world. Ibn Khaldun creates on the political level, through the mechanism of group feeling, a multigenerational cycle in which at the very moment that perfection is attained, dissolution begins.

In the accounts of both al-Ghazali and Ibn Khaldun, moral order is constituted through the harnessing of chaotic powers lying within human nature. This relationship is fundamental within the Arabic poetic tradition as well, but is represented in a different manner. In the foregoing accounts, the harnessing of the chaotic powers is effected by a power or principle within the self that is conceived as having an external relation to the powers that it orders. If we consider the Abbasid panegyric *qasida* (ode), which provided the poetic model for the Arabic poetic resurgence in the late nineteenth and early twentieth centuries, we find that the relationship between order and desire is represented not through the isolation of a single power or principle within the self, but through a structural dialectic of desire and order. Poems of praise of the Abbasid era, composed for Caliphs and lesser figures of political authority and declaimed in formal courtly settings, consist primarily of two parts. In the first part, the *nasib*, the poet grieves the ending of a love affair. The second part, the *madih*, is the praise of the political figure. These two parts are connected through the antithesis between the desolation of failed desire and the fulfillment of sovereign moral order. Stefan Sperl describes the Abbasid panegyric poem as "a formal testimony of the legitimacy of political authority. In its movement from chaos to order, from affliction to deliverance, from isolation to integration, the glory of the social order is proclaimed."[17] In terms of the relationship between the beloved and the ruler in these poems, Sperl says the following: "In the ruler, all the failings of the beloved are countered by virtues, all her virtues sublimated by higher virtues. In turning to him, the individual leaves behind a sorrowful and potentially destructive passion in favor of integration into a justly ruled society."[18] Desire, then, gives way to the justice produced by the ruler's virtue. This justice or virtue is external to desire insofar as they are depicted as antithetical states with opposing outcomes. Yet at the same time, desire is the necessary substrate of virtue. Whereas the poet, in the state of desire, experiences absence of self-control, the untrammeled release of his inner forces, the ruler's justice derives precisely from the mastery and containment of these forces, ultimately embodied in the self-sacrifice that underlies all of the ruler's virtues. Likewise, the poet's desire, awakened by the beloved, cannot be fulfilled except through its constraint in submission to the ruler's order. Love plays the same role here that the lower self plays in al-Ghazali's account of virtue and that group feeling plays in Ibn Khaldun's political theory. All three serve as the underlying, chaotic force whose mastery creates order. The difference here is that what is externalized is not reason or religion in themselves, but the person of the ruler or sovereign figure in his virtuous state. The *qasida* indeed served as a primary means of representing such an individual in many periods of Islamic history.[19]

Part Two: Classical Virtue and Collective Sovereignty

I refer to the externalizing conception of order examined above, in which social order has its origin in the internal order of a virtuous, sovereign figure, as "classical virtue." I mean by this that over a number of centuries, this conception of order and the set of concepts that constituted it retained a normative centrality in many Islamic discourses. Normative change took place in the manner that these overarching concepts were given content and used to justify less abstract norms of political and social order. But it is evident that over many centuries, writers made recourse to a specific set of concepts, a specific model of order, which then underwent rapid alteration in the latter part of the nineteenth century. The aim here is to explain what kind of change took place at this abstract, yet fundamental level. What does it mean that this long-standing set of concepts suddenly transformed into an entirely new conceptual framework of political, social, and moral order? For a sense of the persistence of classical virtue, consider the definition of justice given by the Egyptian historian Abd al-Rahman al-Jabarti (1753–1825), in the early nineteenth century, in his discussion of political and social order in the introduction to his monumental history of Egypt.

> As for the meaning of justice (*'adala*), it is a moral trait of the self, or a character of the soul, which brings about balance, as it is the most perfect of the virtues due to the comprehensiveness of its effect and generality of its utility over all things. The human being is called just in that God has granted him a portion of his justice and made him a means of spreading the abundance of his excellence, and made him his deputy on earth in this capacity so that he may rule among the people in truth and justice.[20]

Al-Jabarti does not deviate in any way from the kind of account given by al-Ghazali and others, attributing the necessity of kingship to the conflict of passions that left to itself would eliminate social order, and affirming a hierarchical social order sustained by figures characterized by internal justice—prophets, scholars, and rulers.[21] Al-Jabarti deploys this model of order to explain and evaluate the actions of elite figures in his society. He can do so only because he takes his fundamental concepts of order to be completely continuous with the more concrete norms of the Mamluk order of his time.

Over the course of the nineteenth century, however, in Egypt and elsewhere, increasing centralization of political administration, the growth of bureaucratic and professional classes, and the formation of centralized public spheres enabled the rise of social discourses that began to invest sovereign attributes of ordering and agency in the social body as a whole. The idea that these attributes ultimately belong to the community had already been present. But sovereignty had been conceived as requiring an externalized figure for its enactment. As social transformation during the course of the nineteenth century progressed, aspirations for social and political reform as well as the new possibilities of ideological articulation arising in the public sphere encouraged the address of society as a moral body that can take actions of its own accord. The idea that the social body is meant to be and act as "a single man" became increasingly prevalent by the end of the nineteenth century. The following example is taken from the anticolonial, anti-British newspaper *al-'Urwa al-Wuthqa*, which was edited by Jamal al-Din al-Afghani and Muhammad Abduh in Paris and clandestinely distributed in various Muslim countries during the year 1884.[22] "The virtues are characteristics of the self that bring about composition and harmony among those who possess them... The virtues are the linchpin of oneness within the social body (*al-hay'a al-ijtima'iya*) and the bond of unity among individuals... such that the mass of people becomes like one of their number, moving with one will and seeking in its movement one goal."[23] This is a frequent theme in the articles of *al-'Urwa al-Wuthqa*, and its aim is to depict the Muslim community as a sovereign collective unit in the manner of a nation whose goal is political dominance.[24]

This raises the question of how collective entities came to be represented as sovereign moral units commanding absolute allegiance. On what basis could an entity like "Egypt" or "the Arabs" come to be conceived as a unified moral agent on the model of a single individual? How could such an entity be depicted as creating the obligation of self-sacrifice? Political poetry of the period shows how the traditional conception of virtue could be invested in a collective entity. The political poems of al-Barudi, on which I will focus, depict an Egyptian community whose authentic condition lies in being a collective moral agent. They do so by linking the moral order of the self—virtue and justice—with the political condition of Egypt. Unlike the hierarchical conceptions of communal order seen previously, in which order is conceived as the proper sequence of subordination within the community, we see in al-Barudi's poems an investment of the ordering capacity in the community as a whole, a community that is Egyptian. This is significant because it is a first step in conceiving of a nation that is an autonomous, self-ordering entity. Al-Barudi's poems show the centrality of the moral process within the self—the conversion of desire into order—in depicting an incipient nationality. The nature of this process was to be transformed in the subsequent development of nationality. Yet the underlying necessity of converting desire into order remained central.

Al-Barudi is credited with founding modern Arabic poetry by rehabilitating the classical Arabic *qasida* primarily as a poetry of public self-display in the context of Khedival Egypt.[25] A member of the Turco-Circassian ruling elite, al-Barudi was an important player in the hothouse of Egyptian politics during the period culminating in the so-called Urabi revolt.[26] Favored by the Khedive Isma'il from the outset of his reign in 1863, al-Barudi "belonged to the inner circle of the ruling class at a young age."[27] He served as a military officer, awarded the rank of brigadier general after the Russo–Turkish war in 1878. He also held the posts of Adjutant-General to the crown-prince Tawfiq (1873) and private secretary to the Khedive Isma'il (1875), before holding ministerial posts during the period of the Urabi crisis, and serving as prime minister in the constitutionalist government of 1882.[28] Unlike his peers of the ruling elite, he threw in his lot with the Urabists, and after the British invasion and defeat of the Egyptian forces, was exiled to Ceylon in 1882.[29]

Al-Barudi's political persona and ambitions are closely connected to the persona cultivated in his poems, both as a heroic figure in war and romance and as a rouser of his community before the onslaught of tyranny. Husayn al-Marsafi, in his then seminal work on Arabic language and rhetoric, *al-Wasila al Adabiya*, published in 1875, presented al-Barudi as an *amir*, or princely/military leader, who, having taught himself the art of poetry, had taken up a poetic style in the tradition of Abu Firas al-Hamdani and al-Sharif al-Radiy, celebrated poet-princes belonging to Arabic literature's bygone age of glory.[30] Al-Barudi and his form of heroic self-representation took their shape in the new social environment created by Muhammad Ali's and Isma'il's initiatives. The incipient Arabophone public sphere, more evident in this period in a burgeoning salon culture than in print media, constituted the social space in which a poetry of self-display could arise.[31] The literary gatherings held at private homes, as well as the various sorts of societies then emerging, formed perhaps the primary venue for the mixing of Turco–Circassian elites with "native" Egyptians in anything approaching a common society. During his career in Egypt, al-Barudi was involved in the intellectual and ideological ferment that took place in the years leading up to the British take over. He held a salon at his house in Cairo during the 1870s, frequented by the luminaries of the day.[32] He was involved in appointing Muhammad Abduh, editor of the official government newspaper, *al-Waqa'i' al-Misriya*, and the two were lifelong friends. Al-Barudi also counted the prominent writer and courtier Abdullah Fikri, and the leading Arabic scholar and teacher Husayn al-Marsafi, among his intimates. Al-Barudi's cultivation of Arabic poetry and his links with Egyptian intellectuals, in addition to his close association with Ahmad Urabi and the Urabist military officers, show that his political aspirations were connected with the rising Egyptian classes rather than with his own Turko–Circassian elite.

In his poetry, modeled on the genres of classical Arabic poetry, al-Barudi depicts himself as a heroic figure who embodies but is external to the social order. His entitlement to political authority arises from his capacity to exhibit desire in its unbounded, externally undetermined form, and at the same time to display the mastery of desire that constitutes order. Through this capacity of self-sacrifice, this harnessing of the power that both threatens society and makes it possible, the virtuous, sovereign figure is ideally capable of keeping society in order. Such a figure is denied political authority only when society is enslaved under the rule of tyranny. The distinctive feature of the poems to be examined here is that the moral order demonstrated by the poet is demanded as well of the community that the poems address. The poet addresses his audience as men who have succumbed to tyranny and enslavement. By heeding the poet's call to overthrow this tyranny, these men will come into being as a corporate body that replicates the moral order and agency of the poet. Egypt in this scenario is not the corporate body itself, the men addressed by the poet, but the entity upon which order is to be imposed by this corporate body. The investment of the ordering capacity in the community is depicted as the capacity and obligation to impose order upon Egypt. In this way, Egypt defines the agency of the corporate body, but only as that upon which this agency is enacted. Al-Barudi's political poetry, then, preserves the traditional depiction of externally imposed moral order while showing its role within an emergent nationality.

We may consider in this regard a poem al-Barudi glosses as "treating of injustice under the despotic government," probably composed either in the latter part of Khedive Isma'il's reign in the late 1870s, or shortly before or during the Urabist split from the Khedive Tawfiq in 1882. It is unclear how wide an audience a poem like this would have had beyond al-Barudi's circle of like-minded friends, which included government officials and intellectuals. Given that the poem's target is not the Khedive himself, but certain unnamed members of the government, and considering the widespread vituperation of government policies even in the press in the period before the Urabi crisis, it is not inconceivable that such poetry may have been widely circulated. The poem follows the structure and conventions of the classical formal ode (*qasida*). It begins with a *nasib*, the conventional lament of love and lost youth, then condemns the condition of tyranny and submission prevailing in Egypt, and closes with a vision of an impending war that will feast on "the hearts of despotic men." The poem's *nasib* is not simply an imitative obeisance to the protocols of classical poetry. It employs canonical motifs of nostalgia and erotic disillusionment to display the desire whose containment is central to the poetic depiction of self-mastery. Here is how the poem begins:

> I settle with what I don't want from this world,
> For what man can lift his arm against fate?
> I seek love's fulfillment but find barriers to entry.
> I want loyalty, but it is contrary to nature.
> I thought love would be easy, not knowing
> its betrayals, how its sport gives way to gravity.
> Sober self-control becomes weightless before it;
> the most obstinate defense submits to it.
> It is astonishing that a rational man
> follows passion just where it contradicts his sense.
> He flees from the ease of solace
> To take refuge in grinding sorrow.
> Love is but an unjust ruler
> who finds none that can thwart his command.
> His army is soldiered by the lovely and tender;
> his troops invade the soul's inner sanctum. (1–8)

To understand the logic behind the depiction of love in this political poem, it is necessary to consider the model of the self that the *nasib* is based upon. In this model, desire is an impulse within the self seeking absolute release, complete freedom from the constraints of the self and its worldly contingencies. In everyday life, however, release from these constraints is impossible. Objects of desire, even if accessible, are necessarily inadequate and thus fail to provide the feeling of completion. The impossibility of attaining fulfillment is experienced as fate, an external power that perpetually thwarts the self. Not only are the external constraints on desire experienced as fate, but empirical desires themselves are forces of fate because they cause enslavement to objects that cannot provide fulfillment and eliminate the sense of lack. Subjection to such errant desires is the condition of ordinary existence, life in "this world" (*al-dunya*).

Passionate love (*hawa*), however, offers liberation from the constrained desire of empirical existence through the absolute release of desire into the beloved. This absolute release of desire is a state of fulfillment and bliss. Love is an "unjust ruler," in the sense that it enslaves the self, but this is an enslavement into which the lover enters willingly and completely. As a result of the lover's absolute release of desire, he is freed from rationality and its constraints, which is to say, from all boundaries of the self. This release and fulfillment provided by love, however, is temporary and illusory. It is subject to fate and death like all other empirical attachments and exposes the poet to death through its dissolution of his self, and to painful sorrow when the beloved is lost. Yet love nevertheless escapes the worldly sense of incompletion and reveals the inner truth of desire as desire for immortality and perfection. This is why, after reaching the dead end of love, and advising others to stay away from it, the poet emphasizes his own failure to do so: "I was the one most in need of this advice, if only my heart had listened, but its pursuit went counter to prudence" (16). The blissful total release of desire results in discontent with everyday existence: "I demand from my days (i.e. fate) what they don't have. And whoever seeks what doesn't exist will be incapable of finding it" (25). The experience of the disorder of ordinary existence, its inherent incapacity to complete the self, sets the poet apart from others. Those who are cowardly and inhibited attempt to content themselves with whatever the world offers them. They remain enslaved to fate and embody the characteristics of fate—mutability, betrayal, degeneration. Since they are too timid to engage in the abandonment of love, they merely make do with the factitious pleasures held in esteem in their particular time and place, while abiding by whatever arbitrary constraints are imposed on them. They thus slowly dissipate, unaware, unto death.

The poet then, because he is willing and capable of complete release in love, is in a position to achieve true freedom as the liberation from desire through self-mastery. Moral order—virtue, justice, reason—consists in the restraint of desire in such a way that it fully turns into order. In other words, it enables desire to achieve fulfillment in its own state of order, so that the self no longer experiences desire for anything outside it, bringing an end to any form of enslavement to fate. Moral order can only exist if desire is implicitly disposed to be ordered in this manner. Therefore, order is the truth of desire but at the same time the opposite of desire as chaos. The resulting paradox is fundamental to the process of self-mastery: the fulfillment of desire is its own negation. Not an arbitrary negation, but one that takes place in accordance with the inner truth of desire, so that it results in the transformation of ordinary, insatiable desire, into an inexhaustible plenitude of order. When desire seeks its own negation, its transformation into order, it becomes free of itself and the self is born as an agent impervious to tyranny. Moral order, therefore, is the truth of the self, the higher state of being to which we all aspire. Orientation toward this moral order is inherently self-sacrifice.

As a result of his enslavement to love that turns into mastery over it, and his resulting condition of freedom from desire, the poet attains a position of moral order external to society that allows him to identify what is wrong with the world as it exists and how to rectify it. In other words, he is able to recognize tyranny and perceive its true nature.

> If I am discontented, it is after companioning an age
> in which the slave angers the free man.
> This age has refused but that its lowest rule,
> and that its scoundrel hold all the keys to success.
> Its foxes among us are howling for blood,
> While its lions, entitled to it, lie sleeping.
> How long shall we stumble in the gloom of persecution,
> while the sword cannot bear its scabbard's confinement?
> If a man does not repulse the grasping hand of oppression,
> let him not weep when it takes his honor.
> Whoever lives abased due to fear of death, his life
> is more noxious to him than his hour of death.
> The most fatal disease is a tyrant in plain sight
> who works ill and whose praises are then sung.
> Why should a man live his time undistinguished—
> does he take joy from the day he spends in the world?
> He sees injustice assail him and delights in it
> like a mangy dog that finds pleasure in scratching.
> If a man faced by a torrent does not turn
> to a solid anchor for protection, he will be swept away.
> To hell with the world if a man cannot live
> heroically, defending truth in battle...
> A defiant soul refuses me any burden of injustice,
> and a heart whose embers flare when compelled to suffer. (33–46)

The poet's denunciation of the condition in which he lives shows his freedom from this condition. He is free because he is willing to die. His willingness to die is the manifestation of his successful negation of desire. These lines pivot on a key trope in the rhetoric of selfhood: fear of death leads to true death, while the willingness to die enables life. Because his desire is properly ordered, the poet is no longer bound to ordinary pleasures. He is no longer enslaved to the limits and desires of his ordinary bodily and social self. Attachment to these results in death, while willingness to give them up confers immortality—subsumption in what is permanent and unchanging, moral order. Al-Barudi generally does not bother to give this principle much content. Here he calls it "truth" (*al-haqiqa*), meaning what is real or actual, as opposed to the chimerical pursuits of disordered desire. Elsewhere he calls it virtue, glory, justice, and reason. It protects one from the "flood" of tyranny, that is, one's own desires, through self-sacrifice in its name. Self-sacrifice through and for the sake of this principle is the opposite of living an undistinguished, insignificant life (*khumul*), contenting oneself with the pleasures offered by ordinary existence, and then dying. Fear of death, therefore, underlies the dissipation of desire in inauthentic pleasures, and thus makes tyranny possible.

The poet's externality and freedom is restated in terms of his social origin. "I am propelled to heights by a lineage whose roots are entrenched in glory and whose star of fortune sparkles" (49). The poet is from a good family, but on an epic scale. His social group has maintained the heroic values necessary for the proper ordering of desire. His people form a free community that determines itself through its fashioning of succeeding generations in its own image. "When one is born among us, his milk is the blood of lions, and thoroughbred stallions his cradle. If he lives, wild deserts are his abode. If he dies, he is left for the vultures" (49, 50). Danger and death in the wilderness, repudiation of any fixed abode or social emplacement is their way of life. The poet attributes to his ancestry, his filiation from this group, his rejection of "the nearer goal," and his aspiration for what is "distant beyond the reach of flight" (51). His social group, therefore, is removed from the condition of society set out in the lines quoted above, untouched by the prevailing moral deformation. It has escaped fate. For this reason, the poet's group has no stake in the petty disputes and corrupt power struggles that attract everyone's attention. The external position occupied by the poet's group affirms his entitlement to sovereign status.

The identity with moral order attained by the poet through the negation of desire is not merely personal, but political. The order that regulates his being is to regulate his society as well. The poet envisions his community as having a self modeled on his own. This is apparent in the lines quoted above, which depict tyranny and enslavement as a moral condition arising from fear of death. We can examine the implications of this collective self more closely by looking at a poem that pictures it in greater resolution. The purpose is served by a more elaborate poem, also calling for political rebellion, said by the author to have been composed during the reign of the Khedive Isma'il, presumably not long before his deposition in 1879. This poem begins not with a *nasib*, but with an anti-*nasib*: an immediate disavowal of passion and assertion of self-mastery. "No belle has diverted me from the pursuit of glory—the pleasure of awareness supersedes that of drunkenness" (4). The anti-*nasib* establishes that the mastery of the self has already taken place, putting the poet in a position outside of the disorder that surrounds him.

> I have sucked out the marrow of this age in experience,
> and I have tasted what it has, bitter and sweet,

And I have found nothing that endures the passage of time
more delightful to the soul than freedom of action.
But we are the quarry of evil in a time
in which those with sense must obey those with none.
An age ruled by a base company,
more painful to the soul than the misery of bereavement;
Scoundrels fit to be spat out of office
and barred from responsibility out of contempt.
After glory, Egypt has been by them abased,
the foundations of its sovereignty disturbed and unsound.
The Cairene state has been brought low
after nobility—what was once a resplendent state.
A band of men who, when they see me approaching
fall silent in anger, their gall boiling in hatred.
If my virtue galls them it is no wonder,
for the shining sun is blinding to the eye.
I am above all that they soil themselves in—
the honey bee scorns the depravity of the dung-beetle.
How wretched a company and how wretched a land Egypt,
become a play-ground for every swindler and prattler;
A land entrenched in tyranny, stricken
from mountain to sea by lightening-bolts of treachery;
Its people enveloped in a black blindness,
in which none can move without stumbling. (19–31)

These lines introduce their depiction of Egypt's political plight by identifying the principle of order that the poet has discovered through his travails as "freedom of action." Apparently, this is something that would obtain under a consultative, constitutional government, if we take the criticisms then being leveled at the Khedive Ismaʻil as our guide. "Freedom of action" is the moral freedom that is impossible in the present circumstances because society is disordered. Egypt is ruled by a band of self-serving scoundrels who have sunk it in an abyss of tyranny. The poem relies here on the classical poetic motif of the "age" (*al-dahr, al-zaman*). The "age" is the corrupt era in which one has had the misfortune to be born, an era in which nothing is as it should be—there is no love, sincerity, loyalty, etc. Talent is not recognized, and meretricious mediocrity is exalted. Everyone pursues his self-interest and fends for himself; no one shows compassion for anyone else, except when it is advantageous. The "age" is the same as fate. Both are designated by the same words. Al-Barudi politicizes the motif by aligning it with a specific ruling order and the policies it pursues. Employing the related motifs of lampoon poetry (*hijaʼ*), he excoriates the leaders of the government. He shows them to be the manifestation of fate by investing them with the characteristics of chaotic desire—particularly fear, greed, inconstancy. As slaves of the age, they are the hand of fate that prevents the social self from achieving fulfillment. This segment of society will disappear when the social self returns to order.

Since society has the form of an incomplete self, one that has not yet achieved agency, the effects of tyranny and enslavement are dispersed throughout. Tyranny and enslavement arise from the same reality. The tyrants are actually slaves. Their apparent willfulness is the passivity of chaotic desire, enslavement to fate. The slaves suffer the same condition. Their master is also fate, which is embodied in the tyrannical rulers. Here is al-Barudi's description, in the same poem, of the people of Egypt:

> Out of cowardice and weakness, they do not repulse
> a hand that violates their honor;
> They fear death and plot against it knowing not
> that death cannot be stayed by plotting;
> How can one accuse his creator,
> when every soul is destined to die?
> Never can a man find peace and pleasure
> without having plunged into a sea of fear. (34–37)

Here again, as in the first poem, al-Barudi invokes the motifs of enslavement to characterize those under the rule of tyranny. Again, fear of death is responsible for their condition. The essence of this condition is indicated in the first line. The word that I have translated as "honor" is "*'afafa,*" more literally, "chastity." The sense is therefore sexual violation, the metonym for any outrageous transgression of the boundaries of the self. The slave lacks honor, meaning that the boundaries of his self are permeable. The site of his moral identity, his self-restraint, which is the underlying meaning of *'afafa*, has no integrity. What should be inviolable is open to violation. His self commingles with its surroundings instead of forming a sealed, autarkic monad. Hence he has no agency, "self-control," for which he compensates by adopting fatalism. Devoting his life to the avoidance of discomfort and death, he "accuses his creator" for his dying condition, his suffering in servitude, when the real fatality is what he brings upon himself through passivity. The clichés of enslavement—ignorance, fatalism, cowardice, and selfishness—are all bound up in the exposed, improperly contained selfhood of dissipation.

The purpose of the poem, however, is not to denigrate the poet's political constituency. It is rather to represent this constituency to itself as a self. The inhabitants of Egypt cannot remain slaves. They must undergo, collectively, a process of self-mastery equivalent to the one undergone by the poet. They must realize their true identity, their identity with virtue, and at the same time with Egypt, through negation of desire. The image of this identity that lies within themselves is the memory of their virtuous forefathers.

> Why then do your souls not scorn to be wronged?
> Why do you indolently suffer unceasing affliction?
> While before you is Egypt, in which war made to perish
> the noblest of your forebears in ancient times;
> A race of men who planted the pillars of truth and held
> reign over mankind, rich and poor;
> They harvested the fruits of greatness with gleaming swords
> and plucked the mountain flower of hope from among thorns;
> Egypt came to flower after lying fallow
> drenched by showers of fresh dew.
> The earth did not sprout until it was leavened
> with blood spilled from necks put to the sword;
> They waged a campaign so frightful it made
> a peace that reconciled the wolf and the lamb;
> Until Egypt became an impregnable fortress
> able to fend off the hand of any foreign enemy.
> Time brought low her champions, and she became,
> after being unassailable, trampled upon by every wayfarer.
> What ignominy do you now bring through lack of ambition
> upon that glory raised to heaven by the sword—
> For if a man has no rational faculty by which to live
> let him then be counted among cows and sheep.
> So take the matter into your hands, before it escapes you,
> and break off the chains of sloth—the world is won with haste. (38–49)

The image of the heroic ancestors and their deeds shows the community as it ought to exist and as it once existed: a collective body constituted through the imposition of order upon Egypt. The poem depicts self-mastery in terms of war. Violence is directed against those who, like the government chiefs denounced above, embody fate through their enslavement to it. They are the tyrants and exploiters who enforce the enslavement of the nation. To oppose them is to conquer fate, to overcome one's fear of death, or in other words, to act against one's own chaotic desire. The sacrifice of the agents of tyranny therefore is an instance of the conquest of desire that brings the self into existence at both the individual and communal levels. The manifestations of achieving existence and agency are peace, prosperity, power, civilization. The community becomes the subject of history instead of remaining its victim. War is the prime metaphor for this process because it most vividly portrays the extirpation of disorder through willingness to die, self-sacrifice for the sake of the community, which is the foundation of social virtue (*himma*). Social virtue, the desire to achieve permanence, glory, power, for the self and the community, is the opposite of the lack of ambition (*khumul*), the undistinguished, complacent life of slavery that results from fear of death. Willingness to die is already death—death of the ordinary self of everyday life through its subsumption in its true identity. In this sense, self-mastery is inherently violent—an externally imposed order, either directly upon the self, or indirectly through the struggle against the forces of enslavement.

Self-mastery is a self-contradiction. Virtue cannot exist by itself, as a self-contained state of being. It is the effect of the restraint of chaotic desire. Therefore, desire can never be fully subsumed into virtue. The two must always be simultaneously present. We see this in al-Barudi's depiction in the lines above, which makes the community that is addressed and Egypt two separate entities. The collective moral agent will come into being through the imposition of order upon Egypt. At present, Egypt is the victim of tyranny, "trampled upon by every wayfarer." The truth of Egypt, however, is to be an "impregnable fortress," a "resplendent state," a peaceful, fertile land. The present condition of Egypt reflects the moral condition of its inhabitants, yet at the same time, the authentic nature of Egypt calls upon the Egyptian community to restore it. In this depiction, Egypt has the status of the desire of the self that is to be ordered and the community addressed by the poet has the status of the agent within the self that is to impose order. What has actually taken place, however, is that the poem has separated the Egyptians it addresses into two manifestations of themselves—one that is passive and enslaved, that is, the present, and the other the potential collective moral agent that once existed in the past. It is only on the basis of dividing the community into that which orders and that which is to be ordered that the poem can invest the Egyptian community with the form of moral order that the poet displays in himself.

Vanquishing tyranny, therefore, is the self-conquest that brings the collective self into being. Even when the tyrant is an "external" usurper that has enslaved the community, an "other," this tyrant is nevertheless nothing more than an emanation of the internal dissipation of the communal self, which for this reason has not yet come into being. Consider the celebrated poem, "Awaken and take heed O Arabs," composed by the Levantine intellectual Ibrahim al-Yaziji in 1883, and distributed clandestinely.[33] This poem is credited with being a founding proclamation of Arab nationalism and its opening verse was made by George Antonius the epigraph of his 1938 book, *The Arab Awakening*. Calling upon the Arabs to recognize their condition of degradation and servitude and rise up against their Turkish overlords, the poem employs the same rhetoric of tyranny and enslavement that we have seen in al-Barudi. In language and form, the poem is classically derived in the manner of al-Barudi's poems and contains many of the same motifs. The primary difference is that in al-Yaziji's poem, the poet's presence is limited to the prophetic voice that occupies the stand-point of virtue and authentic identity, outside of the current condition of the community. Turkish tyranny, in this poem, is the correlate of the current dissolution of the Arab collective self. The poem establishes this Arab collective self by investing Arabness with the externality of traditional virtue, as can be seen in the following passage.

> Your status in the eyes of the Turks is debased,
> And your right by the hands of the Turks is usurped.
> You possess no known stature or honor,
> Nor any existence, or name, or title.
> O to my people and my people are none but the Arabs—
> And never will that identity be lost to them.
> Suppose that you have among you no man of status
> To be given command or endowed with rank,
> Nor any man of resolve and experience,
> To be chosen for setting and unsetting commandments,
> Nor any man of knowledge to adjudicate
> The rules of law though from you came the books,
> Have you no blood ever riled by indignation,
> To fight off this ignominy when it arises?...
> You have nothing left too dear to part with
> Aside from selves sunk in abasement,
> So leap at death and find comfort in it
> From the life of one who dies a death of suffering.[34]

In these verses, the external position of sovereignty that would normally be occupied by a man of virtue capable of imposing order upon the community is placed by the poet within the community itself. The community, which does not exist as a collective moral self in the condition of tyranny and enslavement, is to come into existence, impose order upon itself, by answering the call of its Arabness. This Arabness is the indignation inflamed by injustice. In other words, the capacity to impose order through negating desire for mere existence and bodily sustenance, that is, the capacity for self-sacrifice, lies in Arabness. Therefore, even if the Arabs have no sovereign figures to enact order, this order can be enacted by them collectively by virtue of their collective nature. The Arabs enact moral order and realize their Arabness by dying for for it, by sacrificing their empirical selves, whose correlate is the Turkish tyrant.

The poems of al-Barudi and al-Yaziji show how the conception of order as self-mastery or self-governance was invested in a collective body through the representation of this collective body as an individual agent. The proto-nations that they represent are not fully nations because they consist wholly in the investment of a country or ethnic group with an intrinsic love of virtue. Nationality here is a bare moral command whose sole mode of expression is the rejection of tyranny on a collective level. On the individual level there is no mechanism by which Egyptian identity or Arab identity lifts one into virtue. The manner in which the poet in al-Barudi's poems attains moral order has nothing to do with Egyptianness and is inherently heroic and exceptional in its nature. It is only on the model of this heroic virtue that the nation, as a whole, is shown as attaining virtue and agency in its struggle against tyranny. Since the conception of order in these poems is an external order that is imposed on chaotic desire, there must be something that embodies this chaotic desire. The embodiment exists only on the collective level as the tyrannical usurper and the present condition of enslavement. In other words, it is possible to represent the true nation as external to its present condition of dissolution. But it is not possible to represent an individual member of the nation as external, because the nation is a collective unit that produces its own order. Therefore, these poems project a national self modeled on the man of sovereign virtue, but create a contradiction on the level of the ordinary individuals who make up this national self. Nevertheless, it is only after it has been accepted that the nation is a self, an autonomous moral agent, that this contradiction becomes problematic.

Chapter 2

The Death of the Hero and the Birth of Bourgeois Class Status

By the beginning of the twentieth century, the emerging urban professional and bureaucratic classes characterized by their Western education and Western bourgeois attire (with the important addition of the Fez) had come to occupy a central position in the Egyptian social order by virtue of their domination of the expanding public sphere and of many levels of government bureaucracy. These individuals, who came to be known collectively as the "*efendiya*," enjoyed, as can be seen by this unofficial titular designation, an elevated social status. The most prominent members of this group could come from or intermingle with the large land-owning families, acquire official titles, and occupy high offices of government. Yet at the same time, after the rapid expansion of government schools beginning in the 1920s, the "*efendiya*" came also to be associated with the modest circumstances of the petty bureaucrat or clerical employee.[1] Nevertheless, members of the *efendiya* retained and continued to promote a class status founded on a putative relationship between bourgeois attributes and national representation. The publicizing of bourgeois class status is evident from the end of the nineteenth century. It is seen particularly in the print media in calls for the establishment of bourgeois norms of familial relations and domestic life, as well as of personal education, sentiments, and behavior, and especially in the association of these norms with national revival and progress.[2] The key elements here are the ideal of the conjugal family centered on companionate marriage, and the ideal of self-ordering, autonomous citizens who together form a national "public." Bourgeois class publicity appears as well in the proliferation of charitable and social-service societies, the press attention that such societies received, and the public functions and ceremonies that they convened.³ And it is seen in the rise of prominent, public funeral ceremonies held in honor of bourgeois figures who were depicted in funeral orations and elegies as responsible for the rebirth of the nation through their activity within the public sphere and their exemplary moral attributes.

The emergence of bourgeois class status inaugurated a new form of publicity based not in the exalted personal status of princely figures, but in the projected capacity of a sector of society defined by a set of attributes to represent the order and agency of society as a whole. Through their own being and activity as a class, the *efendiya* purported to reveal to the social community its own inner nature—that is, to make public (manifest) that which is public (belonging to the community as a moral whole). Unlike the Khedive, who was conventionally depicted as embodying this capacity in his person, the *efendiya* embodied it through attributes of moral order that were required of and supposedly attainable by all individuals. The source of bourgeois universality was thus represented as immanent to the social body, rather than hierarchically external to it. This contrast signifies a shift in the nature of publicity and its relation to the social body. It makes possible a form of publicity that is perpetually enacted in a public sphere by the social body as a whole rather than a kind of publicity that appears intermittently in ritualized and spectacular forms.

To understand the nature of the new form of publicity and the bourgeois class status legitimized through such publicity, it is necessary to examine its emergence from then-existing forms of publicity. The universality claimed by members of the *efendiya* for the attributes of their class cannot be attributed to an objective class position within a historical trajectory of social development that would actually endow this class with universality. The *efendiya*, like the "bourgeoisie" or the "middle class," cannot be regarded an objectively constituted class in an economic sense.⁴ These classes have been culturally defined through contrast with other social groups; they are constituted by symbolic capital as much as economic capital, and the meaning of such class categories shifts over time. The categories "bourgeoisie" and "*efendiya*" have indeed ceased to function as class designators. Nor can the nature of bourgeois class status be attributed to the requirements or logic of the Egyptian state. It is certainly true that the centralizing projects particularly of the nineteenth century rulers Muhammad Ali and Isma'il in large part made the emergence of the *efendiya* possible, and that British control, in a more attenuated manner, continued this tendency. It is also true that centralization required citizens and workers with specific types of training and behavioral attributes. State authorities, however, did not ordain the cultural meanings articulated in the public sphere. These meanings developed through a discursive process in which hegemonic claims to status and authority co-opted and manipulated existing cultural meanings for their articulation.[5]

I will argue in this chapter that one of the key elements in the emergence of bourgeois class status was the transference of the existing form of communal status embodied in rulers and other sovereign figures of communal order to the nation as a corporate body represented by the *efendiya*. An externalized, personal form of publicity—constituted by the internal virtue and justice conceived as making a ruler or other sovereign figure external to the community and capable of ordering it—remained culturally dominant in Egypt in the late nineteenth century. In other words, communal unity and order continued to be conceived and represented in the virtue, heroic self-sacrifice, and glory of a figure from whom this order issued. This externalized, hierarchical form of status and publicity was not suitable for the social aspirations and self-conception of members of the *efendiya* because it implies and justifies coercive domination of society. These individuals sought to attain social leadership rather than justify an existing domination, and conceived of their class as the primary representative of a social body capable of generating its own order. This implies that collective order or publicity does not inhere in an externalized figure, but is immanent to the social body, and appears most visibly in the bourgeois classes. Therefore, what was currently accepted as communal order and agency had to be depicted as arising from within the communal body of its own accord and appearing most visibly in the bourgeois classes.

This transference of an external form of order to its immanent appearance in the *efendiya* is seen most dramatically in a form of class publicity particularly prevalent in the early twentieth century—the funeral elegies composed for bourgeois public figures, which were recited in public ceremonies and published in newspapers. These elegies depict the collective mourning of the heroic figure who through his self-sacrifice enabled the existence of the community, which had been his dependent. The actions in which the hero's virtue manifested itself are bourgeois in nature, connected with the hero's profession and public activity. But these actions are depicted as virtuous through their assimilation to heroic acts of warfare. The heroism of bourgeois activity is represented not in an immanent fashion, by contriving this heroism to arise from the nature of the activity itself, but by associating the communal effect of this activity with traditional military heroism. In other words, the dead bourgeois hero is depicted as the equivalent of a princely, sovereign figure from whom the community's order issued externally. The process of collective mourning, however, results in the birth of the nation through the transference of virtue from the dead hero to his mourners. The virtue consisting of bourgeois attributes that enabled self-sacrifice in the hero is reborn through grief over his loss as collective order and agency. In this way, the elegies invest bourgeois activity and those who engage in it with the form of virtue that had formerly constituted personal status and sovereignty. The funeral elegies show that the emergence of bourgeois class status and publicity drew upon an existing form of publicity that was ostensibly incompatible with bourgeois aspirations. These elegies enable an understanding of the origin of bourgeois class status and the basis on which much more radical ways of depicting the immanence of social order could come about.

The rise of the funeral elegy (*marthiya*) as a preeminent genre of neoclassical poetry in the beginning of the twentieth century has been widely noted.[6] Such elegies comprise about a quarter of the collected poetry of Ahmad Shawqi (1868–1932) and Hafiz Ibrahim (1872–1932), almost all of them composed for public figures. By contrast, Mahmud Sami al-Barudi (1839–1904), the preeminent poet of the preceding generation, composed but a handful, and those for members of his family. The volume of funeral elegies found in the poetry of Shawqi, Hafiz, and even Khalil Mutran (1872–1949), a poet much less bound by traditional forms, is great even by classical standards. Only the pre-Islamic period, in fact, bears comparison.[7]

The relative decline of the funeral elegy in the classical period is closely connected with the change in the social function of Arabic poetry once it became a tool of political legitimation in courtly contexts. The impetus behind the elegy composed for a political leader (known as *ta'bin* or praise) and the panegyric poem is in principle the same. The community and its values are exalted in the image of a sovereign leader. This serves to legitimize both the leader and the social structure of the community. In the courtly context, however, the patron of the poet was able fully to co-opt the panegyric by using its confirmation of the legitimacy of the social order for the sake of legitimizing himself.[8] In this circumstance, the political difference between the panegyric and the elegy becomes more apparent. In formal terms, the only difference appears to be that the subject of one is alive, and that of the other dead, or as a tenth century literary critic put it, the poet in the former says "is," and in the latter, "was."[9] This change in tense, however, has important political implications. The elegy, which is similar to the panegyric in its exaltation of a great person, is offered not to that person himself, but to those who mourn his death. The patron who sponsors the poem is not the exalted figure, but those in whose interests it lies that he be exalted. A funeral elegy for a public figure therefore can more readily cast itself as the voice of the community. Moreover, the fact that the hero no longer has political interests allows the isolation of the hero's depicted virtue from such interests. The virtue that is depicted can be cast as belonging fully to the community. In a bourgeois context, the externality of the praised figure to the community dependent upon him, that is, the sovereign status of the praised figure, leads to the extinction of the panegyric as a viable genre. The funeral elegy, however, can depict this kind of externality on the condition that its possessor is now incorporated into the community created through his death.

The funeral elegy took on a heightened public capacity in early twentieth century Egypt in the context of the formation of the public sphere and the political aspirations of the professional and bureaucratic classes.[10] These aspirations involved programs of social and political reform as well as increasing opposition to the British occupation of Egypt. The call for immediate British withdrawal from Egypt, vigorously promoted by the lawyer Mustafa Kamil and his bourgeois followers in the early 1900s, had spread to many sections of Egyptian society by the end of World War I, and is spectacularly evidenced by the riots and strikes of the 1919 revolution. Another important factor in the social cohesion of the new class, and its ideological influence over the rest of society, was the growth of the press. By the turn of the century, the Egyptian press had expanded considerably and continued to grow in size and importance.[11] Most funeral elegies, like other poetry composed for public events, appeared first in newspapers and only much later, if ever, in books. These public events and gatherings, which often combined aristocratic sociality with a bourgeois ethos of public service, proliferated during the early twentieth century. The prominent poets of the period like Shawqi and Hafiz have large sections of their collections set aside for poems recited on such occasions. Of the types of social gathering that seem to have increased in importance after the turn of the century are both the funeral itself,[12] which had always been a public event in Islamic societies, and the *haflat al-ta'bin*, or eulogy ceremony. This is usually held forty days after the death of the important personage (the end of the mourning period, when a ceremony is often held for a Muslim who has died) or on the first anniversary of the death. The *haflat al-ta'bin* ceremony may be then repeated on any anniversary of the death. The ceremony consists essentially of the declamation of funeral orations and elegies. It is usually for this ceremony that elegies were composed and not for the funeral itself. For the famous, these were large public events, well attended by dignitaries and the like. The next day accounts of the event would appear in newspapers along with some or all of the elegies declaimed there.[13]

By the end of the nineteenth century, the traditional panegyric was beginning to open up the domain of political rhetoric that the elegy took over. Under the Khedives Isma'il (r. 1863–1879), Tawfiq (r. 1879–1892), and especially Abbas II (r. 1892–1914), poets maintained the institution of composing panegyrics on the occasions of public festivals and momentous royal events. Panegyrics were often dedicated to the Ottoman Caliph on such occasions as well, which in this case included Ottoman military victories. Abbas II, apparently as part of his effort to bolster his legitimacy and popularity vis-à-vis the British consul Lord Cromer, retained Ahmad Shawqi as his semiofficial court poet during the whole course of his reign. Abbas sought to present himself as the champion of the Egyptian nation and initially allied himself with Mustafa Kamil and his nationalist followers. The effects of this strategy on the self-representation of the Khedive show up in the panegyric poems of the period. The ordering of the community that defines the Khedive's virtue and lordship is increasingly depicted in terms of national progress and development. In other words, the publicity of lordship takes expression in a national, historical manner, aligning it with the form of publicity to be claimed by the bourgeois classes. Nevertheless, this publicity retains its traditional military and heroic nature. Consider the following verses from a panegyric composed by Shawqi in 1893, at the outset of the Khedive's reign.[14] The poem itself fully follows the traditional panegyric pattern and motifs, but contains at its center this passage:

> Lord of the Nile amidst God's creation!
> Free the Nile to water His creation.
> Raise your voice, for your age is a free one;
> it will have no choice but to hear your voice.
> For lordship is that there be a country,
> and that the country through lordship reach glory.
> So seize your path and make succeed
> your subjects in their aim of knowledge.
> Command learning to visit the land
> that humanity has long recognized as learning's cradle.
> Spark electricity there to guide us,
> and empower it over steam to enrich us.
> Reveal the strength of iron there and renew
> the golden age of the builders.[15]

These deeds express the cosmic moral order that vanquishes fate and mortality. "The star's desire is to bow its head before his palace and soil its cheek, / Where time is servile, the fates at watch, and history the army." The form of ordering depicted here, the building of civilization and control over nature, is not foreign to the traditional Arabic panegyric. What is of interest here is the manner in which this type of ordering is depicted as the historical aspiration and destiny of the community. The Khedive conducts these actions as the agent of Egypt, and is exalted in this capacity. This can be seen in the poem's final benediction. "Egypt has, in his living, life extending forever: may he live her life forever prosperous." The publicity of the Khedive is in this way tied to the national status of Egypt.

In the panegyric poem, however, lordship remains the property of the ruler, upon whom glory therefore remains dependent. For this reason, the panegyric was a form of public representation incompatible with bourgeois national aspirations and the transference of lordship to the national community required by these aspirations. Yet the panegyric did at times reveal the tension between the bourgeois claim to national representation and the sovereign status claimed by the Khedive.[16] An instance of this tension can be seen in a panegyric composed by Isma'il Sabri on the occasion of 'Id al-Adha in 1908 and addressed to Abbas.[17] Sabri (1854–1923), who was a government official of high rank (he became Minister of Justice in 1899), composed the poem in response to the pardoning of those imprisoned after the Dinshaway incident.[18] The Dinshaway incident had been seized upon by anticolonialists as an emblem of trampled Egyptian dignity and was probably the single event that contributed most to the upsurge in Egyptian national feeling before the death of Mustafa Kamil. Therefore, the pardoning of the prisoners by the Khedive was greeted with jubilation as at least a partial restoration of Egyptian honor. Sabri's poem is conventional in character in terms of its motifs and structure, but its praise of the Khedive centers on two sections that make liberal demands on the Khedive's authority. In the first section, the poet counsels the Khedive to establish a parliament that will serve as his army. The second section on the Khedive's pardon speaks to the ruler on behalf of the Egyptian nation.

> Egypt has thanked you for the safety of a part of her,
> so that both east and west resound with her thanks.
> She remembers your gracious pardon and ever
> looks toward a matter yet more momentous:
> The judgement of Dinshaway is a sheaf
> which when read aloud causes hearts to tremble;
> Can repose be sought and the mind put at ease
> while the specter of death still haunts its text?
> And while the beds of the sleeping nation are crowded
> with a tortured one dying and another suffering?
> The injured will never be healed entirely
> so long as their injurer, the Indian sword, still gleams;[19]
> So rule without violence and break its sword,
> for restraint is more comely and nobility more fitting.
> Egypt is yours, both her present and past,
> and yours is tomorrow, ordained, inalterable.

It is clear from this section, which calls upon the Khedive to break his sword, and the previous section, which called upon him to institute a parliament as his sword, that the purpose of this poem is not the fulfillment of a ritual obligation of praise. Indeed, there are no other poems of praise for Abbas in Sabri's collected poetry. The aim here is rather the co-optation of the ceremony for the purposes of national representation. Egypt is depicted here as a female suppliant, a dependent of the ruler, but it is evident that the poem is directed to this suppliant as much as it is to the ruler, and embodies the demands of this suppliant more so than the self-image of the ruler. As a result, the externality of the ruler to the community that he rules is undermined.

In terms of bourgeois aspirations to national representation, panegyric poetry is clearly untenable as a means of creating class status and publicity. This form of poetry, however, remained the preeminent cultural representation of communal virtue. Moreover, publicity continued to be predominantly conceived in terms of social virtue, self-sacrifice, and glory. Given this situation, the funeral elegy was able to take over the role of the panegyric. For the elegy is itself a kind of panegyric, but it is a panegyric addressed to the community that sponsors it, not through the person of a living ruler external to the community, but through the person of a dead one of its number, who can be remembered as the living image of all that the community desires and values. In other words, the elegy became the panegyric that the *efendiya* addressed to itself, in order to become itself the bearer of Egypt's glory, as the monarch had been before.

The bourgeois status of the public figure praised in funeral elegies leads to the depiction of communal ordering, the national historical development indicated above, in terms of bourgeois civil society. That is, the realm in which order is enacted, glory attained, and fate subdued, becomes the public sphere. Since this realm is depicted according to the same conventions, however, its meaning and implications remain the same as those of traditional Arabic poetry. That is to say that the work of professionals and bureaucrats is depicted as the work of advancing Egypt's national aspirations within Egypt and internationally. Those who do this work are to be seen as struggling for the glory of Egypt no less heroically than kings and princes. This means, however, that these activities can only acquire their heroic meaning by taking on the traditional military cast of heroism. For the present-day reader, this has a somewhat jarring effect. At the time, however, this procedure not only served as a means of transferring the prevailing form of communal virtue to the nation and its putative representatives, but served to portray a modern-day revival of Arab–Islamic imperial glory. For the poetic styles imitated in the elegies were associated with a former age of high civilization and political domination. The glory claimed by the *efendiya*, therefore, was in a dual respect a borrowed glory so far as it involved the classicizing funeral elegy.

The funeral elegy preserves the structure of the classical panegyric: noble virtue expressed in military action mediates between private passion and mortality on one side (the *nasib*, or in the elegy, the lament), and communal superabundance and immortality on the other. The emphasis in the panegyric is on the transformation of the poet, on a movement from the chaotic desire of unbounded love to participation in the community that depends on the ordering capacity of the sovereign figure. The emphasis in the elegy is on the community itself, showing the manner in which it is brought into being out of a collection of passive individuals. This is effected through the portrayal of mourning. Freud describes what he calls the "work of mourning" undertaken by the ego of the mourner in the following manner:

> Reality-testing has shown that the loved object no longer exists, and it proceeds to demand that all libido shall be withdrawn from its attachments to that object. This demand arouses understandable opposition... Normally, respect for reality gains the day. Nevertheless its orders cannot be obeyed at once. They are carried out bit by bit, at great expense of time and cathectic energy, and in the meantime the existence of the lost object is psychically prolonged. Each single one of the memories and expectations in which the libido is bound to the object is brought up and hyper-cathected, and the detachment of the libido is accomplished in respect of it... [W]hen the work of mourning is completed the ego becomes free and uninhibited again.[20]

In Freud's theory of the formation of the ego, the withdrawal of libidinal energy from the beloved figure is accomplished through the ego's adoption of the beloved figure's attributes, which allows the transference of the libidinal investment to the ego itself. This process results in the alteration and shaping of the ego.[21] Freud's theory, whether or not it has any relation to the actual psychological process of mourning, is illuminating in regard to the representation of mourning. The public funeral elegy is a stylized representation of mourning created for a social purpose. The social purpose of the elegy is the rendering of a myth of the emergence of the community through mourning the life and acts of a figure represented as its founder. In this depiction, the poet is not the primary mourner; the community represented by the poet has this role. The ego, which is here the community as an autonomous corporate agent, a nation, comes into existence through the work of mourning. The absolute libidinal investment made by the mourners in the mourned figure negates itself as unrestrained, chaotic grief by realizing its inner truth as love for the mourned figure's capacity for self-sacrifice. In this self-negation the mourners' own capacity for self-sacrifice arises and the mourners are born as a unified ego, a nation characterized by order and agency. The mourned figure's capacity for self-sacrifice and for sustaining the community has become internalized within the community itself. This is an immanent process of moral self-ordering because it has arisen from an innate disposition of the mourners, their spontaneous grief over the lost hero. But it is dependent upon the original externality of the mourned figure to the community, and will therefore continue to take the form of the lordly, military heroism that imposes order. The process may be immanent, but the content remains external.

We can consider the constitutive capacity of mourning further by comparing the bourgeois elegy with its classical counterpart. For both, the founder of the community, the mourned figure, is initially responsible for the existence and sustenance of the community. In the classical elegy, the loss of the mourned figure is often compensated by a new figure, his heir, who will now take up the role of the sovereign lord that the mourned figure held while alive.[22] The community remains dependent upon this new figure as it had been upon the mourned one. For this reason, classical funeral elegies of the Islamic period often end with praise for the heir or substitute of the mourned figure. Peter Sacks, speaking of the English elegy, refers to this substitute as the "figure for fertility."

> [I]t is worth noting the persistence of the figure for fertility. [M]any of the tropes by which we signify immortality depend in large part on this figure, and upon the images originally associated with it. The nature of the power signified differs according to the survivors, for it depends on the matrix of their needs. But whether such a matrix is that of nature itself, or that of spiritual belief, of fame, or justice, or of social order, the elegy works to create a figure by which that matrix can be refertilized.[23]

The figure created in the neoclassical elegy is not a human successor to the one who has died, but the unified community itself. In it, as in the classical panegyric and elegy, the community is depicted as having been the helpless dependents of the mourned figure. But from the perspective of bourgeois aspirations to social leadership, this was not a true communal existence. It is only once the mourned figure dies, and his dependents, through mourning him, acquire his attributes, that they become consolidated into a community, which is itself capable of the action and the plenitude that characterized him. In the neoclassical elegy, the community itself becomes his heir and substitute, moving from passive dependence to active self-sufficiency.

The structural pattern I have sketched does not appear in bold relief in every public elegy. Its full scope was reserved for figures who were recognized within their lifetimes, or soon after, as national heroes. As the elegy continued to develop in its representation of class status, however, the outlines of this structure became increasingly discernable in elegies for all manner of bourgeois figures. At the same time, their production proliferated. The event that seems to have given the greatest impetus to the rise of the elegy is the death of Mustafa Kamil (1874–1908). It was on this occasion that the elegy first assumed the national role that became characteristic of it thereafter. Likewise, it is on the death of another national hero, Sa'd Zaghlul (1857–1927), that the elegy of the kind being considered here reached its historical culmination. The innumerable post-Kamil elegies composed for other public figures are therefore best understood in light of the master elegies composed for these national heroes.

Mustafa Kamil, considered the father of Egyptian nationalism, was the founder of the National Party (*al-Hizb al-Watani*) and devoted his short life to activism against the British occupation of Egypt. This activism consisted in giving speeches calling for British withdrawal all over Egypt and in Europe, in publishing articles widely in the Egyptian and French press as well as in the influential newspaper that he founded, in seeking and creating alliances with the French and with the Khedive against the British, and in opposing the initiatives of liberal reformers who drew on British support.[24] Kamil was a well-known and prominent figure during his lifetime, the preeminent advocate of Egyptian patriotism, but the massive outpouring of grief and participation in his funeral procession that took place on his death was surprising and unprecedented at the time. The still-raging controversy over the Dinshaway incident, which inflamed anti-British sentiment and raised Kamil's stature, must certainly have contributed to the response. In any case, Kamil's funeral continues to be regarded as the first public manifestation of Egyptian national consciousness on a mass level. As a result, the elegies composed for the occasion of the forty-day commemoration and thereafter were the first to take on fully and explicitly a national public function. All of the prominent poets of the time composed elegies for his death, even those associated with political factions antagonistic to him.[25]

It can appear that the movement of a neoclassical elegy consists merely in an oscillation between grief and praise, which ends with a benediction. In reality, both the grief and praise undergo important transformations through the course of the poem. Generally, the poem begins with a lamentation, which involves, in extreme cases, cosmic and social disruption. Its main part is the portrayal of the distraught throng of mourners at the burial. The lament continues with confusion and disbelief at the mourned figure's failure to answer those who call for him in need. This is followed by a listing of all that the community has lost in losing him. At this point, there is generally a shift from lament to praise. The praise begins with the mourned figure's virtues, then makes a transition to his historical actions—a biographical recounting of the services that he has rendered to his community or nation. It is here that the mourned figure appears as the founder, unifier, or reviver of his community, as the gravity of the situation dictates. Finally, grief enters once again, but a controlled and somewhat detached grief, which enables the community to absorb the virtue and the spirit of the mourned figure by keeping his memory ever alive. It will now be his memory that holds the community together and enables it, as it were, to become his incarnation. This sets up the final farewell to him as he enjoys his well-deserved rest and reward in heaven.

A surprising number of elegies follow this sequence more or less completely. One might expect especially poets with greater aesthetic ambitions to deviate from it, and this is the case, but generally speaking, the greater the communal significance of the mourned figure, the greater the ritual aspect of the elegy. The elegy was not usually an area of radical poetic experimentation. For this reason, the role of the elegy as a form of national class publicity is much more apparent and uniform.

Consider the elegy composed for Mustafa Kamil by Khalil Mutran, one of the three most prominent poets in Egypt at the time, despite his Lebanese Christian origin, and noted for his innovative tendencies.[26] Taking advantage of the fact that his subject's first name, Mustafa ("the chosen one"), is a title of the Prophet Muhammad, the poet treats him as the reviver of Islam as well as the unifier of Egypt.[27] The success of Mutran's elegy is particularly striking, as he was neither Muslim nor Egyptian, nor even a proponent of neoclassicism in poetry. The classical form of the elegy, however, its public, communal orientation, made the use of such thematic material as the revival of Islam wholly appropriate even for a non-Muslim. For this reason, Mutran was able not only to participate in the public grieving of Kamil, but to make a significant contribution to the development of the modern elegy in doing so.

His poem begins, after salutations to "Mustafa" in heaven, with the lament, which is the portrayal of public grieving for the hero. Although Mutran's version of this scene is somewhat restrained, the basic element of social dissolution brought about through unrestrained passion is evident.

> Before you never was a nation seen
> whose men wept untrammeled tears,
> Weighted down by somberness
> carrying a gaunt specter.
> A sea of the living, your bier above them
> a ship shaded by the flapping banner...[28]
> Out of their seclusion the aggrieved women strove,
> sorrow throwing a black veil over all eyes;

> They went unveiled and yet they did not preen,
> in a misfortune of stone-bending grief.[29]

The absence of social order is indicated by the depiction of men weeping and women out in the open. Men have lost their internal restraint and social inhibition, as seen in their display of uncontrolled emotion, as well as their control over the public appearance of their women, which does not stir their jealousy. Women appear unveiled but this has no erotic effect because all emotion is invested in the mourned figure. What Mutran depicts here is filled in with more detail in the elegy composed for the same occasion by Hafiz Ibrahim.[30] In that poem, we find that the day of Kamil's death is as the day on which human society will come to a permanent end, the day of resurrection.

> On the day of his death I witnessed the day of resurrection
> and I learned the hierarchy of greatness,
> And I saw how peoples fulfill for their men
> the right of fealty and the obligation of tribute.
> Ninety thousand around your bier, humble,
> walking under your advancing banner...[31]

In this elegy of Hafiz, the mourning at the burial contains the same elements of the dissolution of society that appear in Mutran's poem. The poet describes the storms caused by the flood of weeping and the winds of burning sighs, bringing the portrayal of mourning to its culmination with the unveiled women:

> So many secluded women, the day death hovered around you,
> rent for your sake their silken curtains;
> They went, uncovered, to bid farewell a nation carried
> upon a funeral bier, not some old story;
> Not fearing the eyes of observers, they rent
> the face of the veil and gave up its shelter,
> For between them and all eyes came to stand
> a curtain of grief and misery.

It can be seen that the public, unveiled appearance of women serves as powerful image of the dissolution of social order. In classical poetry, mastery over desire, symbolized by the control of women, gives rise to social order. Here, however, the investment of the desire of the mourners in its entirety in the mourned figure prevents the social chaos that would normally ensue. Grief for the dead hero, therefore, is an unrestrained desire that causes social dissolution but is at the same time a unified desire that can eventually lead to order. This potential is already apparent in the investment of this desire in "a nation carried upon a funeral bier."

The process of mourning is not limited to lamentation, as is seen in the further development of Mutran's elegy. After the description of the mourning throng, which in this poem is only the first part of the lament, the poem moves to the naming of those who have been bereaved: the youth, the Christians, Jews, and Muslims, and finally Islam and Egypt, which are each given their own narratives. The bereavement of Islam begins with the following verse:

> Who will exonerate Islam of the charges of the enemies,
> and refute the criticism of critics as falsehood?

The actions of the mourned figure are always martial in character, protecting his community (which is under this description the *hima* or sanctuary) and fending off its enemy. The enemy is one of the main presences in this sort of elegy and is indispensable, because the enemy is the agent of adverse fate. The defeat of the enemy stands for the defeat of fate, and thus leads to immortality. This classical framework is used for the sake of a narrative about the past civilization of Islam and Mustafa Kamil's role in its contemporary revival. The narrative is of a piece with the numerous such narratives that found their place in elegies for public figures, recounting the revival of literature, science, medicine, or some other field. All are synecdoches for the revival of the larger community.

The most profoundly bereaved by the death is Egypt, the beloved and lover of the dead hero. Most of the verses in this section begin with the word "Egypt":

> Egypt, whose wounds your two hands washed
> with an outpouring of tears, flowing to exhaustion;
> Egypt, whose most relentless enemies you fought
> going forth a bold target for their archers...

The repetition of the name of the mourned figure is characteristic of elegy in many literary traditions and occurs in the beginning of this poem.[32] The repetition of the name of the bereaved, however, is of special interest because this repetition becomes an echo of the other, creating an identification of the two. Furthermore, the repetition is assertion. The repetition of the name of the mourned is an assertion of his continued existence, a denial of the importance of death. This is akin to another classical device, the piteous command *la tab'ad*, "don't depart," addressed to the dead one.[33]

In pre-Islamic poetry, this command is always given in the paradoxical form, "Don't depart, for all living creatures must die." The meaning seems to be that death should not annihilate those who are dear, as dying is common to all, but all do not "die" in the absolute sense of being effaced from the minds of men. Likewise, repetition of the mourned person's name is an assertion that he has indeed not died in this sense. As for the repetition of the name of Egypt, the bereaved, it can be nothing but the assertion that Egypt exists, that Egypt has identity, precisely *as* the bereaved one, the one most bereaved by the death of Mustafa Kamil. We can see this in the verses which follow:

> Until you proceeded as you wished composing
> of her [Egypt's] members what was not to be composed;
> A hope before which your virtue had fallen short,
> had not your death come to its aid,
> Virtue by which, were it rationed out,
> a just and proud people would flourish.

Here the poem spells out the process that is taking place. The form of community that the hero wished to create could not be created by his virtue alone, but required the transference of this virtue to the community through his death. The meaning of grief on the hero's death is thus revealed. The poem will now proceed to enact the rationing out of the mourned figure's virtue. The community must, as Freud indicated, "psychically" (i.e., poetically) prolong the existence of the mourned figure in order to successfully complete its work of mourning as it successfully completes the emergence of its identity. The poem therefore turns to recounting the mourned figure's virtue in a panegyric mode.

The poem now moves to a fully heroic description in which virtue is cast as courage in warfare, the ultimate form of self-sacrifice. As in classical poetry, valor is the father of all morally desirable traits, and this is the general prelude to the recounting of the mourned figure's deeds, which normally takes the form of biographical and historical narration. In this poem, however, the narrative is only hinted at; the audience is allowed to fill in the allusions to the well-known activities of Kamil's life. In his elegy for Sa'd Zaghlul, Mutran takes the other extreme, making out of his poem a short biography. Here, the poem describes Kamil's writing and oration in a rather classical fashion so that we see him as a figure of old, while knowing the modern form that these activities took. This elegy does not dwell on the function of giving bourgeois activities a heroic portrayal, as was to become the norm later, but fulfills it in a more attenuated manner.

Once the poem has closed its panegyric, it reaches completion by recapitulating itself. Now it is the poet himself who stands before the grave of Mustafa Kamil, desperately desiring to bring him back.

> O sincerest of the sincere upon whom I weep
> as the weeping of Egypt, burning and afflicted;
> Here is your image, present to keep us,
> its veil removed by sorrow, it now looks over us;
> The crescent moon traces a crown for it,
> and the weaver of purity has clothed it.

The sorrow of Egypt brings back his true image that is visible to all who share in this sorrow. The crescent moon of the Egyptian flag, a symbol of Islam, is his crown and he is clothed in virtue. Kamil becomes, as it were, a permanent design on the Egyptian flag. The veil that is now removed does not signify social dissolution but the constitution of society. The reiteration of the poem's structure continues with the final transumption of the mourned figure into the community:

> Let love be as your love of country,
> no falsehood in it nor pretense...
> You have created by virtue of it from fragmented Egypt
> young Egypt, a fortified sanctuary and home;[34]
> You have made of her a nation more generous
> in noble deeds and more disposed to greatness;
> You have taught her people their true value,
> and it suffices their value that it be known.
> The breath of your soul has leavened their souls,
> so that they are what you desire in good times and bad;
> A lofty fortress whose foundations lie
> upon knowledge and which is secured
> from destruction by intellect;
> So rest in your sleep for your Lord has effaced
> the sin of Egypt as you had dreamed and has forgiven.

The birth of Egypt as a nation through the death of the hero is the ultimate redemption of Egypt. This redemption comes about because the audience of the poem, those who mourn, become both Egypt and Mustafa Kamil in mourning him. The poem uses here the figure of the populated abode, peopled with the effects of humanity and culture, which is always opposed to the desolate and ruined abode of the *nasib*, overrun by nature.[35] The glory that results in order and the defeat of mortality is a glory of knowledge and intellect. The following verses from the elegy of Hafiz make more clear that Egyptians can only prove that they grieve Kamil, that they hold his image before them, if they imitate his actions.

> O new generation, follow his path
> and persevere, whether the enemies
>   acquiesce or retaliate;
> For each of you is [the prophet] Mustafa who imitates his deeds,
> and each of you Kamil [perfect] who wards off weariness...[36]
> Sleep now, for you have tired yourself enough;
> we are awake and our body composed.
> This is your banner, flapping, shading us,
> and that is your figure etched in our hearts.[37]

Kamil thus enables the moral perfection of the Egyptian citizen. Grief for Kamil, resulting in the internalization of his attributes and imitation of his deeds, is the conduit by which the citizen achieves identification with the prophet of Islam, the perfect individual. This moral perfection enables the awakening and composure of the Egyptian collective body.

The appearance of the hovering or etched image of the mourned figure, which is equivalent to the *tayf* or semblance of the beloved that continually appears to the lover in the *nasib* of panegyric poetry, indicates the close relationship between the unrestrained grief of the elegy and the unrestrained grief over the loss of the beloved in the praise poem.[38] Freud asserts the psychological identity of the two emotions in his theory that melancholia, which he takes to be the inability to withdraw emotionally from a beloved person or object, is a failed work of mourning.[39] Their literary relationship has been described in the following manner in a discussion of the English elegy:

> [O]ne of the most profound issues to beset any mourner and elegist is his surviving yet painfully altered sexuality. Although it is crucial for the mourner to assert a continued sexual impulse, that assertion must be qualified, even repressively transformed or rendered metaphorical by the awareness of loss and mortality. Indeed our consoling images are most often figures for an immortal but metaphorized sexual force.[40]

The *nasib* centers on the outcome of passionate attachment to a lover in mortality. This becomes the basis of the mastery of desire, which results in the capacity for self-sacrifice. The mastery over desire is external in the sense that it is based on the opposition yet mutual constitution of order and desire. The genre of the public elegy under consideration here has a parallel structure to that of the panegyric. The key difference, however, is that it is not an external mastery over grief that gives rise to order, but the inner truth of this grief that emerges of its own accord. Unlike the passionate love of the classical *nasib*, which is invested an empirical and bodily object of desire, the grief of the elegy is invested in a figure who embodies moral order. Therefore, even though it appears initially that this desire is chaotic, it turns out to be necessary for communal order. This process, then, is a myth of communal self-ordering out of innate desire. Grief for Mustafa Kamil is the necessary condition of nationality, because it is the necessary condition for the moral self-ordering of the citizen.

The harnessing of unrestrained desire for the sake of virtue provides the condition for the importance of the national historical plane of these poems. The martial deeds of the dead hero, conducted in civil society for the sake of Egypt's protection and glorification, are to become the deeds of all who participate in civil society. If they fail to do so, Egypt will revert to the presocial state in which it languished before the hero redeemed it. Such a state is pictured by Hafiz Ibrahim as part of the lament in the elegy he composed a year after Kamil's death. In a long description of the political situation since Kamil died, Egypt is shown to have become a wasteland, a desolate and ruined abode.

> A year has passed and life bears down on us
> at times and at times we suffer calamities;
> The people are in difficulty and fate is severe;
> even those with skill and ingenuity are perplexed.[41]

The agent of fate, the enemy, is the British. The resolve to keep alive the hero's memory changes this, signaled by the replacement of lament by panegyric. Once the internal development of the poem reaches the stage at which the attributes of the mourned figure can be retained by the community through his remembrance, the community acquires the capacity to change the wasteland into fertile land, and this is accomplished in the first place by acts of war.

The transformation of the community's desire into moral, heroic force is tantamount to the attainment of masculinity; this is figured as well in the movement from the dominance of nature in the *nasib* and lament and the dominance of culture in the final union of the mourned and the living. In the lament, one of the signs of the dissolution of society is the feminization of the men: they weep like women, while women come into public without causing an uproar.[42] Such a portrayal is not always developed, but is at least latent in any scene of men lamenting. The following passage, taken from the elegy composed by Muhammad Abd al-Muttalib

(1870–1931) for Sa'd Zaghlul, is a good instance of the manner in which this portrayal can be made.[43]

> In the dark of the night came news of the death of Sa'd;[44]
> O to God how the morning responded;
> Multitudes on the plain, frenzied,
> the open space billowing with them;
> Hearts trembling, bloody
> wounds lacerating their sides;
> Eyelids, their tears dried
> by a grieving, fiery heart;
> Eyes, drunken, unmoving, for them no closing
> on this morning nor opening;
> A night, dark with sorrow and disaster,
> and a day full of fiery winds from burning hearts;
> A valley full of riotous commotion,
> its every plain and expanse suffering its loss;
> As though, without their having touched glasses,
> a wine of grief was being served them.
> Do not blame souls that melted in tears
> the day those beloved departed;[45]
> Will you blame a nation bereaved of her father,
> whose people have lost their wits and wail?
> When they patiently hold in their sorrow,
> the pain of tragedy presses, and they cry out.
> He was a father, without whom they had not known life,
> nor had any scent of freedom reached them.

In the society portrayed in classical Arabic literature, it is the role of women to lament openly, and there were even professional female lamenters hired for funerals (as there have been in other cultures as well).[46] This poem is organized around the trope that Zaghlul is the "father of Egypt," and in the beginning, Egypt is his bereaved daughter. By the time the poem reaches its end, however, the mourners have become the warrior sons of their father, as we have seen in the other poems. They have undergone, as it were, a rite of passage, in which they have shed their feminine characteristics, their excess of uncontrolled emotion, their loss of reason, their passivity, and have become men.[47] This rite of passage is a recapitulation of what happened during Zaghlul's life, for in these poems the state of grief, the state of the hero's absence, is depicted as the same state that existed before the hero's revival. It is only that now the capture and preservation of his memory performs the function that he himself performed during his life.

Indeed, the passage from the absence of moral agency, a state with feminine associations, to the mastered desire of manhood, virtue, and national glory, is one of the dominant motifs of the ideology of cultural revival or *nahda*. The community had been fragmented, passive, vulnerable, and irrational, like the mourners at a funeral, who are together in their common grief, but isolated in that this grief prevents them from coming together as a social body for any unified action. The hero came, and whatever his field of action, brought about within it and through it manhood and unity, virtue and self-control. It is in this light that much of the neoclassical elegiac poetry composed for public figures should be read. The narrative of national rebirth can take its form from any bourgeois field of action, as in the following verses taken from the elegy by Abd al-Muttalib for Atif Barakat Pasha, who had been Minister of Education:[48]

> The man of glory who dies spreads glory
> upon the mass of his people and their leaders;
> And he who perishes spreading knowledge keeps living
> and guiding in the teachers whom he has nurtured...
> Before Atif we had seen the mother of languages
> the prey of a haughty usurper of education;[49]
> Abusing her and carrying her people
> by force into iniquity and injury;
> Her frame bending to the thrusts of attackers
> for want of champions and weakness of protectors;
> We were brought to despair by those charged
> with saving her from injury and warding off enemies;
> But when he took command her star of fortune changed
> to auspiciousness after ill omen.
> Thus she continued until her beauty shone out,
> and she came to rest on the highest pinnacle.
> The sanctuary [homeland] is strong and proud
> when its commander is strong and proud;
> what are goats beside a den of lions?

We see here the nomenclature of lordship of classical panegyric in the use of the terms *'ula* (glory), *qawm* (tribe), *sarat* (nobles of the tribe), *wilaya* (sovereignty or command), and *hima* (sanctuary), within a narrative of military victory and protection. The minister of education becomes the sovereign lord of panegyric poetry upon whom the community was dependent. He is therefore only metonymically praiseworthy, acquiring this status by means of his external association with the power of ordering that is imposed externally on the chaotic forces signified by enemies. This is the sort of order that remains intrinsically praiseworthy; the mourned figure, if he is to be mourned, must be associated with it. The following verses are from Ahmad Shawqi's elegy for Abd al-Muttalib himself:

> He decorated the homeland with a righteous generation,
> and a youth devoted to religion and good works;
> Perhaps [the homeland] will leap forth with them tomorrow,
> as a monarchy leaps forth with its legion army;
> They have made of pens their lances,
> and have used them as spears are used.[50]

The homeland replaces the monarchy, its civil-servant sons replace the army, and their professional implements replace arms. The poet still sings of men and arms, but they are bourgeois men equipped to enter the public sphere.

The paradoxical, transitional character of the neoclassical funeral elegies lies in the disjuncture between the immanent emergence of the nation's capacity for self-ordering and the externalized content of this self-ordering as sovereign authority. This does not mean, however, that the *efendiya* claimed to possess such sovereign authority or that they attempted to base bourgeois publicity in it. Once this type of authority is made immanent to the nation as a whole, it is effectively neutralized as a kind of authority that someone can claim to impose. The type of authority sought in these poems is hegemonic authority—social and moral leadership. This leadership is based in the representation of the bourgeois classes as embodying in the greatest degree the order and publicity arising from the nation as a whole. Anyone in the nation is qualified to lament the death of the bourgeois hero. And indeed, everyone in the nation is obligated to do so. Such grief is the means by which the mourner attains moral order and becomes a citizen. Yet at the same time, this grief affirms the preeminence of the form of activity engaged in by the hero in attaining national glory. The elegy, then, in transferring sovereign order to the nation as a whole through an immanent process makes possible the bourgeois claim to hegemonic order.

The funeral elegy is necessarily a transitional mode of representing class publicity. The immanent order of the nation still depends on an exterior, which is the former status of the figure who is now dead. The elegy is the enactment of the birth of collective agency, which occurs when this exterior is internalized. Such an enaction is a mythic and ritual kind of representation. Grieving the founding hero cannot serve as a depiction of the ordinary way in which citizens achieve moral order. A depiction of this kind requires a representation that contrives moral order to arise from within citizens without dependence on any externality. But for such a representation to come about, it must already be possible to accept that moral order really can arise from within individuals. This acceptance is made possible by the prior acceptance of the nation. Once the nation has been conceived as a self-ordering, autonomous body, it becomes necessary to account for the origin of this order within the nation, and thus to imagine how citizens come into being so as to form the nation's collective order. This is the process that is explained by social and political ideologies and depicted by novels. The neoclassical funeral elegy, however, embodies the earlier moment in which the collective body is initially endowed with the capacity for self-ordering. This can only occur through the investment of the collective body with a form of ordering that is already accepted as such. Neoclassical elegies transfer the existing form of order to the nation, and for this reason cannot represent any other kind of order. But the result is that the representation of more purely immanent types of order becomes possible. This does not mean, however, that elegies of this kind must be temporally prior to more radical representations of immanent order. It is likely the case, however, that the popularity and proliferation of these elegies, at least in the early period of their existence, made it easier for more radical representations to take root and find acceptance. The elegies show how bourgeois class publicity could draw its normative origin and persuasive power from an existing, premodern form of publicity.

Chapter 3

Order, Agency, and the Economy of Desire: Islamic Reformism and Arab Nationalism

We are confronted in the Arabic public sphere as it takes shape by the end of the nineteenth century with discourses grounded in a conception of the communal body as a population that must manage and configure itself in a precise manner to bring about moral integration, and thus the agency of a singular collective will. I will argue here that the moral ideal of nationality makes these discourses possible and endows them with universality by enabling them to depict their forms of order as arising directly out of the individual self. The transformation of virtue into nationality establishes a model of the self constituted by an economy of desire, in which a specific manner of managing and investing desire within the self turns this desire into the capacity for self-sacrifice. In this capacity lie order, agency, power, the endless capacity to grow through the ordering of the external world. The alternative is the mismanagement of desire, the imposition of constraints and avenues of gratification that lead to its futile dissipation. The moral integration of the communal body comes about only as the common order obtaining among all individuals when their internal desire is properly ordered. The social order thus replicates the internal order of the self—the same economy of potential power and its dissipation, the same principle of order that gives rise to will and agency. Indeed, the two levels of the same order are mutually dependent upon each other. Tyranny causes and is caused by enslavement, for they are the dual manifestations of the mismanagement of desires and the death of agency. The properly ordered society, on the other hand, contains the mechanisms that automatically engender order within individuals, whose self-sacrifice in turn enables social order to exist and express itself as power. On this basis, programs of social ordering claim necessity and legitimacy through their depictions of the internal order of the self.

The conception of society as a body of individuals that must be configured in a specific manner to achieve its potential is largely coextensive with Michel Foucault's notion of "governmentality." I am attributing to it, however, a different normative genealogy than the one indicated by Foucault. For Foucault, the modern practices and norms of governmentality, as opposed to medieval "sovereignty," are concerned with the management and cultivation of a population: "population comes to appear above all else as the ultimate end of government. In contrast to sovereignty, government has as its purpose not the act of government itself, but the welfare of the population, the improvement of its condition, the increase of its wealth, longevity, health, and so on..."[1] The management of population, a question of "disposing things" rather than "imposing laws" or any kind of external discipline, is conceived as encouraging and guiding natural processes immanent to the population, which requires "a knowledge of all the processes related to population in its larger sense—that is, what we now call economy."[2] Hence the "insertion of freedom within governmentality," the rights of citizens vis-à-vis the government, as "an element...indispensable to governmentality itself."[3] Foucault finds the crystallization of this new conception of how to increase the well-being and productivity of a population in the laissez faire doctrines of the eighteenth century *économistes*.[4] Yet, in his view, the ultimate purpose of the new governmentality remained the same as that of population management in the preceding disciplinary, mercantilist era: the raison d'etat, the interest of the state in increasing productivity, exports, and thus revenue.[5]

Foucault may well be correct in seeking the origin of what he calls "governmentality" in the logic of the mercantilist state. And in emphasizing the scientific nature and basis of governmentality, he distances the notion from the need for a moral substrate like the medieval "cosmological order." Yet it is at the same time clear that the notions and practices connected with governmentality cannot be justified to the population that is to be thus governed, nor promoted by reformist discourses seeking to influence public opinion, on the mere basis of state interest. Such justification and promotion require a universalizing normative basis, one in which notions like happiness, freedom, and right are the aim of prescribed forms of order rather than epiphenomena of a powerful state. This is true of the physiocrat *économistes* themselves, who present the science of economy as indispensable to "the best possible government" in achieving its purpose of securing the "natural right of man," which is the right to all that is necessary for human happiness.[6] Moreover, we see that the prescription of forms of order involves not just the notion of a *random* population, but a population that is conceived as inherently destined to be a moral unit—a "nation" or a national "society." The origin of these normative notions cannot be explained by the raison d'etat, nor are they spontaneously produced by objective social processes. They are moral ideals that have their own normative logic.

Understanding this logic enables us to understand how specific forms of social order have been justified within the normative framework of nationality. I will argue that the notion of the population that is to form a moral unit is inherently connected with the idea of an economy of forces within this population that realizes its immanent order as collective agency, or "work" on a collective level. In the Arabic context, this relationship can be understood by examining the transformation of virtue into nationality. In Chapter 1, I argued that in the political poetry of al-Barudi and al-Yaziji we see how it was possible to endow a collective body with the sovereign virtue whose locus had formerly lain within high-status individuals. Order becomes a property of the community as a body, instead of merely issuing from those who order it. Effecting this investment of sovereign virtue in the social body, however, required depicting the community as a self that shows its agency in rebellion against tyranny. Only in this way could a form of virtue that is the mastery of desire be shown to form a collective agent. As a result, the collective body is virtuous and self-ordering, but its order cannot be shown to arise from its individual members. The communal body replicates the self, but the self of a sovereign, lordly individual who cannot be the model for the members of the communal body. Nevertheless, this new moral status acquired by the collective body makes it possible to create ways of deriving this status from the individuals members of the community.

This shift that is thus presaged by al-Barudi and al-Yaziji becomes decisive when the collective body is depicted as a bounded whole that generates agency of its own accord out of its own internal order. This means that desire is no longer an overwhelming force that must be contained by an exceptional figure who is partially external to the social order, but has been ordered in each individual from the outset by the very nature of the social order. Each individual, in other words, is to be a morally ordered citizen, whose communion with other citizens in the public sphere automatically results in moral integration and collective agency. Therefore, the principle of order that is intrinsic to the individual self and by which the social body is configured so as to realize its immanent agency takes central importance. I investigate this relationship between the moral ideal of nationality and programs of social ordering in two contrasting political ideologies: the

Islamicly framed republican protosocialism of the Aleppan anti-Ottoman dissident, Abd al-Rahman al-Kawakibi (1855–1902), and the secular, statist Arab nationalism of the prominent Iraqi/Syrian bureaucrat Sati' al-Husri (1880–1968). The heroic republicanism of al-Kawakibi retains the traditional language of virtue but transforms sovereign status into individual moral freedom. Al-Husri, on the other hand, explicitly subordinates individuality to the nation. Whereas al-Kawakibi develops a political economy that makes wealth a manifestation of moral order, al-Husri foresees the reconfiguration of the Arab self and society by the bureaucratic institutions of the state. Nevertheless, the total incorporation of the individual self into the national order is the basis of personal self-completion and social order in both political programs. In both cases, the democratization of virtue means that virtue becomes the product of social mechanisms.

At the same time, however, the shift from sovereignty to nationality in no way eliminates the basis for claims to social and political leadership. Just as the public status of the virtuous, princely figure derives from the communal nature of virtue, and so belongs ultimately to the community, so is the national community seen as containing individuals or classes that represent its immanent order. The claim to this status is the basis of hegemony, and figures prominently in the political programs of al-Kawakibi and al-Husri. In both cases, the present is depicted as a condition of enslavement and moral degradation or psychic pathology. In both cases, a social agent shown to have escaped determination by present social relations is promoted as capable of reordering society and establishing its moral integration. The key contrast between al-Kawakibi and al-Husri arises from the opposing structures of the nation's moral universality in reformist and nationalist discourses. In reformist discourses, establishing a universal principle of order through the enaction of specific reforms brings the nation, as a morally unified collective agent, into being. In nationalist discourses, establishing and consolidating the nation brings order into being, because the universal principle of order inheres in some objective, distinguishing feature of the nation. These approaches have significantly different political implications. Yet the underlying hegemonic basis is the same. In both cases, nationality is an imperative of self-ordering.

Part One: The Political Economy of Tyranny and Enslavement: al-Kawakibi

The Islamic reformist vision of al-Kawakibi has been seen by some authors as enabling the birth of Arab nationalism, and by others as merely an extension of the Islamic modernism of Jamal al-Din al-Afghani and Muhammad Abduh. What I will focus on here, however, is the manner in which al-Kawakibi's writing deploys the rhetoric of tyranny and enslavement discussed in Chapter 1 to develop an immanent conception of communal order. Al-Kawakibi does not merely invest the collective body with sovereign virtue through its capacity to rebel against tyranny, but roots this capacity in a principle of order, "communality" (*ishtirak*), that lies within all human beings and enables collective bodies to order themselves. It is through this self-ordering that tyranny is dissolved. The depiction of an immanent principle of order enables al-Kawakibi to promote and legitimize a political and social order that replicates the order lying within the individual self and brings about the integration of individuals through their liberty. At the same time, however, the nature of this principle as an intrinsic refusal of tyranny allows al-Kawakibi to depict it in terms of the heroic freedom of classical virtue. The result is a social order founded on a form of virtue that is inherently difficult to maintain, a form of virtue constituted through its struggle against the perpetual threat of tyranny.

The widespread deployment of a homogeneous discourse of tyranny and enslavement was a characteristic feature of the Arabic public sphere, as centered mainly in Egyptian publishing, from the late nineteenth century through the 1920s. As an increasingly immanent understanding of moral order altered the conception of the psyche, this discourse was eventually displaced by a new discourse of social disorder and psychic dysfunction. Before the 1920s, classicizing poets as well as liberal intellectuals and Islamic reformers employed the language of tyranny and enslavement to depict the social ills that each one's particular program for reform would set right. A liberal reformer like Qasim Amin, for example, used this language to catalogue the enslaved characteristics of his Egyptian compatriots, even though he had no quarrel with the British rule of his time. Therefore he attributed Egyptian internal enslavement to past tyranny. The moral framework of this discourse, and even the motifs that constitute it, are precisely those of al-Barudi and al-Yaziji and derive from the broader Arabic rhetorical tradition. Yet in the writing of the early twentieth century, the discourse of tyranny and enslavement became the basis of an ideal of individual moral freedom that is immanent to the collective body. This ideal was only to be realized, however, through the particular program of social order that each writer promoted.

Al-Kawakibi's *Tawabi' al-Istibdad wa Masari' al-Isti'bad* (*The Characteristics of Despotism and the Fatalities of Enslavement*), published in Cairo in 1902, takes the prevailing discourse as its point of departure. Al-Kawakibi, born in Aleppo in 1855, belonged to a prominent family of religious scholars who ran their own *madrasa* and played a leading role in local politics.⁷ After graduating from the *madrasa* directed by his father, and editing Aleppo's official Ottoman newspaper, al-Kawakibi tried twice to set up independent newspapers, but experienced repeated difficulties with the Ottoman governor, and was forced to stop publishing by the authorities in each case after only a few issues. Al-Kawakibi's newspapers (*al-Shahba'*, 1877–1878; *al-I'tidal*, 1879), whose stated raison d'etre was "service to the homeland," contained thinly veiled and at times boldly outspoken criticism of Ottoman administration. The Ottoman government tried to mollify al-Kawakibi by appointing him to various administrative positions, including mayor of Aleppo, but he continued to run into trouble due to the enmity of the influential confidante of the Sultan, Abu al-Huda al-Sayyadi, whose headship of the local body of descendents of the prophet was contested by al-Kawakibi's family.⁸ Al-Kawakibi no doubt also attracted official ire by promoting various reform projects and by opening a legal aid office for victims of injustice. His tensions with the authorities culminated in being sentenced to death on the charge of conspiring with a foreign power to overthrow the government. He was able, after much trouble, to have this conviction overturned on appeal, a process which resulted in the replacement of the Ottoman governor. In 1899, after accepting an appointment to a judicial post, al-Kawakibi surreptitiously made off to Cairo, where he began publishing articles and sections of his two books under pseudonyms, and whence he undertook an extensive journey comprising a number of Islamic countries. His unexpected death in Cairo in 1902 took place, his supporters allege, due to poisoning on orders of the Ottoman Sultan.

Al-Kawakibi's passionate interest in despotism is clearly rooted in his experience in Aleppo, where he, like many other reform-minded Ottoman intellectuals, suffered the blunt force of Hamidian autocracy. The distinctiveness of his response, in terms of the political outcome that he championed, is connected with his relatively unique social position at the time. Unlike most other dissidents who fled the Levant in the late nineteenth century, al-Kawakibi was a Muslim religious scholar with significant local political clout. He had no Western style education, and apparently knew no European languages, but read widely in works translated into Turkish and Arabic. His political travails arose from a combination of the ideas that he espoused and the hurly-burly of local politics, which was dominated by his arch-enemy al-Sayyadi, the mystically inclined advisor of Abdul Hamid II. Al-Kawakibi was one the first prominent intellectuals to identify Muslim social and political inferiority with Ottoman, and more specifically, Turkish rule. This comes through most clearly in his work *Umm al-Qura* ("The mother of towns," an epithet of Mecca), which is structured as a conference of representatives from every region of the Muslim world convened in Mecca during the Hajj for the purpose of debating the causes of Muslim malaise. In this work, and in a more subdued manner, in "The Characteristics of Despotism," al-Kawakibi infuses the question of social and political regeneration with an ethnic-national Arab element, the idea that Arabs should enjoy political leadership or perhaps even autonomy. In "The Characteristics of Despotism," this element is linked with a distinctive conception of true Islamic government comprising aristocratic, liberal-democratic, and protosocialist features. The discourse of tyranny and enslavement through which al-Kawakibi articulates his programmatic political conceptions is informed by his experience of Ottoman autocracy, but not derived from this experience. Al-Kawakibi speaks in a language that preexisted him and pervaded his environment. His interest lies in how he anchors in this language an immanent principle of order designed to legitimize the social program that he promoted.

The pervasiveness of the discourse of tyranny and enslavement is not least apparent in the fact that "The Characteristics of Despotism" relies on a European source, an eighteenth-century Italian treatise with similar aims, for its scheme of organization and a number of its ideas and arguments. Sylvia Haim goes so far as to assert that al-Kawakibi's work "is to a large extent a faithful rendering in Arabic of *Della Tirannide* by Vittorio Alfieri."[9] This unwarranted exaggeration obscures the achievements of al-Kawakibi's work on a number of levels. For the significance of "The Characteristics of Despotism" is not *that* it deploys the discourse of tyranny and enslavement, but *how* it deploys this discourse. Al-Kawakibi adopts Alfieri's ideal of a democratic government with separation of powers, but inserts it into an Islamic framework characterized by a mechanism for equitable distribution of wealth. Whereas the atheistic Alfieri finds the provenance of tyranny to lie in monotheism, al-Kawakibi employs the material he lifts from Alfieri to cast the monotheistic prophets as the chief tutors of freedom in human history and to depict modern European liberty as the latest and greatest aftereffect of the Arab-Islamic liberation of knowledge. Al-Kawakibi manages this contraversion of Alfieri's material by deepening the moral substrate of tyranny and enslavement, that is, by developing more fully the enmeshment of this discourse in an economy of desire. Common to both texts is the ruling idea that, as Alfieri puts it, "under the absolute government of one man everything must without exception be disordered and wicked."[10] Al-Kawakibi, however, specifies more fully the relationship between order and virtue, in a manner that allows him to identify these with what he regards to be the true Islamic form of government once instantiated by the early Arab Muslims. The key element in this specification is al-Kawakibi's principle of order, which he designates "*ishtirak*" (association, communality). This cosmic principle is the foundation of all things "except God" and provides the regulative standard by which all human activity is judged. Through *ishtirak* nations achieve prosperity, power, and progress. The realization of *ishtirak* depends on the proper management of desire, resulting in complete freedom and self-sufficiency for individuals, and in complete possession of its citizens for the nation. "The Characteristics of Despotism" is therefore a much more comprehensive work than Alfieri's, providing one of the most substantial sociomoral accounts of an ideal Islamic nation that has ever appeared.

Let us take a closer look at al-Kawakibi's work, considering in turn the depiction of tyranny as dissipated desire, the forms of self-ordering that engender order, the universalizing nation to which the work's rhetoric gives rise, and the unstable alignment of virtue and identity that secures world-historical fulfillment. The book's stated purpose is to address "the social question of the East in general and the Muslims in particular," which is "the reason for decline." The answer to this question comes immediately: "The cause of this illness is despotism and its antidote is the repulsion of [despotism] by means of constitutional representative government (*al-shura al-dusturiya*)."[11] Al-Kawakibi defines despotism as the rule of an absolute government not accountable to its subjects, nor bound in its actions by law, custom, or national will (437). This, however, is only the beginning. Even strictly bounded, pluralistic governments with full separation of powers are nevertheless in most cases despotic, according to al-Kawakibi, because they manage to escape complete national supervision and full accounting of their actions. Every government tends toward tyranny, and it is up to citizens to ensure that that their government follows their will rather than its own. Despotism is therefore nearly impossible to stave off for any substantial length of time, and only the English have succeeded in doing so for more than a 150-year stretch due to their unremitting monitoring of their monarch. Al-Kawakibi's emphasis in diagnosing despotism is not so much on the institutional structure of governance, which he regards as crucial though not ultimately decisive, but on the ideal of a self-possessed, alert nation that relentlessly keeps its government in line. It is already apparent, then, that the slide into tyranny is the symptom of a lapse on the part of the nation, the outward manifestation of an inner moral degeneration. It is to the anatomy of this degeneracy that al-Kawakibi's attention is primarily devoted.

"The illness is love of life and the antidote is love of death" (436). This, one of the many reformulations of the "Eastern question" with which the book is preoccupied, puts us firmly on the terrain of virtue and self-sacrifice. The Eastern question is conceived as a question of will and agency, and ultimately, of existence. The inhabitants of the East can expect to vanish, to be absorbed by others as were the nations of antiquity, "so long as they remain in their present condition, remote from earnestness and resolve, content with amusement and frivolity as palliatives to the pain of imprisoning the self and in habituation to indistinction and abasement" (493). The Easterner is designated by al-Kawakibi as a "captive" (*asir*) of despotism, and the condition of this captive arises from holding his self captive (*asarat al-nafs*) by seeking to propitiate it with the illusions of fulfillment to which the tyrannical order gives rise. The captive of despotism is thus in no way distinct from the despot himself. Both are captives of stray desire. Despotism is defined as "dictating public affairs according to passion," and the fundamental characteristics of both the tyrant and his victim are fear and cowardice (435). Therefore, God "only empowers a despot over despots" (441). The tyrant is not a foreign body that has usurped control over the nation. He is not an alien conqueror who oppresses a powerless population. Or rather, he is these, but is at the same time, and more fundamentally, no more foreign to the nation than misspent desire is to the self. For al-Kawakibi, just as in al-Barudi's poems of rebellion, the tyrant and his victims are the complementary forms taken by the single reality of mismanaged desire.

The mismanagement of desire is simultaneously an individual and communal state of disorder. The captive of despotism has no will (*irada*), which is "the mother of morality" (486). This is because he surrenders to fear; he is not willing to trade his life for freedom. "Flight from death is death, and pursuit of death is life... Freedom is the tree of paradise and is watered by drops of spilled red blood" (513). This is not a call for violent revolution. Al-Kawakibi explicitly rejects that course of action. Rather, it is *willingness* to give up the everyday, bodily desires of life under tyranny that enables self-ordering, and thus agency and liberation. The captive of despotism, however, identifies himself with ordinary desire and is thereby enslaved to it. He leads an animal existence devoted to self-preservation and love of the appetites (484). The only pleasures of the victims of tyranny are "food, drink and the voiding of lust, as if their bodies were containers to be filled and emptied, or abscesses that fill with pus and expel it" (523). Here we have one of the more lurid of al-Kawakibi's hydraulic metaphors of dissipation. The captive of tyranny, as a result of his servitude to fear, his lack of will, has no *namus*, the internal law that creates moral order within the self and determines its obligations (486).[12] Thus, the captive lives a life with no order, as chaotic as the world of tyranny in which he abides, or in other words, a life ruled by fate. The rule of fate, however, is not a condition of unbounded chaos. It is rather a disfigured order that involves a painful caricature of self-ordering determined by contingency. "The laws of the life of the captive are the exigencies of the circumstances that surround him, which compel him to adapt his sensibilities in accordance with them and manage his self as they require" (502). Thus, he must habituate himself to self-abasement, flattery, hypocrisy, blind obedience, surrender of rights. He must numb his feelings and feign ignorance and stupidity—whatever self-abnegation is necessary to persist successfully under tyranny. The captive's condition is inextricably bound to the ups and downs of the wheel of fortune, at times euphoric, due to the misery of others, and at other times wretched, yet at no time is the captive master of his own destiny, in authority over his own self. Therefore the captive is a nonentity that merely takes up space until it vanishes. "The captive of despotism lives undistinguished, inert, without purpose, perplexed, not knowing how to kill his time, going through his days and years as though he were eager to reach his appointed hour and conceal himself beneath the earth" (498). For this reason, he cannot really be said to be living at all; "he is dead with respect to himself, alive with respect to others, as though he were nothing in himself, but something only as an appendage..." His mode of existence is "obliteration (*fana'*) within despots" (502). In this situation, violation of the self is normative. Dishonor, oppression, and dispossession are ways of life. The tyrannical or tyrannized self, therefore, is an unsealed, dissipated entity, like the collective body made up of such selves.

Mismanaged desire on the social level takes the form of inverted values and perverted institutions. Money and appearance are the highest values (475). Falsehood and ignorance prevail (440, 458, 485). The values that ordinarily lead to communal bliss are inverted in order to serve tyranny. Take for example glory (*majd*), which is defined as "securing a position of love and respect in people's hearts" (463). Glory has a spiritual pleasure superior to those of power and wealth and is preferred by those who are free to life itself. True glory can only be obtained through "expenditure for the sake of the community," be this of wealth, knowledge, or one's own self through suffering or danger, which is the highest form of glory. Love of glory spurs men to undergo severe hardships in order to benefit and sustain their nation (464). Despotism, however, promotes "vainglory" (*tamajjud*), which is "to take a flame from the hell of the despot's aggrandizement and use it to incinerate the honor of human equality" (465). In other words, vainglory is the competition for the despot's esteem granted in the form of ranks, titles, and other tokens that signify distinctions in rights and privileges among the despot's subjects. Hierarchy is the means by which despots entice their subjects to work for them and against each other. This is the case whether rank is inherited or conferred for good service. In order to win the top despot's favor, one must become a subordinate despot. Tyrannical relations (*tazalum*) proliferate within society, corrupting every institution. The family becomes a den of brutality and *ressentiment*. What is called glory is nothing more than precedence in iniquity. In this way, the name that should designate the social manifestation of virtue, the means by which nations persist and prosper, under tyranny designates social hierarchy, which is the institutional expression of communal dissolution and the mechanism by which it perpetuates itself. It may be noted here as well that subversion of linguistic truth is a fundamental feature of tyranny for al-Kawakibi and others. In the discourse of tyranny and enslavement, moral terms correspond to moral truth, except under tyranny itself, where only those who have managed to free themselves can assign names correctly.

The primary social institution, and the one that is most profoundly corrupted by despotism, is religion. Here, al-Kawakibi takes over Alfieri's anticlericalism and uses it to castigate what he regards as the reigning defacement of authentic Islam, which would establish a liberty even more comprehensive and enduring than that of contemporary European secular institutions. Al-Kawakibi accepts the arguments against religion put forth by the likes of Alfieri: that God is pictured as a despot and therefore buttresses despotism; that despots control their subjects through priests and superstition; that despots adopt the trappings of divinity, if not divinity itself, to terrorize and subjugate the people. All of this is true, but not of the religion practiced by the early Muslims. What happened, however, is that the Muslim polity fell victim to the inherent difficulties of maintaining freedom, due in particular to the introduction of foreign elements from other religions and the growth of obscurantism and zealotry, all in the service of despotism. "The innovations that have disfigured faith and distorted religions proceed almost entirely one from another and all arise for the sake of a single purpose, which is enslavement" (453). The religious scholars fell to fomenting dispute and division, turning knowledge into a farrago of arcane minutiae divorced from real life. They took over from foreigners religious intolerance, mystical superstitions and hierarchies, and fatalistic doctrines of human impotence. The withering away of the freedom of opinion that had been instituted in early Islam resulted in systematic misinterpretation of the Quran in the interests of despotic rulers. Knowledge cannot exist without freedom. The result is that people came to worship fear, incarnated in the despot, in place of God, whose worship liberates. The paradigm of social order, religion, became under tyranny the framework of disorder.

The means of awakening from the nightmare of despotism is self-ordering. On the level of the individual self, on which the nation is modeled, this means overcoming fear of death and thus transcending the everyday bodily desires that are the be-all and end-all of life under tyranny. Self-ordering comes about by managing one's desire according to the internal moral law that al-Kawakibi calls "*namus*." The result is the state of being that al-Kawakibi calls *"ananiya"* ("selfhood"), a term that means "egoism" in contemporary Arabic but in al-Kawakibi's usage designates self-realization. It comes about when a person "becomes aware of his own existence within the universe and realizes the meaning of selfhood so that his self becomes independent in itself, and he owns his will and ability to choose (*yamlika iradatahu wa-khtiyarahu*) and trusts in himself and in his Lord" (512). Al-Kawakibi puts great emphasis on the self-sufficiency of perfected selfhood. The free individual does not rely on anyone else for anything aside from exchange on terms of equality. He earns his own living and seeks favors from no one. His ties to others are purely voluntary and can be severed whenever his moral sense requires it. "He sees in himself that he by himself is the whole nation" (512). This state of affairs has been realized on the level of social relations only among the English, the Americans, and the Bedouins of the Arabian peninsula—the three peoples who are most free of despotism (439). Al-Kawakibi envisions, therefore, an autarkic, sovereign, morally inviolable individual, so completely subsumed in his own internal order that he is invulnerable to any form of external control. He has conquered fate, or rather, continuously conquers it. Al-Kawakibi sees this ceaseless self-realization as the process of individuation (*shukhus*), the life-process, which he contrasts to the decline or dissolution unto death that characterizes tyranny (505). The law of the individual is his identity in the sense that through it he achieves independent existence as a distinct, self-determining entity.

Yet it is precisely by virtue of the free individual's self-containment and self-sufficiency that he is absolutely and inalienably bound to the nation. He is bound to it from within, at the heart of his being. Virtue always takes the form of social virtue (*himma*), ambition for glory. The last prayer of the virtuous is "long live the nation, long live *himma*" (497). This is because the internal moral law that the free individual realizes is none other than the principle through which the nation itself is realized. Al-Kawakibi describes the man of glory as one who "guarantees with his wealth and his life the nation's *namus*, that is, its fundamental law, and preserves the nation's soul, that is, its freedom" (465). This *namus* or underlying principle of the nation can only demand self-sacrifice insofar as it coincides with the internal *namus* through which an individual becomes himself. Self-sacrifice that does not create individuation and agency is not self-ordering, but some form of enslavement. Self-sacrifice for the sake of the nation is therefore necessary for one to achieve existence as a free, independent being. Sacrifice, not for the existing nation, but for the underlying principle in which the true nation resides. This is how *ananiya* (selfhood) comes about. In other words, the nation is an individual's identity. The true nation is the true self.

Only through the virtue, freedom, agency, of individuals, can *ishtirak* (cooperation, communality), the means of national order and success, take effect. Captives of tyranny are barred from the fruits of communal cooperation. They cannot trust in themselves and therefore cannot trust in each other. They are capable only of deceiving and exploiting each other for the sake of slaking their selfish lusts (489). *Ishtirak*, however, is the accord created through the common devotion of individuals to their inner moral law. Through *ishtirak*, the nation comes fully into existence by realizing its underlying principle, because *ishtirak* is that principle as a process. It is al-Kawakibi's term for communal self-ordering. By means of this process, the nation reaches the point at which "each individual becomes fully in possession of himself and fully possessed by his nation." At this level, willingness to die is fully redeemed in the nation, making actual death unnecessary. "That nation for which each individual is willing to sacrifice his life and his wealth becomes, by virtue of that willingness on the part of individuals, no longer in need of their lives and their wealth" (522). It is only at this point of full alignment between individual selfhood and national selfhood that both individual and nation can really be said to exist as complete beings. They exist through each other, for they are innate to each other. In realizing themselves, individuals realize their nation. In ordering itself, the nation creates virtuous, complete individuals. The two processes are at bottom, one.

Self-ordering on the national level, *ishtirak*, is therefore absolutely fundamental to the elimination of tyranny, the perpetual process of warding off despotism. It is the management of the nation's desire on social, political, and economic levels. Socially, the primary domain of self-ordering is the shaping of individual behavior. This takes place not only through the general conditions of justice, accord, security, and personal freedom prevailing in the ordered society, but more specifically, through the institutions of moral education (*tarbiya*) organized by the properly ordered government. Consider al-Kawakibi's analogy of the gardener and the woodcutter. An individual's moral traits are like a garden. Left to nature, the garden mostly dies, and its strong plants overrun the weak. If it is tended by a gardener who manages it properly, it flourishes and bears much fruit. If it falls to the lot of a woodcutter who plunders it for immediate gain, it is ruined (486). Despotism is nature, or the woodcutter and his "blind axe." Ordered government cultivates the moral traits of its citizens and enables them to become themselves. For al-Kawakibi, moral education is the training in self-ordering necessary for the formation of free individuals. Despotic states cannot have education precisely because their citizens are not free: "How far are those people whose will has been extorted from them, whose hands are shackled, from directing their thought to a beneficial aim like education" (499). The virtues instilled by the correct moral education administered by the government are those of the heroic bourgeois, beginning with efficiency, thrift, adroitness, ending with love of honor, homeland and religion, readiness to aid the weak, contempt for tyranny and for life. The ultimate content of this heroic bourgeois self-negation is work for the simultaneous benefit of one's self and one's nation (498).

The definitive ideological content of "The Characteristics of Despotism" lies in the form that self-ordering takes on the political and economic levels. Politically, *ishtirak* requires and engenders the type of government introduced by Islam, which is, in al-Kawakibi's words, "aristocratic in basis, democratic in administration" (*aristuqratiyat al-mabna, dimuqratiyat al-idara*; 476). What this means exactly is not clear. The Islamic government is based on "principles of political freedom lying between democracy and aristocracy" (447). It is described as "aristocratic consultative government (*shura aristuqratiya*), that is, the consultation of those with authority (*ahl al-hall wa al-'aqd*) in the nation." Administration is based on "democratic, that is, communal, legislation" (*al-tashri' al-dimuqrati, ay, al-ishtiraki*; 450). The constitution of the government is not specified further than this. Al-Kawakibi seems to envision some type of limited democracy in which those who can stand for office must meet a set of moral and social criteria. Despite the "aristocratic" aspect of this government, al-Kawakibi emphasizes that it fosters justice, equality, fairness, and brotherhood. It is self-governance *par excellence*, wherein each member of the community is responsible for the community. Islamic rule is thus founded upon political values similar to those of liberalism. These values were properly understood during the early centuries of Islam, but were later subverted or divested of their political content. For example, religious scholars now use the word *'adl* to mean "rule according to law" and interpret *qisas* as meaning "retribution," whereas the primary Quranic meaning of both terms is "equality" (449; 504). Similarly, they obliterate the political intention behind the Quranic duty of "commanding the good and forbidding the evil," which is the establishment of a body, such as a parliament, that holds the ruler to account and prevents him from engaging in despotism (449, 451). Although the political liberty created by the early Muslims could not last, due to the seeping in of despotic practices by way of foreign elements, the legacy of the Islamic liberation of knowledge enabled Europeans to throw off the yoke of religious and monarchical tyranny and realize the principle of *ishtirak* in their own political institutions. "They replaced the tie of cooperation in obedience to despots with the tie of cooperation in public affairs, that cooperation from which love of homeland arises" (491). For this reason, Europeans are vastly superior to contemporary Muslims with regard to social virtue, and their societies are immensely more organized, powerful, and progressive than those of the East.

The self-negation of Europeans, however, is not complete. They tolerate a domain of dissipated desire that threatens their global preeminence. They remain in thrall to economic tyranny, which fatally vitiates the social order of European nations. This judgment proceeds from the protosocialist doctrine that al-Kawakibi articulates, which is perhaps the most innovative aspect of his Islamist ideology. Al-Kawakibi converts the moral economy of tyranny and enslavement into political economy by making money or wealth (*mal*) the correlate of desire. If the nation's wealth is properly managed, the wealth of individuals properly disciplined, excess wealth is subsumed into the nation resulting in prosperity, order, and power. If, on the other hand, individuals are left unrestrained in their quest for accumulation, the result is public and private moral corruption, the despotism of wealth exercised by the few over the many. According to al-Kawakibi, the relationship between wealth and despotism is "closely connected to the innate tyranny of the human soul" because wealth is nothing more than the means of obtaining pleasure or avoiding pain (474, 475). It is "drawn from the bounty that God has placed in Nature and its laws and may only be owned, that is, made exclusive to a person, by virtue of work exerted upon it or in exchange for it" (475). The only ways of producing wealth are the securing of natural materials, the processing of these materials for human benefit, and the distribution of finished products. Any other means of producing wealth is extortion, either by force or by fraud. Extortion converts one man's work into another man's pleasure. In other words, it is the conversion of negated desire (beneficial, legitimate wealth) into dissipated desire (excess, illegitimate wealth). Extortion of wealth is therefore extortion of personhood, of agency, and in this way, despotism. Accumulation of wealth is unnecessary in an ordered society and should be permitted only in a limited and strictly regulated manner. "Excessive wealth destroys a person's moral traits" and engenders social hierarchy (479). The desire to accumulate has been fostered in human beings by the tyranny of nature or of despotism (476). Accumulation of wealth "much beyond the amount of need" always finds immediate expression as dissipated desire, excess pleasure. As the equivalent of desire, wealth is the substance from which order is made, and when this substance is unnecessarily expended, order seeps away with it. Wealth is to be liberated from the circuit of pleasure and pain by becoming work for the nation: the work that continually produces the nation and in which national agency inheres.

According to al-Kawakibi, the basis of economic despotism lies in unjust division of labor, beginning with the deception practiced by women so as to enthrall men to them and thereby avoid work and other hardship. The more advanced the society, the greater the domination of women; modern Europe is a "feminine civilization" (475). Other unjust divisions follow, with the result that a small number of idlers appropriate the wealth produced by the majority. Moreover, even those who provide society with genuine benefit, such as merchants and scholars, are awarded far more wealth than their contribution justifies. If the poor were allowed their legitimate rights, vast disparities in wealth would cease to exist. The essence of despotism is plunder, the power to violate the moral economy by creating excess wealth in the hands of individuals, which can only come about through illegitimate means. The benefit of excess wealth can only be realized at the national level in the form of increased national prosperity and freedom. This is why the political order in Europe is threatened by social movements ranging from anarchism to socialism (477, 480). While European countries have much greater national wealth than Eastern countries, and are thus more independent and powerful, they nevertheless continue to tolerate a despotism of wealth that creates severe social inequality and corrupts the morals of both rich and poor.

It is in the ordering of economic relations that the superiority of the authentic Islamic social dispensation becomes apparent. "Islamism (*al-islamiya*)[13]... established a law for mankind based on the principle that wealth is the value of work and does not accumulate in the hands of the rich except by means of domination and deception" (476). Economic order comes about through *ishtirak*, which is in this domain near in meaning to *ishtirakiya*, the Arabic term for socialism. The main mechanism by which Islam creates this order is the yearly 2.5% tax on capital, known as *zaka*. According to al-Kawakibi, the purpose of this tax is to redistribute half of all profits, assuming a 5% rate of growth. Furthermore, "Islamism" stipulates that agricultural lands are not to be privately owned, but held in common by the nation, while income from these lands goes to those who cultivate them. Al-Kawakibi implies that this arrangement applies to the other means of production as well. In addition, all able-bodied individuals are to work for their living. The strict labor theory of value of course precludes many of the financial transactions and mechanisms, such as interest, that are fundamental to capitalist economies. These precepts, al-Kawakibi argues, fulfill the demands of the movements in Europe for social justice. They create a society in which individuals, families, towns, and regions enjoy complete autonomy within the nation and belong to the nation voluntarily.

Self-ordering in the economic domain replicates the logic of subsumption within the nation underlying the discourse of tyranny and enslavement, but this time in opposition to Europe rather than in alignment with it, as in the political domain. It is by virtue of its blueprint for economic organization that the Islamic dispensation will create an emancipated society that supersedes Europe in driving human history toward perfection. Al-Kawakibi's form of self-ordering, which he calls "public order" (*al-intizam al-'amm*) or *ishtirak*, creates simultaneous individual and national freedom. Just as individuals become agents by subsuming their desire into their internal principle of order, which is at the same time that of the nation, the nation itself attains freedom by subsuming its own desire, in the form of surplus wealth, into its internal principle. The excess desire of individuals, whether in the form of excess wealth or other types of pleasure, must be reinvested in the nation or else is squandered. Payment of the *zaka* tax is an act of self-sacrifice that brings individual agency into being, just like the broader struggle against tyranny to which this duty belongs. The same goes for, say, contributing to the national library. The basis of al-Kawakibi's political economy is that work is desire negated according to a principle of utility, thereby generating an intrinsic use value, which is simultaneously a moral value. The principle of utility is specified no further than "benefit to others," but we are told that a baker is superior to a poet, because his occupation is more useful (521). Work, therefore, is the activity that creates the self and the nation, and brings about universal human progress (*taraqqi*). But only the Islamic order manages and disciplines human activity such that it fully achieves its destiny as work.

Islam for al-Kawakibi is justified on a secular basis.[14] The principle of order that it enshrines, *ishtirak*, is the universal foundation of social freedom and flourishing. Any nation that has thrived and advanced human progress has at least partially realized this principle; the Islamic social dispensation fully realizes it. Al-Kawakibi defines progress on the national level in the same way that he does on the individual level: as the process of individuation, which is identical to *ishtirak*, and which is opposed to dissolution and dispersion (505). In other words, a nation progresses, and advances human progress, by becoming a distinct, self-determining, autarkic entity, the manifestation of its internal identity. A nation dies when, as a result of its disorder, its alienation from its identity, it becomes vulnerable to external forces and loses itself in its surroundings, usually absorbed by other more powerful nations. The basis of identity is moral and universal. This is why a mere return to authentic religion cannot cure the illness of the East unless preceded by a moral transformation. "Religion effects social progress when it encounters innate moral traits that are not corrupt, in which case it flourishes through them (*yanhada biha*) as Islamism flourished through the Arabs—that florescence (*nahda*) that we have been seeking for a thousand years in vain" (494).[15] "Islamism"—the Islamic social dispensation—is the social framework that most efficiently harnesses individual self-ordering at the national level. Islam frees humankind because it allows no authority above reason, and requires people to think for themselves, never submitting to any power other than God.[16] The primary vocation of the prophets was in teaching men how to be moral, how to own their will (490). At the same time, Islam, as a religion, motivates people to engage in self-sacrifice for the common good more effectively than mere love of country or of humanity, and this self-sacrifice is essential to nationhood and progress. In any case, the underlying difference dividing the believers in God, the materialists, and the "naturalists" (*tabi'iyun*) is a mere quibble over names (509). The inescapable conclusion, therefore, is that European nations can only succeed in defusing the social conflict that threatens them by adopting the precepts of authentic Islam (517).

Islamic identity, the institutional form of individual and social virtue, is universal—it is everyone's identity. But al-Kawakibi introduces an element into the ultimate identity to which he appeals that is not universal, and this is Arab ethnicity. The language of tyranny and enslavement relies on the opposition and unity of the despot and his captives. In speaking this language to depict the moral debasement of both, al-Kawakibi implicitly identifies the despot with the Ottoman Turkish government, and explicitly identifies the captives with the inhabitants of the East, or with contemporary Muslims in general. Al-Kawakibi refers to the Arabs and Arab ethnicity only in conjunction with another opposition that cuts across the first one. This is the opposition between the existing morally debased community, and the ideal, true community that lies within it. In other words, even though Arabs are among the captives of despotism, al-Kawakibi does not invoke the name "Arab" except in connection with virtue and self-ordering. This allows al-Kawakibi to take advantage of the self that is split between the actual and the real so as to align Arab ethnicity with freedom and agency. Even when he does mention the Arabs in the context of captivity, it is not to excoriate their moral condition as captives, but to withhold them from the ranks of the true captives in consequence of their enduring moral nobility. Thus Arabs, unlike other groups, are incapable of internalizing or successfully conforming to the rules of survival under despotism and therefore suffer the most under it (502). Otherwise, al-Kawakibi invokes the Arabs under two descriptions—as Bedouins of the Arabian peninsula, and as the masters of the early Muslim polity. Bedouin Arabs, by virtue of their individualism and freedom from central rule, are the only people in the East that have avoided despotism. Due to their remoteness and their innate qualities they have managed to escape fate (439–440). They are therefore not only the original Arabs, the most Arab Arabs, but the most free. As for the early Muslim Arabs, they are the ones who created an exemplary free polity and liberated knowledge for all humankind. Islam is the key to social order, but in al-Kawakibi's account, this order comes about only when the Arabs are in charge. In this way, al-Kawakibi invests contemporary Muslims with the attributes of lack, mistaken identity, dissipated desire, while reserving the name "Arab" for the attributes of negated desire. The effect of this strategy is that the moral transformation that eliminates despotism requires the reinstatement of Arab political leadership in the Muslim community.

On the collective level, the logic of self-ordering ultimately ensures that the disorder of despotism neatly parallels the order of freedom. In other words, the structure of oppression and self-ordering, of self-abnegation, and self-negation, of absorption and autarky, are the same. Only the content differs. We can consider this with respect to "foreign" rule, which is always rooted in the self, but which may be characterized as belonging either to the true self or to its enslavement to desire. In the case of Ottoman rule, the foreign element is depicted as the locus of the self's dissipation, which will lead to non-existence and absorption unless brought under control. The process of reforming or eliminating Ottoman rule, as much as the outcome itself, constitutes the self-ordering that restores order. This is because foreign rule merely manifests the condition of the people subject to it. The imposition of foreign rule, however, may itself be a form of self-ordering. "When a nation does not rule itself properly God subjugates it to the rule of another nation, just as the law empowers a guardian over a minor or incompetent" (534). This is the necessary consequence of the universality of virtue and identity. Hence, "individuals and collectivities under ordered governments progress in knowledge and wealth, and thus have natural authority over the individuals or nations that have been sunk by ill-omened despotism to the depth of ignorance and poverty" (522). The rule of foreigners is, in this case, the rule of the true self rather than that of the dissipated self. The order of the self is in this case completely externalized.

Despite their structural similarity, freedom and despotism are antithetical conditions immediately recognizable to those who are themselves free. It is up to the enlightened inhabitants of a despotic state to awaken their compatriots to the conditions of their existence and spur them to change it by stirring their national feeling. "The single effective means of disabling despotism is the progress of the nation in awareness and feeling and this only comes about through education and emotional inspiration (*tahmis*)" (531). Who are the enlightened inhabitants? Broadly speaking, they are the intellectuals who study the "sciences of human life" (*'ulum al-haya*), and thereby serve in the perpetual war between knowledge and tyranny. "The intellectuals strive to enlighten minds while the despot struggles to extinguish their light. The two sides compete over the public (common people: *al-'awamm*)" (458). This is, once again, the classic hegemonic struggle over an inert mass ready to fall in line behind whichever side gains the upper hand. Not all intellectuals, however, fight on the right side. Many, or even most, serve despotism one way or another. Those who have managed to embrace freedom, who are qualified to lead the people, must have moral qualities that enable them to do so. One way in which this status comes about is through lineage. According to al-Kawakibi, most self-sacrificing lovers of glory under despotism come from "rare houses protected by chance from the eyes of humiliating tyrants, or are of the noble men of houses whose line of righteous warriors has not terminated and whose old women have not ceased mourning them" (464). These are men of innate nobility who, like the Bedouin Arabs, have managed to defy fate. Al-Kawakibi himself can probably be counted among their number, since he informs us that he has spent thirty years of his life seeking a remedy for the illness suffered by the Muslim community, risking his life in the process (431). Those qualified to awaken and lead their captive compatriots—whether men of al-Kawakibi's ilk, the Bedouin Arabs, or even the Arabs in general—are characterized by some manner of isolation from ordinary people and ordinary life, some kind of proximity to death, resulting from a combination of innate moral traits and propitious circumstance.

In al-Kawakibi's combination of classical virtue and self-governance with an immanent principle of social order, the key point of articulation is the idea that the virtuous citizen "sees in himself that he by himself is the whole nation." In this way, the citizen occupies a position that is akin to the externality of the virtuous sovereign figure. This autonomous position allows the citizen to recognize tyranny and refuse it without making him the source of an order to be imposed on others. For the consequence of this position is that "each individual becomes fully in possession of himself and fully possessed by his nation." This freedom anchored in each individual's embodiment of the moral agency of the nation is in al-Kawakibi derived from classical sovereignty but has become an immanent principle that makes a non-hierarchical integration of individuals on the basis of their internal order possible. The tenuousness of this balanced position staked out by al-Kawakibi is apparent. The political hegemony of the Arabs or even that of the enlightened intellectuals is difficult to distinguish in al-Kawakibi's depiction from the external imposition of order. Virtue is often difficult to distinguish from the sovereign status derived from the mastery of desire. Social hierarchy, though it is inveighed against, seems to be instated in the "aristocratic democracy" of al-Kawakibi's virtuous republic. Moreover, the constitution of "communality," the principle of individual and social order, through its intrinsic freedom from injustice and oppression, allows the deployment of the classical language and motifs of tyranny and enslavement in the depiction of the contemporary social order. In all of these respects, al-Kawakibi's conception of communal order is inherently continuous with traditional sovereign virtue. Nevertheless, al-Kawakibi's social order replicates the internal order of the individual, not on the basis of a hierarchy of powers within the self, but on the basis of the investment and management of desire that results in productive, ordering activity in all individuals. This is the basis on which al-Kawakibi's program for political and economic order acquires its claim to legitimacy.

Part Two: The Nation Without Qualities: Sati' al-Husri

Tyranny and enslavement is a rhetoric of moral condemnation that takes a virtuous standpoint outside of the corruption of society. As increasing responsibility for the moral order of individuals is placed in the structures and mechanisms of the social order, the enslavement of individuals to desire comes to be increasingly cast in terms of psychopathology rather than moral failure. This trend becomes clear in the reformist ideologies that emerged after World War I, and particularly with regard to Sati' al-Husri (1880–1968), the most well-known expositor of Arab nationalism.[17] Al-Husri consistently presents the reality of the Arab nation as an inescapable sociological fact backed by the empirical evidence of dozens of other nations whose formation al-Husri tirelessly details. He adopts the style of an academic researcher rather than that of a fiery orator. Although he often casts his conclusions in the form of memorable slogans, he mainly avoids heroic rhetoric and outright moral condemnations. Moreover, he makes no appeal to Islamic texts and doctrines, preferring to support his arguments with references to modern European scholars and thinkers. Nevertheless, an underlying rhetoric of national selfhood, with its logic of self-negation, remains constitutive of his nationalist vision. The moral economy of desire, with its intrinsic principle of order, continues to be the matrix from which the nation is produced. In al-Husri's thought, this principle of order is social organization, which is the means of self-preservation and the key to power, freedom, and progress. The ability to enter into social organization, "sociality" (*ijtima'iya*), is the essential nature, the identity, of human beings, and can be fully realized only in the nation. Al-Husri is an Arab nationalist in that he founds identity in Arabness. But the importance of Arabness for him is not its positive content, but simply that it is what makes a distinct nation possible. What is of ultimate importance to al-Husri is the social form of the nation, which he sees as the origin of moral order in individuals and in society. Therefore, the social element that will order Arab individuals and their nation is not one that embodies Arabness per se, but the one that embodies the social form of the nation—the state-bureaucratic institutions. The result of al-Husri's abstract, universal form of identity, is that the sole purpose and function of the nation is the production of ever-increasing degrees of social organization. The essential elements that distinguish one nation from others, common language and history, are only of value in that they make this end possible. The marks of national distinction are simply the fundamental universal means of transforming desire into order.

Al-Husri's doctrine of nationality is simple and well-known, stated and restated by him in dozens of lectures and articles, reprinted in almost a score of books. The nation is a "living social being" (*ka'in ijtima'i hayy*), made up by all those who share a common language and common history, whether they are aware of their nationhood or not. Nations are "natural kinds," like animal species; they are objectively given. A nation dies if its language dies, and new nations are born with the birth of new languages. New nations can be born as well when the speakers of a single language split into isolated groups and develop separate histories, although al-Husri does not clearly specify the criteria for what constitutes a separate history. A nation exists whether its members form a single polity or not, and whether they govern themselves or are incorporated into one or more foreign empires. Nevertheless, each nation harbors an innate impulse to form a single self-governing polity and cannot realize its powers until it does so. Any other political arrangement is unacceptable and must be resisted. The ties that bind together the members of a nation exist on the mental-emotional (*ma'nawi*) plane rather than in material factors such as kinship, race, economy, and way of life. Nor is religion an essential binding element. The common language is the nation's being, without which it would not exist. Common historical memory is the nation's feeling, its self-awareness, and self-love, without which it would be paralyzed and insensate. Thus, a nation is a single organism, living and feeling, though spiritual (*ma'nawi*) in nature rather than physical.[18]

William Cleveland has suggested that al-Husri was impelled to adopt the abstract conception of nationhood that these claims add up to by, at least in part, his lack of rootedness in any specific Arab social network. Al-Husri was brought up mainly in Istanbul and trained for a career in civil administration. He then served as a high-level Ottoman bureaucrat in the field of education, achieving fame as a brilliant reformer. He did not settle in any Arab land until the collapse of the Ottoman empire in 1919, in his fortieth year, upon which he went to Damascus and entered the service of the newly installed King Faisal, whom he accompanied to Iraq after the French put an end to Arab government in Syria. In the various high offices that al-Husri held in Iraq and later in Syria, through which he shaped educational policy in these countries, Cleveland argues that he sought to stay aloof from factional politics and focus on the big picture of Arab unity. "[A]l-Husri's espousal of a broad Arab nationalism...was at once cause and effect of his socio-political ambivalence..."[19] Cleveland also emphasizes al-Husri's thoroughly secular and European education, and his lack of grounding in traditional Arabic and Islamic intellectual culture, as crucial factors in the form of nationalism that he developed.[20] In the present discussion, I will not elaborate al-Husri's nationalist doctrines per se. Rather, I will show that al-Husri structures and legitimizes the form of nation and national institutions that he calls for by systematically anchoring them in the moral order of the self. For al-Husri, this means making the objective, distinguishing feature of the nation—language—the means to humanity and universality. I will conclude by showing how al-Husri invests the state and its institutions with the nation's power of self-ordering, and thus national agency, imagining the politically unified nation as the ultimate machine of modernity, the device that unleashes endless order.

For al-Husri, like al-Kawakibi, mismanagement of desire lies at bottom of the "Eastern question," resulting in the dominance of egoism over national loyalty, self-sacrifice, and incorporation. Let us begin with the foundation of this mismanagement as al-Husri presents it in a piece entitled "The Concept of Happiness and the Spirit of Activity Among Us and Among Westerners."[21] Al-Husri argues here that happiness can be conceived as the proportion of pleasure to pain in a person's life. The difference between "us" and westerners is that we seek to achieve happiness by minimizing pain, while they pursue happiness by maximizing pleasure. In order to avoid pain, we are willing to forgo pleasure, while they are willing to risk pain in order to augment pleasure. The result is that we are drawn to minimalist "static pleasures" (*al-ladhdhat al-sukuniya*), which are "negative" in nature, whereas they pursue maximizing "active pleasures" (*al-ladhdhat al-fa'aliya*), which are "positive" in nature. We like to lie about in gardens, listen to music, watch dancing, eat, and drink. They like to exert themselves in strenuous exercises, which are no different from hard work in terms of application and activity. We are correct in our perpetual refrain that we are men of "indolence and indistinction" (*kasal wa khumul*), whereas they are men of "earnestness and action" (*jidd wa nashat*). We are far off the mark, however, when we explain this by saying that we, and not they, are devoted to pleasures and amusements. We must admit that they are devoted to pleasures and amusements even more so than we are. But they are possessed of a "penchant for pleasure, tied to movement and activity," rather than a "penchant for pleasure, tied to idling and indolence." Therefore, "we must say, 'Europeans are people of earnestness and work, to the extent that they are devoted to amusement and frivolity (*lahw wa taraf*)', not 'They are people of earnestness and work, despite their immersion in amusement and frivolity.'" Herein lies the secret to European success. We are sunk in stasis and indistinction because we extirpate our children's natural impulses towards activity, which we see as signs of vulgarity and disrespect. We train them, through our errant attitudes and repressive social customs, to love indolence and to be devoid of ambition. Once we reform these attitudes and practices, once we succeed in completely changing our understanding of happiness, there will be born within us "a great force which will free us from the swamps of stasis and indistinction in which we now flounder and lead us to hard work and exertion with zeal and joy."

We see here that al-Husri accepts the general premise that Easterners dissipate their desire in passive pleasures, forms of enslavement, while Europeans convert their desire into active social virtue and rule the world. But whereas many other authors find scope for criticizing Europeans with regard to their distinctive and well-known "pleasures and amusements," or feel the need to apologize for them, al-Husri is able to do one better. Generalizing European amusements under the description "strenuous and active," he analyzes European recreation as the paradoxical negation of desire as the *attainment* of pleasure. In other words, Europeans are superior to Easterners because for Europeans, the self-ordering that leads to power and dominion does not result from the repression of desire, but from its release. European pleasures are emblematic of the proper arrangement of the European self, such that desire naturally expresses itself as order. Easterners, on the other hand, due to their internal disorder, find pleasure only in unproductive passivity, and are averse to the naturally exhilarating exertions of the body. In the beginning of the article, al-Husri avers that happiness is the proportion of pleasure to pain, because the total elimination of pain is an impossible fantasy. His depiction of active amusement belies this claim, in a critical sense, because the pain suffered in European exertions produces pleasure and power and is thereby fully redeemed, while Eastern pains cannot be redeemed by negative pleasures, which add up to nothing but national stasis. This is why transforming negative into positive happiness leads to the undertaking of hard work with "zeal and joy." European desire is fully subsumed in self-mastery, in work for the nation. Eastern desire is squandered without issue.

Europeans have achieved this subsumption not because they are inherently morally superior, but because they have adopted the nation as their form of social and political organization. Only through the nation can the self and society be configured so as to enable the realization of the self in society. The reason for this is that the human essence or identity, that which distinguishes human beings from other animals, lies in rationality (*'aqiliya*) and sociality (*ijtima'iya*), both of which arise from the capacity for language.[22] Language enables human beings to form large societies in which most people never see each other, or have direct connections with each other ("imagined communities," in Benedict Anderson's phrase). Human beings are distinguished from animals by language, and in turn are distinguished from each other by the specific languages that they speak. The language spoken by a group of people creates within this group shared sentiments, thought, and ideals, causing them to regard themselves as a unified body. Al-Husri concludes from this, citing Herder, Fichte, and others, that the speakers of a single language form a natural social unit, a body with a common "heart and soul," and must have their own state. Languages have not given rise to self-governing nations until modern times because increasing social complexity, with its demands for more intensive communication, popular participation in government, and so forth, makes it necessary for the modern polity to operate on the basis of a single language. "The events of the 19th century did not create nationalities, and did not engender national feeling, but rather provided the circumstances that allowed national feeling to effect the formation of states."[23]

In this discussion, al-Husri designates sociality as the main principle of human identity, and finds it to be located in the human capacity of speech. Then, performing the slippage that is necessary for linguistic theories of nationality, he transfers this human identity from language as the capacity for speech to the specific language that an individual speaks. And he treats this specific language as a standardized national language, ignoring the vernaculars that people may actually speak. In this way, the human capacity for speech generates sociality, which is the principle of human identity, and the nation, which is the social form in which this identity is realized.

The casting of sociality as the principle of identity has far-reaching moral consequences. It means that whatever traits and behaviors bring about the realization of sociality constitute virtue, and whichever ones inhibit or impair it are vicious. Thus, for al-Husri, the primary moral failing, the one that underlies virtually all undesirable attitudes and actions, is egoism (*ananiya*). Egoism is a concept to which al-Husri has frequent recourse in his lectures and writings. It is al-Husri's term for the misidentification of the self as its illusory desires, resulting in the dissipation of desire. Consider this description of egoism's anti-moral nature:

> This excessive individualism which thinks of nothing but itself, which avoids all forms of exhausting effort, which seeks the greatest possible

amount of pleasure, and which concerns itself perpetually with its own health and comfort, whoever scrutinizes these characteristics, must admit with me that they point to one thing, and this is "moral disintegration" and it leads necessarily to one result, "social dissolution".[24]

Although the language here is not as colorful as that of al-Kawakibi, the rhetorical structure is the same. Immersion in everyday life, in the petty concerns and pleasures of one's personal and bodily existence, in the conditions of life as one finds them, is the loss of the real self, the surrender of one's agency to the tyranny of the given. Order, value, and freedom require the negation of this ordinary dissipated desire. But al-Husri is no moralist in the conventional sense. His concern is not so much for personal morality, but for virtue as the means for social incorporation. For him, as is apparent in the quotation above, the linkage between moral integration and social integration is absolute and definitive. The provenance of this quotation is a 1941 lecture entitled "On the Collapse of France." In it, al-Husri argues that France fell so quickly to German forces because of the spread of egoism among the French in the period after World War I, leading to factionalism, disunity, and indifference to the national cause. Once the French were conquered and lost their national freedom, their selfish pleasures were no longer so abundant or appealing. The moral is that the nation must come first. Nationalism is synonymous with moral and social integration, because the nation embodies sociality, the principle of human identity. It is for this reason that the nation attracts desire and turns it into motivation for virtue. "The nationalist idea possesses a subjective force; it motivates action and struggle when it enters minds and seizes souls. It is one of the '*idées-forces*' which stimulate ambition for glory (*himam*), move the masses, and motivate people to expenditure and sacrifice when necessary."[25] Nationalism, therefore, is the antithesis of egoism. Whereas egoism dissipates desire, nationalism turns it into virtue. In the nation, desire finds its own internal principle of order in which it can be subsumed, and thereby becomes free of fatal egoistic attachments.

Egoism, therefore, is mistaken identity, the failure to recognize one's authentic human identity in the nation. As such, it underlies all political orientations and attachments that go contrary to Arab nationalism. Espousing the wrong ideology, the wrong political identity, means that one has chosen self-interest instead of virtue and true identity. Consider the arguments al-Husri makes in an article entitled "Between Patriotism and Cosmopolitanism."[26] Here al-Husri seeks to defend patriotism against what he calls two of its most dangerous enemies—egoism and (Marxist) cosmopolitanism. Patriotism, according to al-Husri, is fully opposed to egoism because it promotes the high ideals of altruism and self-sacrifice.

The same might be said of cosmopolitanism, which rejects nationality and holds the unity of all human beings as its ideal. In theory, cosmopolitanism does not contravene moral values as egoism does. But the cosmopolitan ideal is remote and "negative" in nature. People may believe in it, but unlike patriotism, it "does not require individuals to undertake immediate action and actual sacrifice." Only patriotism commands direct self-sacrifice for the sake of others. Cosmopolitanism, therefore, becomes a pretext for refusing the sacrifices called for by patriotism and adhering to a life of egoism. It serves as nothing more than a hollow justification for the pursuit of selfish interests. The result is that the nation becomes weak and vulnerable to foreign conquest. Al-Husri offers the example of the pre-Napoleonic Germans, and particularly Fichte, who espoused cosmopolitanism until the French invasion, upon which he became a chief advocate and philosopher of German nationalism.

> The enlightened German intellectuals saw with their own eyes that while they were sunk in dreams of humanity and cosmopolitanism, their country was conquered by the armies of a foreign nation remote from those dreams and suffused with the spirit of patriotism in its most intense and powerful form. This nation began to rule them, enslaving them and humiliating them and driving them forth as it pleased.

Thus, cosmopolitan ideals led, not to world peace and universal enlightenment, but to the reduction of the Germans to the status of cattle in their own country. The German intellectuals responded by adopting patriotism and promoting it among their countrymen, leading to independence and national renaissance. Only native patriotism can successfully oppose foreign patriotism. Moral ideals that do not extirpate egoism in such a way as to lead to national unity end up strengthening egoism. They are chimeras that do not correspond to the natural form of human sociality.

It can be seen that the fate of foreign conquest is one of the chief bogeys of al-Husri's discourse. For him, as for others, the nation that has not yet unified is perpetually under threat of dissolution and absorption into alien others. Foreign conquest, however, is no less phantasmic in al-Husri's thought than it is in other versions of national selfhood. It is an emanation of the egoistic self, rather than a mere external reality. This is most apparent in al-Husri's linkage of regionalism in the Arab world with colonialism.[27] According to al-Husri, the existence of many Arab states instead of a single one is due to no natural or necessary factors, but is the outcome of historical accident. The Arab lands "split into numerous states because of the agreement of states that coveted them ... they split up in fulfillment of the desires of illegitimate occupiers."²⁸ The new countries are embodiments of colonial greed and there is no reason for their continued separation. They fail to unify, however, because of regionalism, which al-Husri defines as the "tendencies to preserve the status quo." People become attached to their local country, its state, its tangible particularities, simply because these occupy their everyday lives, while the Arab nation, though primary, remains only a mental and emotional phenomenon, bereft of material manifestation. Vested interests take root in the artificial polities. Foreign powers "exert their utmost efforts to provoke the spirit of regionalism in different countries," because fragmentation is conducive to colonial interests. Hence, regionalism, the complacent attachment to existing Arab countries, is in reality attachment to colonialism. In other words, love of one's local nation is a form of egoism, and as such, encourages, enables, and is content with foreign subjugation. Such love betrays a colonized soul. Therefore, "it is necessary for every Arab individual to fight regionalism as he fought colonialism, first within the recesses of his self, then among the people of his nation, with all of his powers." The rhetorical structure at work here is crucial to al-Husri's depiction of the nation in general and reappears in numerous contexts. Egoism and colonialism are two sides of the same coin. The nation eliminates colonialism by eliminating egoism. That which opposes national unity, in this case regionalism, is one of many forms of egoism as foreign tyranny that the self must overcome. Foreign rule is the tyranny of one's own desire. It is the investment of desire in a manner that surrenders it rather than in a manner that redeems it.

Yet on the structural level these two investments are parallel. The line between tyranny and self-realization is an elusive one. Consider the following statement:

> Whoever does not sacrifice his personal freedom for the sake of his nation's freedom—when circumstances require it—may lose his personal freedom along with the freedom of his nation and homeland. And whoever refuses to 'obliterate' himself in the nation to which he belongs—on certain occasions—may be forcibly obliterated in foreign nations that may conquer his homeland some day.²⁹

Obliteration in the nation means freedom and agency, even though it may involve bodily death. Obliteration in a foreign nation means slavery and extinction, even when the body survives. The first should be voluntary, because it corresponds to the truth of desire. The second is always involuntary, because it results from the failure to master desire and attain agency. The two forms of self-obliteration are the antithetical realities that structure al-Husri's rhetoric of nationhood. Yet the use of the same term to designate them indicates the tenuousness of their opposition. And the instability of this opposition is inscribed in the very heart of the nation. For the Arab nation itself is the result of the conquest and absorption of non-Arab linguistic communities, nations by al-Husri's definition. Arab existence has come about by the very process Arabs must be willing to die to prevent. Calls for the revival of those extinct nations, often associated with regionalism, attract al-Husri's sharpest condemnation. In this way, foreign conquest may really be self-conquest, just as foreign tyranny is enslavement to one's self.

The present reality of multiple Arab countries is therefore an expression of the bifurcated Arab self, whose truth lies in the unified Arab nation. The primary site of the bifurcated self, however, is the Arabic language itself. For in it lies both Arab identity and the extinction of this identity. According to al-Husri, the Arab nation exists because it has a single language. But this language is "unified and unifying" only in its written form.[30] The dialects of spoken Arabic, if promoted as languages of writing and public communication, would lead to the disintegration of the Arab nation. This fate was averted during the medieval periods of Arab disunity and weakness only because the preservation of classical Arabic was guaranteed by the sacred status of the Quran.[31] For the modern period, al-Husri articulates the linguistic divide to the history of colonialism.[32] The promotion of different forms of spoken Arabic in various regions belongs to a long line of colonialist policies and stratagems designed to spiritually subjugate colonized peoples by keeping them divided and cutting them off from culture. Colonialist deceptions have convinced a number of Arab intellectuals of the supposed benefits of replacing standard Arabic with spoken forms. Though this policy has not been adopted by any government, the use of spoken dialects in public contexts, particularly in radio and television broadcasts, film, theatre, and so forth, poses a grave danger to the standard language. Therefore, "it is incumbent upon every Arab intellectual to fight against the spoken language, in which colonialists see great benefit for their politics, at the cost of great harm to the interests of the Arab nation and its future."[33]

It can be seen then that although al-Husri places the essential nature of human beings in their ability to speak (*natiqiya*), their exercise of this ability may alienate their nature if it in any way impedes the formation of a nation on the basis of a standardized written language that need not coincide with their speech. Language provides human beings with their social destiny and enables them to fulfill it, but at the same time may prevent them from doing so. This contradiction arises from al-Husri's transference of human identity from language as the ability to speak, to language as a national language, the kind that is instituted, standardized and taught to an entire population by a modern state. The contradiction is "resolved" only at the rhetorical level, in terms of an economy of desire. The use of the vernaculars in public contexts is a manifestation of misplaced desire, of residual colonial self-enslavement. To "fight against the spoken language" is to engage in self-ordering, to bring about the true self, by strengthening the national language that unites the Arabs and enables their social communion. Unlike many other intellectuals, al-Husri has no particular concern for classical Arabic per se. His chief desideratum, rather, is that there be a homogeneous national language, preferably in speech as well as writing, and if this can be created through the infusion of written Arabic with shared elements of spoken dialects, then so be it.[34] He wants a language that makes the Arab nation transparent to itself. What this means is that the source of Arab identity, the "unified unifying" Arabic language, has as yet only an ideal presence. The nation exists and is known through its language, even if this language does not yet fully exist. In this way, the Arabic language mirrors the Arab self—its present disordered reality must be subsumed into its true identity. It must be ordered so that it and the nation it engenders can come fully into being. "Modern history is full of eloquent examples of the tremendous efforts which have been and still are exerted by more than a few nations and states in this cause, in order to set the ground for their independence, or secure their unification."[35] The human faculty of speech, therefore, can properly constitute human and national identity only so long as it is governed by the nation, which creates itself, as well as fully realized human beings, in the process.

The nation has precedence over individual existences because it is the nation that brings fully realized individuals into being. Personal freedom is only valuable insofar as it can be subsumed in the nation. "Freedom is not a self-standing goal, but one of the means to the higher life."[36] This is the life of social organization and world-historical progress. The organization of individuals afforded by the nation brings out the hidden powers of these individuals more completely than any other means. In other words, it enables their self-negation. Since the Arab nation has not yet fully come into being, Arab individuals cannot realize themselves and remain enslaved to untamed desire, thereby subject to diverse forms of deception and servitude.

> I know that the illness of egoism is epidemic in all of the Arab countries, and solidarity for the sake of the common good is almost unknown in them. I am not unaware that the dominance of egoism creates fertile ground for nourishing plots and conspiracies which very often sacrifice the common interest on the altar of personal gain. I know as well that the nationalist and patriotic impulse has not yet acquired—in any Arab country—the necessary power to suppress the violence of lusts and egoisms.[37]

Al-Husri argues that the "moral defects" of Arab society are the result of colonial rule, and are similar to the sort of bodily and psychological disturbances experienced by pregnant women, teething children, and pubescent girls. They are deeply ingrained "base dispositions" implanted in the selves of those who surrender to colonialism as well as those who rebel against it. They do not vanish immediately after the overthrow of colonial rule, because they are perpetuated by persisting practices and conditions, which can be extirpated only through a new form of struggle. "This internal struggle that must be undertaken against existing conditions and entrenched habits is no less difficult than the struggle undertaken against foreign rule, perhaps more difficult."[38] Such a struggle will eventually lead to "psychic and social ferment." Intellectuals are in the position of the physicians who treat feminine and infantile maladies, and must therefore adopt the perseverance and optimism of such physicians. In this depiction of the condition of the Arab nation, al-Husri intermingles medical and moral tropes, alternately splitting and unifying the national self. "Internal struggle" applies to the nation as a unified subject, whereas medical treatment is performed by the intellectual stratum upon the passive, ill, feminized body of the nation. The rhetorical equivalence of these two images of the national self enables al-Husri to move agency away from individuals who would realize the nation by transforming themselves, and place it in a specific sector of the nation responsible for transforming the whole—most often, the educational and military institutions of the state.

It is the function of the state, and particularly the school and the barracks, to root out an individual's egoism, his (colonial) self-enslavement that leads to social division, and replace it with "the spirit of solidarity, obedience and sacrifice, which would secure for him success not only as an independent individual, but as a person serving his nation as well."[39] This comes about through "social education," also known as "moral education."[40] Al-Husri believes that emotions "work as the true motor of behavior, and the underlying impulse of will," whereas cognition "does not move the will, but illumines the paths and by-ways for it."[41] Hence people cannot be virtuous, which is to say, socially incorporable, unless they are trained to love society and social existence above all, and habituated to social discipline. In an article entitled "Social Education,"[42] al-Husri argues that the difference between the West and the East is that in westerners, orientation toward the "we" is predominant, while easterners suffer from excessive orientation to the "I." For this reason, westerners have greater social virtue, as evidenced in the proliferation of social organizations and institutions among them. Easterners, however, are self-centered, as is apparent in their appalling lack of concern for the rules and etiquette of public behavior. The underlying cause of these Eastern "defects" is the self-enclosed nature of the eastern family, due to the exclusion of women from public life, which creates a different social "morphology" from that of the West, one leading to social stagnation and atrophy.[43] The purpose of social education is to remedy the resulting defects, not only by imparting the correct beliefs to children, but more crucially, by inspiring them with the right emotional attachments and implanting in them the right habits and traits. Social education is effected not only through compulsory schooling, but through compulsory military service.

> I know of nothing that equals military life in its influence on social traits. Military barracks are tantamount to social schools that connect the individual to his nation and insert him into the most important link of the social chain, give him a vivid impression of the nation and homeland, and habituate him to true sacrifice in different forms...for the sake of the nation and homeland.[44]

The idea here seems to be that although social structure is responsible for the ills of Arab society, state institutions can counteract the effects of social structure, and set in motion its transformation, through direct action upon individuals.[45] What al-Husri emphasizes in this regard is the creation of stable "social traits," which ensure automatic self-negation, rather than the freedom and agency that self-negation requires and engenders. Al-Husri is quite similar to al-Kawakibi in terms of the critical function that he assigns to national education (notwithstanding their antithetical views on military service), and even with respect to the importance of inculcating correct habits and traits. Moreover, both writers see individual self-realization as occurring in conjunction with national self-realization. The emphasis for al-Kawakibi, however, lies in the capacity for freedom that proper education creates in an individual. For him, freedom is the key to social cooperation, even though his "freedom" is structurally indistinguishable from al-Husri's "social discipline." Thus, he retains a heroic language of the individual achievement of self-mastery. Al-Husri, on the other hand, by depicting self-mastery more as a product of state institutions, turns virtue into an ensemble of bureaucratically designed and administered procedures.

The state bureaucracy, therefore, is the primary site of national agency in the present condition of unrealized Arab unity. In order to endow it with this function, al-Husri must separate it from the disorder, dissension, and self-interest of society as a whole and identify it with the real national will. He must make it a liminal, ordered entity that operates at a higher moral level than that of everyday life. This is in spite of the fact that the state institutions of which he speaks belong to *regional* Arab governments, whose mere existence embodies egoism and colonial manipulation in his view. What enables bureaucratic transcendence for al-Husri is the formal nature of state institutions. It is by virtue of their intense degree of social organization, into which they incorporate individuals and thereby train them to be incorporated, that these institutions lift themselves and those in their charge above the disorganization of ordinary life. Thus, a fundamental function of the properly designed school is the placing of students in contexts in which they must work together to achieve a single end. Hence, he lays great emphasis on the contribution of group sports to socialization.[46] The virtue of life in military barracks is that in it "the disciplinary regime (*al-nizam*) has first place in everything."[47] For al-Husri, social incorporation requires self-sacrifice, no matter at what level this incorporation takes place. It is all at bottom a form of military life. In addition to this point, al-Husri insists that educational institutions remain completely free of ordinary politics. He distinguishes between "the lofty, fundamental aspect of politics," and "the everyday, subsidiary aspect of politics."[48] The former is nationalism itself, and has a definitive role in education. The latter is party politics, and must be kept out entirely. The issues at stake in this form of politics are too close to us, involve private interests and sentiments, are subject to rumor and manipulation, and it is therefore nearly impossible to know the truth of them. Schools must maintain a position of complete neutrality with respect to everyday political conflicts and the parties involved in them. Thus, the moral and epistemological degradation of everyday politics makes this realm inimical to the nature of educational institutions. The morally universal and transparent nation, however, is not only central to these institutions, but the very provenance of the values that they serve. As long as educational institutions are structured by the nation and oriented toward it, they embody a universality that lifts them above everyday life, and enables them to transform it by creating virtuous individuals.

Al-Husri's conception of "social traits" (*al-sajaya al-ijtimaʿiya*) encapsulates his representation of the nation as the site of ultimate selfhood, revealing the manner in which the nation, rather than the individual, is the primary matrix of the economy of desire. The transformation of egoism into patriotism unleashes the inner forces of individuals only when this transformation occurs on a simultaneous collective level. Whatever private benefits an isolated individual might gain from virtue are of no consequence to al-Husri, because he understands individual self-ordering solely as the capacity to be productively incorporated into society. For al-Husri, true moral value lies in the "positive" and "active" virtues of social participation, rather than in the "negative" and "reactive" virtues of restraint and self-abnegation.[49] Such virtues take the form of firm "character" (*sajiya*), which is composed of strength of will and enduring affect. This character is what enables self-sacrifice. It is the product and producer of the transformation of egoism into patriotism. The social traits that make up character enable the formation of social institutions and organizations. Such social bodies are of paramount importance in modern life. They are the equivalent, on the mental-emotional (*ma'nawi*) plane, of the technological machines and devices that have transformed modern life on the material plane. Just as the latter harness powers from material bodies that otherwise remain hidden in them, so do social organizations "bring out powers hidden in selves and magnify the effect of individuals stupendously."[50] These powers are precisely the desire that was formerly dissipated in egoism. The creations of modern technology themselves, and in particular, the machines of modern warfare, "conceal a stupendous array of mental-emotional powers" to which these machines owe their design, manufacture, and coordinated operation. The most important of these powers are "the spirit of patriotism," and "the spirit of organization."[51] As we have seen, the nation is the fundamental form of social organization, and patriotism is desire subsumed into the nation. Hence the nation is the modern machine par excellence; it comprehensively harnesses human powers and thereby makes possible the endless proliferation of social and physical machines that replicate it. The meaning and purpose of human desire lies in the unlimited order and power that it becomes in creating and surrendering to this ultimate machine of self-ordering.

Al-Husri's nation, then, is the highest form of the will to order. It is modeled on, as Foucault puts it, "that coldest of cold monsters," the state bureaucracy. It turns its citizens into a "system of levers," which firmly interlock in an embrace of efficiency. This nation is distinct and impermeable, with the solidity of "hard stones," yet has no essential content other than difference. Al-Husri's nation is constituted by the common language and common history of its members. But this common language may change in any way whatsoever so long as it remains a unifying national language distinct from other national languages. Similarly, national history contains no essential, definitive content, other than the formation of the nation itself as a group of people who speak the same national language. Aside from the moment of birth, there is no specific historical event or context that al-Husri designates as crucial to national identity. He sees the value of history, rather, in its inspirational capacities for creating attachment to the nation and conviction in its greatness. "The most important impulse we should derive from history is in my view faith in the vitality of the Arab nation and in its capacity for achieving a renewed glory that is no less momentous than the glory it achieved in by-gone times."[52] Therefore, what is of importance in national history is not its specific factual content, but its moral-emotional effects. Whatever the past holds that is deemed important for this purpose should form the focus of national history. Similarly, al-Husri designates no features of Arab culture or ethnicity as essential to Arab identity. The existence of a distinct national language will always engender a distinctive culture, but there is nothing in particular that must be preserved or that should be regarded as the Arabs' unique contribution to humanity. Unlike other proponents of nationalism, al-Husri refrains from elevating the Arabs above other nations in any significant way. He does not claim that the Arab nation is destined to redeem humanity. He claims rather that the modern nation is destined to redeem the Arabs, just as it has redeemed the rest of humanity.

What al-Husri accomplishes with his definition of the nation is the delineation of what sort of social group is capable of achieving agency through self-negation. The only group so capable, according to him, is the one composed by the common language and common history of its members. Groups composed on the basis of any other factor—including religion, ideology, race, economic interest—cannot achieve this sort of agency. Whereas social and political reformers called upon their audience to unite and achieve national agency once again, they more or less took existing social structure and political boundaries for granted. They promoted a specific form of self-ordering that, if effected, would give rise to national agency. The issue of who does or does not belong to the nation did not usually occupy central importance and was often left vague. With al-Husri, however, it is precisely the "objective" features that distinguish one nation from another which give rise to order and agency. Therefore, he and other nationalists change the polarity of the reformist call to nationhood. Instead of calling for order so that there can be an undefined national unity, he calls for a defined national unity so that there can be order. In both versions, order and unity should actually come about simultaneously, and each one fully requires the other. Nevertheless, logical precedence is crucial. The belief that if people enact a specific form of order, a unified nation that is a moral agent will come about, has political consequences far different from those of the belief that society can only attain order through the formation of a specifically defined nation-state.

There is a significant intellectual and cultural distance between al-Husri and al-Kawakibi. Al-Husri was the product of a secular, Western-oriented education while al-Kawakibi was educated in a traditional *madrasa* to be a religious scholar. Whereas al-Husri spoke in the academic tones of a sociologist, al-Kawakibi proclaimed the indignation of an Islamic moral reformer. While al-Husri resorted to a medical language of psychopathology in depicting social ills, al-Kawakibi saw love of pleasure and called for willingness to die. Nevertheless, both promoted programs of social ordering aimed at lifting the Arabs and the Muslims out of their present condition of backwardness and fragmentation. These programs correlate the present collective condition with moral dissipation, egoism, and enslavement, said to characterize the selves of contemporary individuals. The forms of social order envisioned in these programs are on this basis legitimized through their replication of an economy of desire within the self through which desire is transformed into order. This replication consists in the idea that order on the collective level is of the same nature and generated through the same process as order within individuals. Through this means, the two writers depict and justify two radically different forms of social order. This is due largely to the difference in the historical circumstances in which they wrote and the political aims that they pursued. Yet despite their different political orientations and attitudes toward religion, and despite the different forms of social integration that they envision, there is a deep continuity between them. A secular nationalism like that of al-Husri can only find an audience once writers like al-Kawakibi have established the possibility of attaining moral universality through the empirical, defining features of a collective body. Once these features are no longer mere accidents that are irrelevant to what is really human, but become attributes that enable the attainment of humanity, forms of nationalism become possible. Nationalism, like liberalism, is one of the inevitable outcomes of the democratization of virtue.

Chapter 4

The Moral Transformation of Femininity and the Rise of the Public–Private Distinction in Colonial Egypt

The public sphere in Egypt began to undergo a rapid expansion in the 1890s, resuming a trend interrupted by the imposition of British control in 1882. One aspect of this expansion was a proliferation of publications calling for the reform of the traditional regime of female seclusion and promoting new ideals of womanhood and of family life within the private home. In many respects, the bourgeois ideal of the private sphere, with its nuclear family centered on a parental couple bound by romantic love and mutual respect, who perform distinct but complementary roles in securing familial fulfillment, became normative for the literate classes during this period. A body of recent research has documented the emergence and content of these new ideals and representations through examination of the books, pamphlets, speeches, journals, newspaper articles, and iconic images in which they appeared.[1] This research has shown the valorization of child-raising and household management as distinct, feminine social roles and areas of expertise requiring women to possess specific virtues and educational qualifications for their successful performance. Moreover, this research has emphasized the critical role played by nationality within the new discourses as the source of legitimacy for the reordering of domestic life and thus for empowering women with the status, rights, and education necessary for this reordering. It can further be seen that this ideal of domestic femininity established a new image of the woman as beloved—a refined, literate, sensitive human being, who stimulates love, a morally ordered affect, in the heart of her suitor or husband. This ennobling beloved, the same woman who is a rational mother and an efficient manager, is likewise shown to be indispensable to national advancement. In these primary dimensions, the emerging feminine ideal defines the new private sphere and links it to the state of the nation.

To understand the nature of this linkage, and why it is to have a binding, legitimizing effect, it is necessary to understand what the nation is, how it can make morally obligatory demands, and what femininity can have to do with this kind of moral obligation. Since people do not naturally adhere to the nation, know what it is, or in what adherence to it lies, it is necessary to inquire into how the nation is represented such that individuals should be willing for the nation's sake to disrupt and rearrange their social practices and gender relations in manners formerly repugnant. In other words, it is necessary to find out what place femininity is given within the normative structure of nationality such that femininity acquires nationality's moral force, its binding legitimacy.

I have argued in previous chapters that nationality is an ideal of a collective body with order and agency that comes about when individuals achieve the state of order, their higher self, within themselves. This means that to acquire the moral force of nationality, femininity must be linked to this state of order in a manner that makes femininity indispensable to individuals in realizing their higher, national self. I have argued, moreover, that the moral order of nationality is depicted as the outcome of the process of the negation of desire, which lifts individuals out of the state of egoism and makes them capable of self-sacrifice. Therefore, whatever can be represented as bringing about the negation of desire within individuals becomes the foundation of personal completion and fulfillment in national self-realization. On this basis, I will argue here that discourses endow the imperative of reforming gender relations with hegemonic status—that is, they make it the key to the realization of national order and agency, and thus comprehensive of other ideologies of national advancement—when they show that femininity in the current state of affairs is prevented from performing its definitive role in lifting individuals into the higher moral condition of nationality. In endowing femininity with this critical function within the self, discourses and representations vary in what they depict individual moral order and national order to lie in. As a result, they vary in their image of the ideal woman who gives rise to this order.

I will argue, then, that the transformation of the normative meaning of femininity that takes place in the colonial period occurs through the placement of the feminine ideal in a new position within the self, as the mechanism that enables the national self to come into being. To characterize this transformation and its implications properly, it is necessary to understand its relationship with existing representations of femininity in the Egyptian context. Just as nationality cannot become a new communal ideal without intrinsic connection to existing communal ideals, so also femininity cannot change in meaning without beginning from and drawing upon its prior meanings. If the new ideal of womanhood had no linkage with existing ideals, people would have no basis on which to understand it and even less basis on which to adopt it. The claim that there is a radical, absolute disjuncture between bourgeois Western norms and the premodern norms of the non-West means that no mind or society could move from one to the other without first annihilating itself. On the contrary—not only does articulation to existing ideals enable the new meaning of femininity to come about in the first place, but the nature of this articulation reveals the normative structure of the bourgeois "Victorian" private sphere in relation to the ideal of virtue that preceded it. Moreover, the articulation of the new feminine ideal to an existing one brings into question the Habermasian account of the natural emergence of the public sphere out of the rational humanism supposedly engendered in the private sphere of the bourgeois conjugal family.

To gain a perspective on the emergence of a new ideal of femininity, I will examine the relationship between classically derived poetic representations of femininity and the representations of femininity put forward by reformers who promoted a new vision of women's social status, functions, and rights. On this basis, I will argue that the movement from the heroic virtue of the literary tradition to the nationality depicted by reformist writers involves a moral transformation of femininity. In the former, femininity embodies the primordial, chaotic desire that must be symbolically displayed in order to motivate its negation and concealment. In the latter, femininity is linked to desire that is always morally ordered from the outset, completely absorbed into the public–private national order, such that the appearance of any stray chaotic desire is not heroic transgression but deviance and depravity. In other words, the classically derived beloved embodies the desire that must be negated, but must nevertheless be always present, while the new woman stands for the negation of desire, the moral process itself. In this transformation of meaning, femininity moves from one side of the moral divide to the other, while the nature of this divide itself shifts. The private sphere emerges, therefore, in its normative dimension, as the site in which the new woman engenders the ordered desire of national agency.

For this reason, the moral transformation of femininity is the central element in the rise of a public–private order based on the reciprocality of its two spheres. The representation of a collective agency that does not issue from a figure who embodies and displays the values of the community but which inheres in the site in which the community displays itself in its daily, collective self-ordering—the public sphere—requires a new relationship between desire and moral order. The citizen and his desire must be preconstituted as subsumed into the higher order from the start. The love that a man feels for a woman, and the love that a woman feels for a man and for her children, can no longer be depicted as elemental and unmastered, but should be infused with moral control and purpose. This cannot be represented, however, unless the meaning of femininity as well as marriage is altered. Marriage, as a fully human, moral relationship, can now stand as the home of the desire that is subsumed into the community, rather than standing for the chaotic desire that has been negated in and through its concealment. Marriage and the women who are or are to be married (to bourgeois men) are in this way brought into the light of publicity as constituting a private sphere that is the origin of public order and are no longer defined as the bearers of a sacrosanct, hidden relation.

Understanding the basis of the new normative order in the movement from virtue to nationality enables us to understand how the emergence of the private sphere creates the possibility of bourgeois feminism, while at the same time making possible the confinement of women within their private role. There can be no demand for the social and political equality of women without the norm of morally ordered private citizens, and in particular, without a norm for the process by which such citizens come into being. How the nature of women's agency in this process is depicted determines how permeable is the boundary between private and public. And the role of women in this process enables us to understand the logic behind the pervasive requirement that women embody, over and above men, specific "traditional," national characteristics seen as definitive of the public order.

In arguing for a normative transformation, rather than a birth *ex nihilo*, I do not claim that the reconfiguration of social relations and institutions that began taking place during the colonial period was brought about by a mere reshuffling of representational categories irrespective of social, economic, and political forces. What I argue, rather, is that these forces and their effects were experienced as meaningful, and took social form in the context of this meaning. There is no such thing as a social form that first exists and then gives rise to its own meaning. Even motherhood can have a wide range of social meanings and normative content, as we can see in its transformation during this period, and none of them is automatically generated from a zero-point out of the relation itself. Nor is there any reason to believe that romantic love, domesticity, or the sentimental novel are the automatic by-products of the "bourgeois conjugal family" purely in virtue of its structure as a living arrangement. Similarly, social forms cannot simply be imported from the West, already constituted in meaning and structure, without articulation to existing forms. In this view, the history of all modern societies is European history.

To capture the underlying logic of the moral transformation of femininity, necessarily in a somewhat abstract and limited manner, I focus on writings of three Egyptian intellectual figures who represented femininity in a sustained and probing manner. The poetry of al-Barudi, with its extensive depictions of erotic desire on the basis of centuries-old classical models, was taken as a point of departure by poets of the following generation all over the Arabic-speaking world. His body of poetry may therefore be taken to instantiate a culturally powerful mode of representing femininity and its relation to moral order that rapidly began to undergo modification as well as come under attack in the following generation. Most prominent among those who attacked this mode of representing femininity was the Egyptian jurist Qasim Amin (1863–1908). His work reveals, in an intensive manner, how the centrality of the public–private division within the moral ideal of nationality formed the initial basis for the representation of feminine order and agency. Moreover, his work reveals how even a radically liberal, Western-oriented social vision drew its legitimacy from its linkage to the kind of heroic virtue depicted by al-Barudi. The Egyptian feminist Malak Hifni Nasif (1886–1918) promoted a vision of the public–private division couched in Arab–Islamic rather than Western-oriented cultural terms. Her writings show how investing the new ideal of femininity with "traditional," culturally "authentic" markers of moral order could make these valued markers modern signifiers of moral universality, civilization, and progress. This strategy enabled Nasif to outflank the critics of Amin and win many of them over, showing the way for many subsequent developments in the representation of femininity.

Virtue and the Maiden

To get an idea of late nineteenth century representations of femininity in its relation to virtue, I will consider poetic texts of Mahmud Sami al-Barudi (1839–1904), the general, statesman, and Urabist leader discussed earlier in this book. In reviving poetic styles of early periods of the literary tradition for his own self-presentation as a heroic figure, al-Barudi brought the depiction of the female beloved into renewed prominence. Not only does this depiction form a major dimension of his poetic production, but he adopts the antiquated practice of naming the women he describes and in some cases giving them dramatic dialogue. In a number of his poems, the beloved is endowed with an exalted personal and Arab tribal nobility corresponding to the poet's own heroic status. It may be surmised that the ethos of the heroic poet adapted by al-Barudi from Abbasid period poets like al-Mutanabbi, Abu al-Firas al-Hamdani, and al-Sharif al-Radiy, is connected with the formation, during the nineteenth century, of the Turko-Circassian elites into an administrative, military, and landowning aristocracy within an emergent public society in which Egyptian commoners increasingly came to the fore. Al-Barudi was distinctive in his cultivation of deep ties to prominent figures belonging to these rising social classes, and his literary activities played a central role in this.

In order to make any use of al-Barudi's poetry for present purposes, it is necessary to consider what kind of relationship it may have had to the ideals and practices of its audience with regard to gender relations. There is no doubt that the specific norms governing expectations, behavior, manners, practices, rituals, institutions, and the like, among the various groups of the rising and upper classes at the time, would not only have differed from those of the much earlier and geographically distant social groups among whom al-Barudi's poetic styles initially developed, but would have shown substantial variation even among social groups in Egypt. The same goes for the specific constitution of the regime of female seclusion itself. Al-Barudi's poetry can tell us nothing of the norms that directly governed actual social practices. In this, it is no different from the traditional Arabic poetic genres in all historical periods. These genres operate at a high level of representational abstraction. One cannot draw conclusions from them about actual social life. They are not mimetic genres but depict objects, persons, events, and states of the self through manipulation of a system of value-laden motifs and symbolic relations in a highly structured and stylized manner. Poetry like that of al-Barudi, therefore, indicates only overarching valuative relations to which many different types and levels of concrete social norms can be articulated. This is perhaps partly responsible for the remarkable longevity, expandability, and exportability of the classical literary system. In any case, these overarching value relations, though lacking social specificity, reveal the logic operative within concrete social norms and practices nonetheless. We see, moreover, that the traditional poetic modes of representing femininity, love, and virtue dominant into the beginning of the twentieth century were increasingly attacked, modified, and pushed out as social change and new ideals advanced. The transformation in the meaning of femininity required a struggle over representation, and this struggle was directed for the most part against traditional poetic modes of depicting women.

In many of the poems that established al-Barudi's reputation, published before his exile from Egypt in 1882, depictions of entanglements with a female paramour play a key role in the poet's self-presentation as a figure of heroic, military virtue. Al-Barudi's cultivation of this kind of poetry ought to be understood in the context of the incipient Arabophone literate public domain, both in terms of publishing as well as the rise of salons. The self-presentation in these poems publicizes the poet's embodiment of communal virtue through his personal capacity to negate his rampant desire and engage in self-sacrifice. This is a communal publicity, therefore, that inheres in the poet himself, in his nature as an exceptional, complete individual, and his lordly status among men derives from this nature. The contrast, therefore, between the chaotic, free, externally unrestrained desire to which he succumbs completely, and his miraculous ability to order this desire for the sake of the community, is central to the depiction of this kind of personal publicity. As the poet says, "Were I not possessed of a free character, I would not craft poetry nor fall in love."[2] This "free character" (*shima hurra*) is his moral freedom from external constraint, his refusal to yield to any such constraint, which is both the source and sign of his elevated personal status. For this freedom is at the same time the character of the community in its ideal, realized form.

The display of unrestrained desire in juxtaposition with its negation in virtue is therefore the organizing axis of much of al-Barudi's poetry. Their relationship is expressed in different forms, depending on the nature of the poem, but in each case, desire must be present and absolute in nature, while at the same time ephemeral, ultimately unfulfilling, and requiring negation. The fundamental feature of love as experienced by the poet when under its sway is its inherent boundlessness. "All things have a limit, however long they persist, but passion has no limit."[3] Love always takes the form of the freeing of the self from internal as well as external constraints, as in the following opening line of a poem: "I became ecstatic, dream-images and drunkenness overcame me, and my character was no longer held back by forbiddance."[4] In this state, the poet is "prostrate to passion." He no longer has rational self-control. "The people say that magic has deluded him, yet it is but a glance that is beyond magic. / How can people rebuke me when I have not, nor has anyone, the power in love to command and forbid?" Love cannot be repulsed, even with the weapons of war, and its heat is of an absolute intensity.[5] This description of love, which is typical and has numerous parallels, gives us a state of the self in which the self, in all of its empirical contours, is effectively dissolved, and its desire has been set completely free. The nature of love is precisely this absence of control; no one can command or forbid themselves while under its sway. Nevertheless, immediately after this description, it suddenly transpires that desire may actually be brought under control. "Yet I concealed in my breast its fire of passion that no breast can conceal, / And I held back tears that, had I left open their channels to pour onto the earth, no one had doubted were the sea, / Out of modesty and pride lest it be said that love overcame him or that his blade was blunted by separation" (lines 9–11). In other words, the poet has enclosed the infinite, bottled the ocean, squared the circle, by establishing control over chaos from its midst, and thereby creating himself as ordered, negated desire. This is the basis of his political primacy over men, asserted in the succeeding line and the subject of the rest of the poem. "I am a man to whose sovereignty (*sultan*), were it not for adversities, both war-like bedouins and townsmen would yield" (line 12). Only the disorder of the present age prevents the recognition and establishment of the poet's innate hegemonic status. He himself is not to be mastered or constrained by anyone or anything other than virtue, because he has within himself that which is unmasterable except in his own virtuousness.

It is crucial to this representation of virtue and innate status, therefore, that the unmasterable nature of desire be both displayed and mastered at the same time. While it is in effect, that is, in its actual depiction, desire must be inherently boundless, in order that virtue be depicted as the containment of this boundlessness. This may occur in the most direct possible manner. In another poem, the description of the poet's erotic transgressions with his paramour climaxes in the following line: "I dwelled in union with her in a garden whose boughs had ripened with the fruits of intimacy and affection." In this line, the fulfillment of love is absolute, a paradise of complete release and bliss, in which one would wish to stop for eternity. Yet the next line immediately reframes the situation. "I allowed the eye to take enjoyment in her, but I restrained the hand of youthful passion from the clasps of garments."[6] Now we find that the state of bliss has been turned into an assertion of self-mastery. As the poet says in a similar situation, "a man may be proud when he renounces despite his power."[7] The power contained in virtue consists precisely in the renunciation of the immeasurable power of desire.

In the balance between desire and renunciation, therefore, both are, in principle, equally vivid and present. This balance may be weighted in deference to thematic priorities. In two of al-Barudi's notable political poems, for example, heroic self-display takes the renunciation of desire as its point of departure.[8] In many other poems, however, the depiction of love takes the upper hand over its renunciation. In these poems, the description of the female beloved becomes the medium in which love takes form. The descriptive techniques of classical poetry associate the meaning of love with the various elements of the beloved's appearance. This meaning includes bliss and release, as seen above, but also the negative dimension of this bliss, its linkage with fate, death, and enslavement. Consider the following lines from the description of a fair maiden: "She turns her neck like a faun yet her glance is more lethal than a *coup de grâce*; / She renders healthy souls sick with love, and does what the weapons of war cannot do; / I lowered before her the wings of my affection, and surrendered to her eyes, as fate (time, *al-dahr*) decreed."[9] The conventional parallel between bodily destruction in war and the suffering of love is not mere hyperbole, but again indicates the intrinsic relationship between virtue and desire. Love is more lethal than warfare, and for this reason enables the lover who fully surrenders to love, yet is able to master it, to surrender himself happily in war. The overcoming of love, the false promise of empirical existence, grants freedom from fate (the law of time), death, nature, the body, enslavement to external forces, and so forth. Love is the fatality of empirical existence in its most bewitching appearance, that of a beautiful woman.

Love, in both its positive and negative dimensions, finds its central manifestation in attachment to a beautiful woman. This love, however, is not limited to beautiful women in its object. We are speaking here of all varieties of love, including love between parents and their children and love between friends. There is no specifically sexual predominance in the love that can be signified by attachment to a woman, or which finds its primary embodiment in that attachment. Love for other objects is expressed in the same terms of boundlessness and loss of rationality and self-control. The grief felt on the death of a loved one is expressed in the same manner.[10] The beautiful female beloved is the primary means of evoking bliss and loss, and imparting this situation and its meaning to other phenomena. It can be seen, then, that in this representation of love, emotional and sexual dimensions are not differentiated. There is no separate "lust" as a motive within love. The dangerous and sacrosanct nature of love lies not in its sexual element per se, but in that it is a boundless, inherently ungovernable total attachment of the self, characterized by loss, enslavement, and death. Yet at the same time, its mastery is the virtue that gives rise to a morally ordered community. In this way, the woman whose beautiful appearance embodies the meaning of love stands in a metonymical relation to the virtue that founds the community. She is indispensable to the virtue that founds the community in that this virtue comes into being through her displacement.

If love may be symbolically displayed in a manner that reveals the necessity of its negation and concealment, the same logic may apply to women insofar as they signify love. In other words, the presence of virtue, by this logic, requires the confinement and concealment of women in some manner so long as love is a primary sense of womanhood.[11] The *rabbat khidr*, or concealed upper-class woman, whom al-Barudi speaks of and addresses in many of his poems, is revealed in a manner that shows why she ought to be concealed. On the one hand, she is inaccessible to anyone lacking in the daring of total abandonment demonstrated by the poet, and so is necessary for this demonstration. Others are too timid, too inhibited, too weak in desire to contemplate such a violation. This violation and display, however, may be understood only as fulfilling a symbolic function. On the other hand, the poet's experience of love justifies the beloved's concealment. Whereas initially she was portrayed as the object of desire wrongly withheld from her seekers, she is now shown to be incapable of redeeming the abandonment to which she gives rise. The confinement and concealment of women, therefore, and of the realm of desire in general, whatever form this takes in an actual social regime, signifies that desire has been negated and disciplined and that virtue reigns.

This confinement and concealment, however, does not constitute a private sphere in the sense that is complementary to the public sphere. The linkage of femininity with love and its negation does not determine the role or activities of women in the home or anywhere else in the manner of the notion of the private sphere. That the home is the site of disciplined desire does not determine the nature of life within the home, or set up an ideal for this life. Moreover, it is important to avoid confusions resulting from the multiple meanings of the term "private" and their far-reaching implications. When Jürgen Habermas, for example, speaks of the bourgeois private sphere, he emphasizes its publicly oriented nature. The public sphere was the "expansion and at the same time completion of the intimate sphere of the conjugal family" because the latter engendered an "audience-oriented subjectivity," which was "the source of privateness in the modern sense."[12] This private domestic sphere consists of the drawing room and dining room, but not the bedroom or the toilet. The private in this sense is the family life that can be displayed to outsiders and freely spoken of or represented. It is the realm of the "common humanity" of family relationships and excludes those functions and activities that are not audience-oriented. In contrast, another common sense of the term "private" refers precisely to this excluded realm. One's "private parts" are not audience-oriented, nor is that which must be conducted "in private." The publicly oriented private sphere is constituted by the exclusion of this other "private," thereby defining the true nature of the home as the site in which humanity and moral order are fostered, while relegating the bodily dimension of domestic life to silence. Of a piece with this exclusion is the separation of sexuality as an independent motive, an autonomous domain of the self, that enters publicly oriented privacy only in its silent subordination to moral order, but which, insofar as it exceeds this order, occupies domains and discourses specifically devoted to it.[13]

The mistake, then, is to understand the concealment from publicity of the domain of love and domestic life in prebourgeois social regimes as the relegation of this domain in its entirety to the excluded private. It is a misunderstanding, in other words, to believe that the dimension of life corresponding to the bourgeois private sphere in these societies is assigned wholly to the realm of the bodily and for this reason is kept off-limits and unrepresented in a publicly oriented manner. If this were true, the domestic domain as a whole would have the same meaning and valuation in these societies that the bedroom and the toilet had in polite Victorian society. As I have argued, however, the relationship between the concealed realm of negated desire with public yet personal virtue is different from the bourgeois distinction between private and public. The realm of controlled desire is closed off from the public display of virtue but is sacrosanct in that it is the interiorized obverse and source of this public display. As such, it is entirely absorbed within the personal status of the male overlord. This does not determine, however, the specific norms of domestic life or the ways in which it is valued, nor the specific regime of formalizing the "confinement" of this realm. Nor is this realm a private sphere in the sense of being closed off from external society. Women's society may be as extensive as male society, with the household serving as a node of interaction in both. Most fundamentally, the logic of virtue and desire by itself generates no norm that separates an individual, personal domain from the common domain. On the contrary, the perpetual presence and danger of desire, made manifest in gossip and scandals, justifies the nature of the social order. There is no publicly derived right to privacy because the category and status of the "private citizen" does not exist. Rather, it is up to a person's public status, or honor, to establish its inviolability (*hurma*) through respect or fear, and the degree to which it can do so is precisely its measure. Moreover, if desire is the underlying social reality, and its control necessary for social order, then its escape from control is of utmost public interest. The logic of the literary representation of publicity, therefore, indicates a publicity of moral order, and a negative publicity of disorder, but does not demarcate an audience-oriented or socially excluded private domain.[14]

It is paradoxical, however, that al-Barudi's revival of classical, early Islamic literary representations of status publicity actually belongs to the incipient formation of *bourgeois* publicity in the Arabophone Middle East. Al-Barudi's revivalist turn, which became dominant in the following generation, played a role in the normative transformations then taking place by reasserting culturally prestigious forms of femininity and masculine publicity at abstract, relatively content-free levels of representation. This is perhaps not surprising given that the emergence of an increasingly integrated and politically significant Arabophone public created the audience for al-Barudi's deployment of a long-antiquated heroic style of self-representation. The hegemonic orientation of his political poetry projects an audience, often addressed as "Egypt," that can respond to it and that is capable of acting as a collective body. This initial representation of the moral ideal of nationality in terms of classical virtue sets the stage for the internal transformation of the moral ideal. We see in al-Barudi the process by which the publicity of status, by shifting emphasis to the *collective* body whose values it publicizes, begins to anchor publicity in this body itself.

This process is evident in the renewed importance of female figures in al-Barudi's poetry and in the incipient appearance of a classical feminine form of publicity that was taken up directly from early Islamic sources by women writers of the following generation and transformed by them into a bourgeois ideal. One of the key features of al-Barudi's neoclassicism is the centrality of the female beloved in his poems and his revival of an emphatically heterosexual norm in the depiction of love, in contrast with the long-standing trend of depicting the beloved abstractly and gender-neutrally. In a number of instances, al-Barudi brings back the pairing of the heroic lover with a high-status beloved parallel in personal nobility and exaltedness to himself. This depiction is seen especially in Umayyad love poetry and sporadically thereafter. Moreover, al-Barudi's *diwan* contains an elegy on the death of his mother, and rather remarkably, a significant elegy on the death of his second wife, an exceedingly rare phenomenon in the Arabic poetic tradition. In all of these instances, the social status of the female figure corresponds to her personal capacity to embody the sublime desire of the poet. An intrinsic linkage emerges between love of a queenly woman who is inaccessible to the ignoble, and the heroic publicity of virtue. Nevertheless, the exalted female cannot symbolize public virtue in herself because this virtue comes about only when she, that is, the desire that she signifies, has been subsumed within the person of the lordly male and no longer appears. The kind of publicity that such a woman can possess is derivative of her relation to the high-status male who is worthy of control over her. It is derivative, in other words, of her status as *to be controlled only by virtue*. The same is true of virtuous men, except that the sovereign male lord is the source of his own virtue and thus in charge of his own desire. As the eleventh century Andalusian author Ibn Hazm put it, the virtuous man controls his self by avoiding temptation, whereas the virtuous woman is the one who, "when she is controlled, she comes under control" (*idha dubitat indabatat*).[15] This subtlest of discursive distinctions, based on the use of an active but nonagential verb form, ensures that in the final instance, agency does not belong to the woman. It is precisely the fine yet radical moral line here separating the sexes that becomes subject to manipulation in the normative transformation of femininity. The metonymical relationship between femininity and moral order, therefore, derives from the promise of fulfillment contained in the female beloved in balance with her embodiment of fate, which finds its irredeemable manifestation not in her but in the political corruption of the age. The reassertion of this metonymical relationship in the name of a male publicity of personal status as an incipient form of nationality is a key step in the emergence of the bourgeois feminine ideal.

An important instance in this regard is the depiction of femininity put forth by the Egyptian reformer Rifaʻa al-Tahtawi (1801–1873) in his work on education and moral cultivation, *Al-Murshid al-Amin li al-Banat wa al-Banin* (*The Trustworthy Guide for Girls and Boys*, 1873). This work is rightly recognized as one of the earliest to advocate a full education for girls.[16] Indeed, al-Tahtawi introduces a number of new elements in his depiction of femininity. He argues that women are as intellectually capable of benefiting from education as men. He emphasizes the role that women should take in the household, thus presenting marriage as a complementary division of duties between husband and wife.[17] Moreover, he advocates a companionate relationship for the married couple based on friendship and mutual respect, resulting in a "virtuous, beneficial love free of passion."[18] Like the reformists of the generation to follow, he posits a necessary role for mothers in the socialization of children and extols the power of the beloved to inspire men in seeking glory. Nevertheless, these elements remain subordinated to a framework in which femininity ultimately signifies desire and its control. "Although women are created for the pleasures of men, they are, *aside from these pleasures*, the same as men."[19] Thus, the inherent "weakness of women" is precisely their virtue, "modesty" (*haya'*), through which they "rule the hearts of men," while the virtue of men, courage, is strength.[20] Feminine weakness, cultivated through confinement to the household, is the capacity for self-restraint (*hilm*), but is passive in that it is defined by obedience rather than agency.[21] Women are therefore incapable of acting within the public sphere in al-Tahtawi's view, and he affirms the rights of the husband to the concealment of his wife, and the necessity of women's seclusion in general.[22] It can be seen then that the framework in which masculine desire must be present and available for the sake of preserving the community and its order, while femininity signifies the control of this desire, is still intact. This enables al-Tahtawi to cite copiously the medieval Arabic literary corpus, including hundreds of lines of poetry, in support of his doctrines. Like al-Barudi, al-Tahtawi relies on the literary tradition to foreground the social significance of femininity. In doing so, he promotes new norms of domestic happiness. Yet he does not portray a publicly oriented private sphere, because he does not transform the moral status of femininity in a manner that would make the agency of women in some way central to the creation of public order.

Femininity, Publicity, and Privacy

The transformation of the meaning of femininity consists in the recasting of the position of femininity within the self. This recasting was part of and central to the broader realignment of social norms that took place in the context of the emergence of a public society. Concurrently with the rise of the professional, technically educated classes in Egypt, the development of a socially integrated, Arabophone public domain, the increase of social participation, directly or indirectly, in governance, and the influence of European values and lifestyles on some sectors of the population, issues of the status and role of women in society began to take a prominent public place. This is evident to a limited extent in the years leading up to the so-called Urabi revolt and British takeover in 1882, but is much more evident in the rapid expansion of the Egyptian press and publishing beginning in the 1890s. During that decade, significant works addressing women and women's issues began to appear, women's journals began to proliferate, and the general press showed increasing interest in gender topics. By 1900, with the appearance of Qasim Amin's controversial books, the complex of issues surrounding women's capacities, status, social role, education, and rights had become established as a center of public debate and contention. The promotion and establishment in public discourse of bourgeois norms regarding family relations, domesticity, love and marriage, and child-rearing, developed rapidly from this period, to the extent that "conservative" positions on women's issues a generation later were articulated on the basis of rather than from outside the bourgeois normative regime. By the 1920s, the discursive realignment of the position of femininity in the self had become established nearly across the board among a wide range of heterogeneous attitudes toward and representations of women. The meaning of womanhood had changed irrevocably, as had the model of desire and communal order within the self.

As a striking indication of this change, consider some verses from a poem addressed by the renowned poet Ahmad Shawqi (1868–1932) to an audience of women convened for some philanthropic purpose in 1924.[23] Shawqi's poem, composed in the classicist idiom, repudiates any urge to look to the West, celebrates the past greatness of women in Islamic history and extols the assembled ladies for their beneficent efforts, culminating in the framing of these efforts in terms of nationality.

> Egypt renews her glory through her self-renewing women...
> They breathe into youths the spirit of courage and resolve.
> They long to kiss the sword and to feel the embrace of the lance.
> And they deem, even in dreams, the kisses of men to be forbidden.[24]

This representation is striking not so much in its adaptation of the poetic motifs of antique warfare to contemporary bourgeois virtues and activities, a specialty of poets of that generation, but in the application of these martial motifs to respectable ladies. Military combat is the principal manifestation of self-sacrifice in the Arabic poetic tradition and the ultimate form of agency. The readiness to die for the sake of moral order is the internal achievement of moral order. Desire has turned away from ephemeral objects of attachment, thus embracing its own negation, and in so doing attained to the immutable moral condition of nationality. So long as "our cause" of Egyptian independence, for which these ladies are zealous combatants, has not reached fulfillment, their sexuality will take expression as a passion for self-sacrifice. The ladies, then, have attained the ultimate masculine state of virtue, and this is seen in their public, national activity. Yet they have done so in a manner that is distinctively feminine. For the poet links their philanthropic efforts with their maintenance of womanly modesty, the sign of their self-negation, and with their motherhood, which is not a mere biological function, but consists in the investment of their sons, the rising young warriors (*fityan*), with the capacity of self-sacrifice. And their withholding of "kisses" from the men folk, which signifies the morally ordered nature of their love at the expense of sexuality, will have the same effect. Though the women have actually participated in the battle, as the poem tells us, they have clearly done so to impel men to win the battle.[25] The ladies' philanthropy, therefore, does not in itself achieve the collective order and agency of the nation on the world-historical level, but is *the public manifestation of women's capacity to enable men to achieve the nation*. Nevertheless, this depiction of femininity, though it remains on the same classicist representational terrain as traditional depictions, has decisively altered the position of women and the love of women in relation to desire and order.

The female agency depicted here, an internal moment of the overarching agency of the national self, has an intrinsic relation to a form of publicity that is itself new. The poem indicates the subsumption of the bourgeois public–private circuit and the role of women therein within the moral ideal of nationality. The women's private role and nature takes a public, national manifestation in their civic actions. It is necessary to consider how this new normative logic of public and private incorporates femininity in a manner distinct from that of status publicity.

The push for social and political significance by the bourgeois, professional classes led, as seen in previous chapters, to a new way of representing sovereignty and social order. Social order began to be conceived not as an order imposed by sovereign, virtuous figures, but as an order that arises out of the collective body itself. Publicity, the manifestation of society's order, was no longer seen to be located in the virtue of sovereign figures and their spectacular acts of imposing order, but in the public sphere: the collective activities of citizens that maintain and enhance the order of the collective body. This national public is made up of private citizens who achieve integration on the basis of their common humanity. Nationality is a universal ideal in the sense that the value of the nation lies in its contribution to and recognition by humanity as a whole. National agency brings about national glory on the world stage. This means that the collective order shown in public is a human order that advances human history. The "common humanity" of the private citizens that makes them a public, therefore, consists in whatever is represented as the moral order that brings about national agency and advances humanity.

Unlike the publicity of status, therefore, in which certain exceptional individuals embody communal values, national publicity requires that all private citizens, in order to form the public, be already in their private state morally ordered by public values. They should already be characterized by the moral order that they will express in their communal activity in the public sphere. In other words, the private must be already public, as the public is merely the manifestation of what is present in private. This is why Habermas characterizes bourgeois privacy as "audience-oriented" and sees the public sphere as the "expansion and at the same time completion" of the private sphere. The private, in this normative logic, is defined by its public nature, its origination of public order, to the exclusion of whatever is regarded as outside this function. It is on this basis that the role of women, under the description of belonging to the "private" sphere, becomes a public issue.

My analysis here focuses on how the moral ideal of nationality and its internal normative logic gives rise to a form of publicity that is related to but different from status publicity. In this sense, my analysis is different from that of Habermas, who sees the bourgeois ideal of the public sphere as arising directly from the "patriarchal conjugal family." In his well-known work on the topic, *The Structural Transformation of the Public Sphere*, Habermas argues that the "public's understanding of the public use of reason was guided specifically by such private experiences as grew out of the audience-oriented subjectivity of the conjugal family's intimate domain" (28). The bourgeois notion and experience of "humanity"—autonomous individual subjectivity conceived as free of external (economic) necessity—is according to Habermas the "interiorized human closeness" of bourgeois family life.[26] The space of this family "was the scene of a psychological emancipation that corresponded to the political-economic one" (46). The emancipated internal sense of humanity found its spontaneous expression in literary writing and criticism, the "republic of letters," where it fully realized its inherently public character. "[A]s the subjectivity of the privatized individual was related from the very start to publicity, so both were conjoined in literature that had become 'fiction'" (50). By the "public" character of bourgeois subjectivity Habermas means its intrinsic orientation to rationality. Because it was conceived as autonomous and human, it provoked and submitted to open rational argumentation. It is for this reason that it necessarily gave rise to "the public sphere of a rational-critical debate in the world of letters within which the subjectivity originating in the interiority of the conjugal family, by communicating with itself, attained clarity about itself" (51). Habermas, therefore, sees the literary representation of private life as the spontaneous, transparent expression of private experience. Moreover, he sees the Enlightenment ideals of humanity and rationality as the direct offspring of bourgeois family intimacy.[27]

Habermas's view takes literary representations of the human sentiments and ideals produced by bourgeois family life at face value. It is now commonly understood, however, that literary depictions of social phenomena are structured to achieve specific ends. They *show* readers what sort of experiences they should have and desire to have by investing such experiences with normative content. In doing so, they employ literary devices, structures, genres, in contrived and purposeful manners that create conflicting and competing pictures of social life. In short, these depictions are carefully constructed normatively oriented models of experience and subjectivity rather than direct expressions of them. The same issues of representation apply to the representation of ideals like humanity and rationality. It is clearly in the interest of the bourgeoisie to depict its way of life as the one most infused with humanity, just as it has been in the interest of every social group seeking to ground its hegemony. More fundamentally, it is unclear how the social experience of family intimacy can directly generate abstract ideals such as "humanity." Ideals are linguistic, conceptual categories, and new ideals, like all new linguistic forms, arise as modifications or transformations of existing categories or forms rather than issuing spontaneously from some kind of pure experience. Novel experience is always already interpreted and laden with meaning, even when it is characterized as "meaningless." We see moreover, particularly in the case of Egypt, but in European contexts as well, that the call for the institution of the conjugal family and its norms issued insistently from an already existing public sphere, and that this call was given justification through appeal to nationality. This shows that the "private sphere" is an ideal rather than an empirical reality. It is a way of understanding, representing and assigning value to domestic life in terms of a norm. Most often, this norm was used to deplore existing family life by casting it as a deficient private sphere. Whatever was the actual nature of family life in the late nineteenth century, reformist discourses and fiction show that the public ideal of nationality was the central means of promoting the *ideal* of bourgeois family privacy.

Humanity, as well as nationality, which is intrinsically connected to humanity, are hegemonic moral ideals. The ways in which they are given content justify specific forms of social and political order, and define authentic emancipation by delineating the forces of repression. It has been widely recognized that depictions of the family, as the microcosm or metaphor of the nation, are means of endowing humanity and nationality with content. In this way, these depictions legitimize particular forms of social order as well as the pictured form of family order itself. Representations of family life, in their particular delineations of moral freedom from economic as well as bodily necessity and the agency and social integration in which this freedom consists, define the content of an authentic humanity that is to be realized in collective incorporation. Such representations, in other words, seek to establish the nature of the self-negation that gives rise to individual and collective order. They make the family home the fundamental site in which the disposition to self-sacrifice arises in the displacement of egoism, and in picturing this moral polarity, configure contemporary society as a whole. The public character of privacy lies precisely in deriving public order from a private moral process, a derivation which takes different forms in different representations.

In investing the family with this representative and hegemonic role, bourgeois writers not only drew legitimacy from nationality, but established its structure as a communal moral ideal. By depicting the private family, they defined the nature of national publicity. As pointed out above, the continuous enactment of order and agency by private citizens who have come together to form a public requires these citizens to be already morally ordered in their privateness. The relationship between the private and public spheres is therefore immanent. Moral order must be depicted as arising directly out of private experience, which requires new forms and strategies of representation. Classicizing poetry like that of Shawqi cannot represent such an immanent and continuous generation of moral order, because it creates meaning through the association of phenomena with a preconstituted, conventional array of value-laden motifs. It can clothe the activities of bourgeois women in the conventional imagery of martial glory, but has no means of showing how this glory arises necessarily out of the nature of such activities. Intellectual discourses and narrative genres like the novel take up the task of theorizing immanent order and creating the semblance of immanent meaning. By depicting the private sphere in this manner, they project a form of moral order that constitutes and is continuously enacted by a uniform and totalized collectivity.

The Reinscription of Femininity within the Self

The central element in the discursive creation of a private sphere was the recasting of the position of femininity within the self. Whereas femininity had formerly signified the chaotic desire that enslaves until brought under control, it now came to signify the means by which freedom from chaotic desire is secured. Whereas in the literary tradition a (high-status) woman under the control of virtue could at times stand as an image of freedom, it now became the norm in public discourse to portray women as possessing a particular form of agency that would lead to the agency and freedom of all, as individuals and as a collective body. In other words, femininity came to be represented as the catalyst within the self of self-negation. Under this norm, hegemonic contestation centered on what femininity and self-negation should be seen to consist in, how they are intrinsically connected, and what sort of order, freedom, and agency issue from them. This was the terrain of struggles over the nature and scope of feminine agency and a key battleground of struggles over the nature of authentic social and political order.

The most fully elaborated and influential reformist account of the role of femininity within the self was set forth by the Egyptian jurist Qasim Amin in *Tahrir al-Mar'a* ("The Liberation of Women," 1899), and particularly in *Al-Mar'a al-Jadida* ("The New Woman," 1900). At the time of their publication, these writings aroused bitter controversy and provoked a flood of acrimonious rebuttals and attacks on the author's character.[28] Nevertheless, they had immediate effect in thematizing and framing the issue of women's status within the Arabic public sphere, though they were by no means the first to raise or treat this issue. By foregrounding linkages among the status of women, the nature of European modernity, and the meaning of national self-realization, Amin's works became the standard point of reference for future debate. Despite the politically inflammatory nature of Amin's views, his works played a critical role in laying bare the public–private normative logic that was unfolding in many writings and debates of the time.

Before moving to the analysis of Qasim Amin's account, it is instructive to consider the manner in which his mentor, the Islamic reformer Muhammad Abduh (1849–1905), took up the task of reinscribing femininity within the self in Islamic terms. Abduh published articles on the social role of marriage and the family when he was editor of the official Egyptian government newspaper *al-Waqa'i' al-Misriya* during the period of the Urabi revolt (1880–1882), and sporadically expressed his views thereafter in articles, legal opinions, and in his Quranic exegesis.[29] It seems reasonably certain that Abduh had some role in the composition of Amin's book *The Liberation of Women*, which relies heavily on Islamic legal textual arguments, whether this role was merely advisory, or extended to the actual writing of the chapters that engage the Islamic legal tradition, as some suspected at the time and as some commentators have continued to argue (Amin's own legal training was secular).[30] What is of interest to me here, however, is the different techniques deployed by the two reformers for the common purpose of establishing the moral meaning of femininity.

In his interpretation of the Quranic reference to the "inviolable covenant" taken by women from their husbands (4:21), Abduh argues that the Quran teaches that the bond between man and wife is intrinsic to the self (*fitri*), moral in nature, and the basis of social integration. It lies within the self "beyond lust" and consists in "divine intellection and intrinsic feeling," which lead women to desire marriage in preference to the security of their families. This bond is human in nature and is perceived through "human feeling." "What is the value of one who does not fulfill this covenant and what is his status as a human being?"[31] Since this bond belongs to the human, moral order of the self, its violation leads to individual and social disorder. "The tyranny of husbands over their wives corrupts more profoundly and devastates more rapidly than the tyranny of a ruler toward his subjects, because the bond of marriage is the most deeply rooted bond in the self" (26). Like other contemporary writers, Abduh expresses the linkage of disorder within the self with political disorder through the discourse of tyranny and enslavement. "Let it be known that the men who seek to be lords in their homes by oppressing their wives are doing nothing more than fathering slaves for others" (69). It can be seen here that Abduh is transforming an accepted form of authority into a form of tyranny, a dissipation of desire, whose effects are manifest throughout society.

On this basis, he depicts domestic relations as a private sphere that should be under public regulation. Opposing the canonical Islamic legal framing of marriage, in which a wife's sole spousal duty is providing unlimited sexual access to her husband, Abduh argues that the marital regime enjoined in the Quran is a balanced division of rights and duties between husband and wife, such as to make the family a joint partnership under the husband's leadership. "This is the foundation and the natural (*fitri*) division on which social well-being (*maslaha*) stands" (61). Moreover, Abduh argues for legislation hindering ease of divorce and delimiting rights to polygyny and concubinage. For these practices have lost their original social function and have become detrimental to social order. Regarding men who practice polygyny, for example, he says that "they have not understood the purpose of God in permitting it, and have taken it as a means of satisfying lust and obtaining pleasure, nothing more" (135). Abduh gives public authority wide-ranging powers in altering canonical legal precedents for the sake of regulating "social well-being." It is evident, however, that his conception of social well-being derives directly from the kind of moral order that he places within the self, whose key element in this regard is an innate human bond between man and woman that lifts them above "lust." Together they form a private sphere characterized by companionate marriage that enables social order. On this basis, Abduh is able to cast formerly legitimate authority and order as tyranny and enslavement, to which he then articulates a series of signs of social dysfunction.

Abduh's aim in these occasional writings is limited in ambition and lacking in full development, giving only an inkling of the possibilities of his endeavor. Qasim Amin's project is much more ambitious in that it seeks to inscribe femininity into the self in a manner that supports an extensive ideology of human liberation and national self-realization through the power of critical rationality, explicitly associated with Europe. In a recent reading of *The New Woman*, Lisa Pollard has pointed out the national orientation of Amin's call "to transform the state of women and society," characterizing it as "an example of a gendered, nationalist discourse in which the virtues and victories of the public realm—the victories and sentiments of men—were wholly dependent upon the politics of the families from which those men came." She shows that the role Amin envisioned for women was the "creation of a new man" who, having imbibed from his mother modern bourgeois attributes and patriotic sentiments, would have the capacity "to put an end to tyranny in the public realm." The purpose of Amin's project, Pollard argues, was to create the basis of a new, modern Egyptian order.[32]

The argument made by Pollard that Amin's primary interest lay not in liberating women but in modernizing men is somewhat misleading in its emphasis.[33] Amin indeed aimed at establishing a model of the morally ordered citizen, whose full instantiation is conceived as a male. But so also did his political arch-adversary, the nationalist leader Mustafa Kamil, who rejected calls to abolish female seclusion and focused on the sentiment of patriotism for his purposes. Amin, however, sought to place femininity at the heart of citizenship and make patriotism contingent upon femininity. In order for women to be seen themselves as morally ordered citizens who create the agency of the collective body and are thereby entitled to political rights, femininity must first be disassociated from chaotic desire and linked with collective moral order. I will argue here that Amin effected these steps by making femininity the catalyst of moral order within the self. In Amin's depiction, the moral order of the rationally autonomous citizen gives rise to the same kind of heroic self-sacrifice glorified by al-Barudi. By making feminine agency in the private sphere the means by which innate human emotions and impulses turn into the capacity for self-sacrifice, Amin and other reformers fashioned a feminine ideal associated with moral order and the negation of chaotic desire. Analysis of this mode of representation as it is extensively displayed in Amin's work shows how instituting the public–private relation made possible the emergence of bourgeois feminism.

I will suggest, moreover, that the specific manner in which Amin places femininity within the self is designed to authenticate the Eurocentric ideology of rationalism that he promotes by casting it as the means of human liberation. His book *The New Woman*, I will argue, provides both a general model of the recasting of womanhood so as to generate a publicly oriented private sphere, as well as a specific example of how this hegemonic model may be invested with content. It will be seen that the way in which women's function in the private sphere is depicted—their role in effecting self-negation—determines the nature of feminine agency and the degree of permeability between the public and private spheres.

The central thesis of *The New Woman* is that Europeans are dominant because they are morally superior to Egyptians and other Easterners, and that if Egyptians do not raise themselves to the European moral level, all of their efforts to lift Egypt out of its state of decadence will be futile. Europeans enjoy this superiority because they have autonomy as individuals, meaning that their higher, rational selves have broken free of all domination and attained self-rule. The rational selves of European individuals are impervious to the enslavement of irrational forces due to the autonomy of women in European societies, for the relationships of motherhood and marital love order the self by orienting desire toward truth so decisively that any desire for mere pleasure vanishes or is ineffectual. The result is that European nations are themselves autonomous and well-ordered, and thus advance human civilization. It is therefore both right and necessary for Egyptian men to follow Europeans in granting women autonomy by eliminating the practice of seclusion and providing women a full education.

The New Woman, in justifying the adoption of European norms on the basis of European moral superiority, makes a fundamental departure from Qasim Amin's previous book, *The Liberation of Women*, which had taken an Islamic revivalist line by arguing that granting women autonomy fulfills the trajectory of early Islamic society. *The New Woman*, though it does not in any way impugn Islam or Islamic law, explicitly repudiates the view that the Islamic civilization of the past can offer any model for the present by pointing to serious shortcomings in its institutions and intellectual culture. Nor does the book offer any kind of specifically Egyptian element in its vision of the future order. The effect of this is that the "new woman"—the ideal woman to be inscribed within the Egyptian self—appears to be a European woman.

Amin was not a nationalist, but a liberal reformer who sought to articulate his ideology to the moral ideal of nationality. His goal was to move Egypt out of the East and put it in the West. "Egypt" was for him nothing more than a collective ideal of order and freedom. He did not seek to unite Egyptians on the basis of any objective criterion of Egyptian identity, nor did he regard Egypt as in some way distinguished among nations. Nor did he ever call for Egyptian independence from British rule, which he regarded as conducive to freedom. Amin belonged to a group of prominent associates of Muhammad Abduh, including Sa'd Zaghlul and Ahmad Lutfi al-Sayyid, who in the period before World War I collaborated with British rule and opposed the nationalists led by Mustafa Kamil. The problem for Amin was not foreign tyranny, but the internalized tyranny of Egyptian society, the absence of liberal autonomy, embodied in the degraded condition of women. Amin sought, therefore, to confer hegemonic status on liberalism by making it the content of nationality through the medium of the female role in the private sphere. Internalizing liberal values is for him the only means of attaining national order and freedom, and otherwise, independence from colonial rule would be the victory of tyranny. "If the Europeans desire to harm us then all they have to do is leave us to ourselves."[34]

The New Woman situates Egypt within a moral-historical framework in which the liberation of women is the liberation of humanity. Amin employs the categories of "decadence" (*inhitat*) and "progress" (*taqaddum, taraqqi*) to establish the equivalence of humanity, freedom, and femininity. When women suffer the condition of decadence so do their societies, and when they progress society does as well. This seen in "the correspondence of the political condition with the familial condition in every land, for in every land in which man has debased the status of woman and treated her as a chattel he has debased his self and deprived it of the sensibility (*wijdan*) of freedom, and conversely, in lands in which women enjoy personal freedom men enjoy political freedom, so the two conditions are linked completely" (426). This has not merely political but universal significance. "Freedom is the basis of the progress of the human species and its ascent to happiness" (437). The West has reached the highest stage of progress and freedom, in that it has "liberated human reason from the authority of illusions, fancies and superstitions and turned over to it the guidance of itself" (420). The "new woman" is the product and sustainer of this stage of perpetual progress. It is clear, then, that the humanity to which the new woman is linked has a specific sense: the reason or intellect (*'aql*) in which human freedom inheres, which comprises not simply the traditional notion of reason as the capacity of self-restraint, but critical rationality in the Enlightenment sense.

Just as reason is the site of human freedom, the institution of female seclusion, *hijab*, is the site of its repression. The Arabic word *hijab* denotes a curtain, a concealing barrier. In *The Liberation of Women*, Amin distinguished between "Islamic *hijab*" and his contemporaries' usage of the term. While accepting that "*hijab* is a basis of propriety," he extensively argued that *hijab* in Islamic law refers only to modest dress, and not to segregation of women and full concealment of their persons from men, which is a customary, religiously unfounded, and historically primitive practice. In *The New Woman*, Amin leaves "Islamic *hijab*" in the background and reserves the term for the despised practice of seclusion. The "concealing barrier" becomes in his rhetoric the barrier that obscures and represses the inner humanity, the critical rational self, of Egyptians. "The concealment (*hijab*) of women is the cause of the decadence of the East, and the absence of concealment is the secret of the progress of the West" (508). In this way, Amin fundamentally alters the relations among femininity, concealment, and moral order. Whereas formerly, femininity signified the desire whose control and concealment give rise to moral order, Amin makes it signify the moral order whose repression and concealment result in slavery—not just for women, but for society as a whole. The result is that the nature of moral order itself is altered in a manner that allows it to take the form of liberal autonomy.

As a result of female concealment, Egypt is a decadent society, whose operative principles are tyranny (*istibdad*), enslavement (*isti'bad*), and passion (*hawa*). It is instructive to note that Amin's first book, written in 1894, presented a rather different picture. This book, written in French and titled *Les Egyptiens*, was a response to a scathing description of Egyptian society issued by a French traveler, the Duc d'Harcourt. Amin, defending his countrymen from many of the same charges he himself would later level at them, presented Egypt as a well-ordered society whose institutions, including sexual segregation and polygyny, held moral advantages over those of Europe. He explicitly repudiated the charge that Egyptian women were somehow enslaved, maintaining that "all that we men may do, women may do as well, and they do so."³⁵ In *The New Woman*, however, repression takes centerstage, and the logic of tyranny and enslavement governs the depiction of Egyptian and other Eastern societies. "If you look at the Eastern lands, you find the woman enslaved to the man, and the man enslaved to the ruler, so that he is an oppressor in his house and oppressed when he leaves it" (426). Political enslavement, however, is not the current problem in Egypt. "Our laws are those of a free nation, but our morals are still those of an enslaved nation!" (433). Egyptians were handed freedom, they did not achieve it, and therefore they have not internalized it. They do not esteem it, love it, or respect it in others. Free women would create such feeling in them, but because men are enslaved they want only to tyrannize their women. The result is that Egypt is sunk in decadence. Whereas Europeans enjoy historical agency in the sense that they critically evaluate and rationally determine their social norms and institutions, Egyptians and Easterners are gripped by prejudice, ignorance, superstition, unable to distinguish nature from custom or self-interest from truth. They are led by passion, blind to reason. Europeans, in their deliberate and dispassionate pursuit of truth, understand Egyptian history and society better than do Egyptians themselves, and this is what led to colonial conquest.

The rational autonomy of Europeans does not consist in cognitive or intellectual abilities, but is a moral capacity. The fundamental difference between Europeans and the East is that the former are capable of negating their desire, ordering their selves, integrating into the collective body. The act of self-sacrifice is the meaning and form of this condition of simultaneous individual and collective agency for Amin just as it was for al-Barudi. Or in other words, it remains that there is no other agency than self-sacrifice. Thus, Europeans, even their upper and lower classes, who are more prone to corruption than the middle class, are categorically on the other side of the moral divide from Easterners.

> This corruption...has not weakened in them the social virtues that are the firmest foundation of the edifice of nations, and the expenditure of self and wealth that arises from these virtues. The lowest man in the West is like the highest in that when he is called to an attack or a defense or to a beneficial work he quits all of his pleasures and forgets them, rises in response to the call, risks his life and gives of his wealth until the nation achieves what it willed. So what comparison can there be between these two classes of Western nations, in respect of these glorious virtues, and the state of an Eastern nation? (504)

The European "rises (*yanhad*) in response to the call" just as al-Barudi's virtuous hero rises: "If a man does not rise (*yanhad*), sword in hand, would that I knew how truth were defended."[36] This kind of rising for the sake of fulfilling moral order, negating thereby every impulse to passivity, comfort, self-preservation, constitutes nationality, the collective form in which humanity is realized. Without this kind of rising, there is nothing but tyranny and slavery, ignorance and falsehood, the dissipation of desire. Amin's decisive formulation of what Europeans have and Easterners lack illustrates the full articulation of his moral ideal to that of traditional representations. However distinctive is the actual content of this ideal, it upholds the value and retains the meaning that it has held in the past. It is the basis on which the transformed nature of moral order—liberal autonomy generated in the private sphere, and the transformed manifestation of agency—critical-rational participation in the bourgeois public sphere, are to be accepted.

The private role of free women is the "most important and beneficial of any living human being on the face of the earth" because femininity induces the moral condition of collective agency. "The work of the woman in the social body is the formation of the morals of the nation, those morals whose effect upon society, in respect to the ascent and decline of nations, is greater than the effects of institutions, laws and religions" (474). Europeans so honor their mothers and wives because "they know that whatever virtues and good qualities they have are from their mothers, who deposited in them the best portion of their souls" (473). To endow women with this role, Amin must show them to possess agency and humanity in the specific manner that will give rise in the collective to the form of agency and humanity that he is promoting. In the case of Amin's liberal project, this means that he must show them to be capable of an agency and humanity that is nearly indistinguishable from that of men. The "freedom" that women should be granted is the same liberal autonomy that men require. "The sound conscience will judge that anyone who does not have complete control over his thought, will and action is a slave!" (438). Amin argues that women are entitled to such autonomy by establishing their capacity to participate fully in the *public* sphere, citing their achievements in the West. He points to examples of famous women in the arts and sciences, women's participation in the workforce, their political movements, and the success of women's suffrage in the American states where it had been permitted. He argues that women will soon attain full political equality in Europe and America. The *capacity* to act in the public sphere is in Amin's presentation the criterion of women's full human status and entitles them to the same kind of freedom and education enjoyed by men. Whether they should actually be granted full public rights at the present time in Egypt is a separate issue.

The displacement of femininity across the moral divide between desire and order means the repudiation of traditional representations of femininity and the woman who conforms to them. It means replacing "the animal being that was enveloped in ornament, attired in finery, and sunken in frivolity" with the "sister of man, partner of her husband, cultivator of children, refiner of the species" (421). To do this, Amin denatures the former meaning of femininity by turning chaotic desire into mere sexuality. In this regard, Amin relates a verse of poetry whose image of womanhood, he expects, will be held up against his own: "Upon us was ordained war and struggle—and upon lovely maidens, trailing the trains of gowns" (456). This verse evokes the conventional relationship between heroic agency and the desire that must be displayed and controlled. As discussed previously, the signification by femininity of this desire creates a relationship of status and incorporation between the masculine and the feminine. But this meaning of femininity does not specify any particular social role or function for women, nor project any necessary sphere of women's action. This is precisely the basis on which Amin repudiates the verse's image of womanhood. For even if it corresponds to the state of the women that the poet saw, "it is not the true image of woman, because it is not an image of a human being, nor even of an animal!" It has no connection with the tasks and functions necessary for women to perform in life, which may include those of the public sphere, as women lawyers and lecturers in Europe have shown. It is an image, therefore, that strips women of their humanity, the autonomy to which they are entitled, for the sake of men's passions. Thus, the celebrated ability of women to enthrall men to their wishes is based not on men's respect for women as human beings, but on nothing more than ephemeral lust (441). The lordship (*siyada*) currently exercised by men over women is a dehumanizing tyranny that enslaves women by making their existence dependent upon and for the sake of men (440). The concealment of women (*hijab*) is the symbolic vestige of men's ownership of women in ancient times. Amin, like Abduh, reduces the existing gender regime and the meaning of femininity within it to the unrestrained sexuality of Egyptian men. What was formerly represented as desire now becomes concupiscence. The result is that the traditional meaning of femininity can be in no way connected with virtue, but is based upon and perpetuates the egoism and dissipation of men, thereby making them incapable of autonomy, agency, and incorporation into the nation.

The repression of women's autonomy is the repression of the specific function of femininity in the psyche of all individuals, particularly men, that engenders rational autonomy. Women's private roles, especially as mothers but also as wives, give rise to and cultivate the mental-emotional faculty called by Amin the "sensibility" (*wijdan*), which aligns emotional attachment with rational order, thus making it possible for individuals to be free of the rule of egoism and passion. This is precisely the "sensibility of freedom" lacking in Egyptians despite their actual freedom. The fundamental problem of the East, Amin argues, the underlying cause of its decadence, is the dormancy of this faculty among its peoples. For it is the presence of noble emotions, love of perfection, that impels individuals to act in the name of noble values. Thus we see that youths in the present day are provided with the most thorough education and trained in the highest of values. Yet when they become men, "Alas! Our hopes in them are disappointed, and we see in these educated youths withered hearts, small aspirations (*himam*), weak resolves, and as for emotions, they are nearly extinct" (480). They are not moved aesthetically or morally nor can be stirred to beneficial action. In other words, they *know* rational autonomy and its values without actually possessing it. "This has no cause but that their early cultivation has not addressed their sensibility, *this sensibility that is the sole motor of action*, and which is not exposed, strengthened or nurtured but by cultivation within the home, whose only agent at home is the mother" (481, emphasis added). By this means, mothers inculcate in their children love of all noble values. Thus we see that whereas Europeans feel intense patriotic emotion, even as children, Egyptians are devoid of such emotion, as shown by the memoirs of a prominent figure quoted by Amin. In sum, "the decadence of the Egyptian arises from his deprivation of this primary cultivation" (481). The psychic role of women is quite similar to that of fine art, held by Amin to be as important as knowledge in education. For art, in Amin's view, embodies perfection in its form, and by presenting perfection directly to our senses, causes us to perceive it and love it in a manner that cognitive knowledge of it cannot effect (490). Thus, femininity is responsible for the spiritual, affective substrate of rational autonomy, which is the higher emotion that is rationally ordered and motivates rationality. It is, in other words, the means by which raw emotion, chaotic desire, negates itself and becomes love of its own ordering. This, and no longer chaotic desire itself, is the love that ought to bind mother and child, man and woman, and is the love that will make the private citizens who form the public sphere.

The private role of women is therefore publicly oriented in that it is the origin of public order. It is the lynchpin of the reciprocity and complementarity of public and private that defines both. In Amin's account, the separation between the public and private spheres is not rigid; there is a great degree of permeability between the two. This is effected through the depiction of women's agency as equivalent to public agency. I have indicated above Amin's insistence on women's full capacity for participation in the public sphere. It is precisely this full capacity that is necessary for women to fulfill their role in forming the self in the private sphere. In other words, the full degree of moral order required for agency in the public sphere is required as well for women's agency in private. Instilling the capacity for self-sacrifice within children requires itself an "indescribable" effort of self-sacrifice, as does companioning a man in a manner that impels him to the highest deeds (473, 478). To be capable of successfully undertaking these critical roles, women must not only be fully autonomous, but must have the full educational qualifications and social experience required by men as preparation for public participation. Anything less redounds to the harm of the collective body. To act in private, women must be fit to act in public. This means that in Amin's account there is no natural barrier to women's movement from private to public.[37]

Nevertheless, Amin has placed the definitive function of femininity in the private sphere. Moreover, he does not demand the immediate elimination of all social and political inequalities between the sexes. Although he argues extensively that women must be qualified to work outside the home should they find it necessary, and that numerous professions would benefit from female participation, he still envisages that the destiny of most women will lie in the home. Nor does he believe that Egypt is yet ready for women's political participation (457). In any case, by defining femininity in terms of a private role, regardless of other potential roles, and in defining feminine agency in terms of a gender-specific function, despite its moral equivalence to and necessity for masculine agency, Amin preserves a moral distinction between masculine and feminine that seems at odds with the tenor of his liberal project. It has been argued that this is because the ultimate aim of Amin's project is to reshape masculinity and the public order, for which the discourse on women is merely a means, and that Amin cannot therefore be regarded as a "feminist."[38] This claim, however, implies a notion of feminism that is not applicable or analytically useful in a context in which the private sphere is not yet an accepted norm. Feminism, if it is the struggle for the legal and political equality of women with men, can only take place in the context of an established bourgeois public sphere, in which a norm of citizenship based on common humanity is in effect, as well as an ideal of women's autonomy, however limited, based on their participation in this humanity in some way. All of this requires the ideal of a reciprocal private sphere from which private citizens emerge and in which women play a humanizing role. Without the prior establishment of women's moral agency through the ideal of the private sphere, there is no accepted moral basis for bourgeois feminism to launch its struggle. It is in establishing the ideal of the private sphere that representations of femininity move femininity across the moral divide and make it publicly oriented, even though they do so by subordinating it to an existing ideal of collective agency, which serves as the anchor for this move. This is precisely what we see not only in Amin's writings, but in those of his contemporaries, women as well as men. The publicly oriented private sphere is the platform from which women's entry into the public sphere can be demanded, even though it is at the same time the site in which women's public contribution can be confined. Therefore, activists like Nabawiya Musa, who called for women's entry into the workforce, and Inji Aflatun, who called for women's right to suffrage, were not mistaken in referring to Amin as a major antecedent who helped lay the groundwork for their political demands.[39]

Amin depicts feminine agency in a manner that makes it necessary for collective agency by inscribing femininity into the self as the catalyst for the self-negation of desire and thus accession to the moral condition. In this, he is no different from many other writers who helped establish the norm of the private sphere. Yet there are different ways of depicting femininity such that it performs this function, resulting in different types of feminine agency and different ideologies of moral order. Rational autonomy, in the liberal sense, powered by an aesthetic, feminine substrate is not the only possibility for creating a private–public nexus. Other modes of depicting the nature of self-negation and the feminine role in it can result in much more rigid barriers between private and public and in forms of feminine agency that are much more distinct from masculine and national agency. An extreme contrast is provided in the novel *Return of the Spirit* (1933), to be discussed in a later chapter, in which feminine "agency" performs its definitive moral function in men but turns out not to be an authentic form of agency at all, thus confining women to a private existence. In this case, the ideal woman's moral effect arises naturally from her *being* rather than from her performance of active self-sacrifice. For Qasim Amin, on the other hand, women must engage in such self-sacrifice, yet its nature still has some connection with their feminine being. Absolute permeability between the private and public spheres is only established in accounts that define women's agency as a direct catalyst of national agency without the intermediary of the individual selves that women will form. This is seen in the writings of feminists of later generations, like Inji Aftlatun, who argued that the persistence of colonial domination required and perpetuated the disenfranchisement of Egyptian women. Among those writers who ascribe moral value to femininity through a private function, a position within the individual self, there are many distinctions to be made regarding the nature of feminine agency, the degree of its difference from masculine agency, and the form of national order that arises from it. These distinctions hinge on the depiction of the moral process in which agency and order are anchored.

The outpouring of denunciation that attended the publication of Amin's books can be seen not only as evidence of the social conservatism of his contemporaries—which is amply evident in their arguments for the necessity of women's seclusion—but as repudiation of the political stance that Amin promotes. Amin's account is structured in a manner that not only places femininity in a decisive position within the self, but at the same time places Europe in this position. This is not only because the European woman is the universal ideal of the new woman, but because Europe is necessary for Egyptians to achieve the state of moral order. Amin's account establishes a circle of decadence from which there is no exit but the direct imitation of European practices. Egyptian men are enslaved because they have not been formed by relationships with free women. As a result, they are egoistic tyrants who will not grant women their liberty. Egyptian women, since they are enslaved and denatured, are incapable of fulfilling their role in liberating Egyptian men. The way out of this impasse, Amin argues, is for Egyptian men to recognize that Europeans have advanced the furthest on the path of human development, they have understood the laws of this development, and they have rationally chosen their social practices on its basis (508). For the sake of lifting Egypt out of its decadent condition, Egyptian men must overcome their prejudice and egoism and imitate Europe in granting women autonomy. To struggle for the sake of Egypt and save it from oblivion, or in other words, to achieve national integration and agency, Egyptians must become European. Europe is the moral and historical ideal that has always been implicit in human nature. The new woman is the European woman, she makes good the deficiency within the Egyptian self, and if Egyptians do not fix their aspirations on her above all else, they are doomed to perdition.

The Arabo-Islamicization of Femininity

Qasim Amin appeals to nationality as an abstract moral structure that is devoid of national content. For Amin, the nation is nothing more than the collective level at which order and agency are to be attained. There is nothing distinctively Egyptian that enables this order and agency to come about. In other words, there is no fundamental national identity other than human identity. This takes form in his purely human ideal of femininity, in which differences of ethnicity, language, and religion, are merely incidental (517). The reason for the absence of national content in the ideal woman and in the nation to which she gives rise is that there is no concrete national dimension in the manner in which women enable men to achieve self-negation. Neither

Arab, Muslim, or Egyptian identity play any role in a woman's capacity to propel men into the condition of moral order, nor do these identities affect the quality or nature of moral order in the self. The European way of life, on the other hand, is intrinsically linked to this order.

The result is that Amin's program is apolitical and orientalist in character. It implicitly justifies colonial domination. It casts authentic resistance as the struggle against Egyptian custom and prejudice rather than any kind of opposition to British occupation. At the same time, its linkage to existing moral ideals occurs at an abstract level. It promises Egyptians the collective agency so highly valued in their cultural representations at the expense of the cultural symbols and forms in which this agency has traditionally appeared. Values associated with Islam and the Arab heritage are stripped of ultimate human significance and are in many cases aligned with tyranny and enslavement. This put Amin's program in direct conflict with the anticolonial movement, as well as with the most firmly entrenched normative forms and symbols of Egyptian society. The normative transformation of femininity and the promotion of the private sphere, however, did not require linkage to Eurocentrism or to Amin's radical form of liberalism, and many reformists were loath to disable their efforts by provoking outraged opposition. They sought rather to distance their project from such linkages by aligning it with colonial resistance and articulating it to hallowed normative symbols. They did so by making Arab and Islamic elements fundamental to women's role in effecting self-negation and engendering moral order.

We can get an idea of this process by briefly considering a dramatic instance—the transformation in the meaning of the term *hijab* over the course of the twentieth century. For Amin and his contemporaries, as previously indicated, the term denoted the institution of female segregation and concealment, cast by Amin as the fundamental site of repression and tyranny. Yet Amin's attempt to reverse the moral valence of the term faced a difficult struggle, as its association with moral order was deeply entrenched. Consider, for example, the opening lines of a humorous poem narrating a love adventure by Abdullah Fikri (1834–1890), a prominent intellectual, official, and friend of al-Barudi:

> A belle of European extraction whose *hijab*
>   was for those seeking her favors in love, easy.
> I fell for her and there was no guardian
>   to worry about nor was she inclined to be stingy with a lover...[40]

The *hijab* here is the restriction of access to pleasure, the barrier concealing the self's chaotic desire, instantiated in the desirable lady. To say that her *hijab* was easy is equivalent to saying that she was a woman of "easy virtue." Her meaning is thus the unleashing of the desire whose confinement gives rise to virtue. There is, moreover, an implicit association of the unconstrained European woman with this kind of release of desire. Even though the poem is merely an exercise in transgressive frivolity (*mujun*), we see here a fundamental equivalence between *hijab* and virtue, both absent in the European woman. We have then a rather different set of associations from those later promoted by Amin, and in the long run, the notion of *hijab* retained its equivalence with virtue even though its moral content changed. The transformation in the *denotation* of the term *hijab*, from the regime of seclusion to the "Islamic" headscarf, a process completed much later in the twentieth century, had its origin in Amin's (and Abduh's) arguments for a true Islamic *hijab*, but was made possible by a profound transformation in the conception of moral order and feminine modesty. For *hijab* in its latter-day incarnation no longer signifies the confinement and concealment of chaotic desire, but is the marker of the moral order of a normatively Islamicized private sphere. It is fully publicly oriented in that it exists only for showing adherence to this order in public. Whereas *hijab* in its former sense could denote the face-veil, as the most prominent marker of the regime of seclusion, the means by which women stayed out of "public" even when outdoors, the new *hijab* is precisely what enables women to inhabit the public sphere while still characterized by their adherence to the norm of the Islamic family. In this way, the new *hijab* belongs fully to the private–public order, while at the same time preserving the inadvertent distinction of the older *hijab* vis-à-vis Europe, turning this distinction into an explicit marker of moral superiority over the Western private–public order. The new *hijab*, therefore, like the old one, signifies a normative Islamic relation between moral, social order, and feminine modesty, but the nature of this relation has been drastically altered.

The evolution of the meaning of *hijab* belongs to the process of depicting a new woman in whom an Arabic and Islamic character is necessary for her moral and social function. This process was an integral dimension of the general emergence of the norms of the private sphere and took a great deal of impetus from the writings of Qasim Amin, both in developing his themes and in staking out opposing positions. The writer and activist Malak Hifni Nasif (1886–1918), who took the pen-name Bahithat al-Badiya, was one of the key figures who can be cited in this regard. The daughter of the prominent Egyptian man of letters and judge, Hifni Nasif (1855–1919), who was, like Amin, a close associate of Muhammad Abduh, Malak Hifni Nasif was a prominent public advocate of women's issues in the early twentieth century.[41] Nasif was one of the first group of women to graduate from the government teacher's college, and enjoyed an accomplished mastery of classical Arabic in addition to her familiarity with European thinkers. She founded women's organizations, gave public lectures to female audiences, and published numerous articles in the press.[42] Unlike Amin, Nasif did not provoke controversy, but drew the acclaim of both conservative religious figures and liberal reformers. She takes the tone in her writings of a high-minded moralist concerned to defend Islamic values and the Arabic cultural heritage while at the same time seeking to remove the ills and injustices of present-day society. The Eurocentric liberal ideology promoted by Amin plays no role in framing her discourse, which aligns itself with anticolonial sentiment and espouses no explicit social ideology. Although at bottom, her reformist demands were not fundamentally different from those of Amin, she incorporated them into a rhetorical framework that invests Arabic-Islamic identity with moral universality and that manifests this identity in a feminine subjectivity of tragic seriousness.

The key difference between Nasif's reformism and that of Amin was that she sought to establish the norms of a bourgeois private sphere without calling for the immediate abolition of the institution of sexual segregation. On the level of actual social life, the abolition of female concealment is a momentous transformation both symbolically and practically (de-veiling began to become a social norm in Egypt after Nasif's death, in the 1920s, initiated by the feminist Huda Sha'rawi). The difference between its "abolition" or nonabolition on the discursive level, however, is not necessarily as momentous. This is so in regard to Nasif's writings because she does not reject the social mingling of the sexes, but argues that it is an ideal condition for which Egyptian men and women are not yet morally ready. Nor is Egyptian society yet strong enough to resist Europeanization and its excesses should it adopt this course. She calls, therefore, for "a middle way between Western non-concealment and the antiquated Egyptian segregation, so that we suffer neither an excessive mixing and vanish into the Europeans, nor a confinement which constrains the body and forfeits social welfare."[43] This middle way is the practice of the early Muslims who allowed supervised contact between men and women under certain circumstances, particularly for the sake of ensuring the compatibility of prospective spouses. The rhetorical strategy pursued by Nasif in her writings can be seen in this instance. In every case, actual Egyptian practice and actual European practice are forms of excess characterized by tyranny and dissipation, while the correct morally ordered golden mean is the authentic Islamic practice. This strategy is not peculiar to Nasif; the positing of an Islamic ideal that resolves what are cast as opposing moral failures of East and West has been and remains a pervasive discursive phenomenon. On this basis, Nasif seeks to preserve Egypt, as a collective body brought into being by its Arab–Islamic character, from twin threats of extinction: world-historical oblivion, resulting from the decadent Eastern perversion of Islamic practices, and absorption into the West, resulting from the surrender of Islamic practices in slavish imitation of Europeans.

Nasif's equivocal position on feminine seclusion is the result of her attempt to subordinate the institution to the logic of the publicly oriented private sphere without explicitly calling for its abolition.[44] In this way, Nasif was able to show her moderation, avoid controversy, and focus on what she regarded as more urgent matters—the call for women's education and for reform of the marital regime, both of which would entail the moral transformation of Egyptian men and women. These reforms aim at the replacement of male lordship with a monogamous companionate marital norm in which morally ordered women are able to play their proper social role in giving rise to Egyptian agency. Nasif represents this as the humanization of domestic life, which in this respect fully corresponds to the bourgeois ideal of familial privacy. But she at the same time endows the bourgeois ideal with an Arab–Islamic character as its central element. This is seen most fundamentally in the manner in which women enable men to achieve the national self.

Unlike Qasim Amin, Nasif does not elaborate a developed account of the process by which women enable men to achieve self-negation, for her reformism centers on no ideology of the nature of moral order corresponding to Amin's liberal autonomy. Yet she insists upon this effect nonetheless. In a speech entitled "The Influence of Women in the World," Nasif agrees with male reformers that the cause of Egypt's backwardness is the "decadence" of its women, although she criticizes them for putting off their own action until women are capable of inspiring them. Women are necessary for the inspiration of such action, she argues, but men must at the same time make themselves capable of responding to this inspiration. Nasif defines the fundamental function of women, beyond their social necessity for childrearing and household and family management, in this way: "Above that, they have complete power over impelling men to sublime deeds and turning them towards momentous affairs" (115). This is "the use of their God-given influence over men to impel them to beneficial work that uplifts the nation towards progress" (116). Here Nasif uses the same term for "arising" to create moral order and collective agency that appears in al-Barudi and Amin. This capacity to effect self-negation within men is for Nasif "women's greatest weapon." "The nature of this influence is unknown because it belongs to the special properties that God has placed in the essence of substances." But it is akin to the emotional effect of "beauty and sublimity," as well as eloquent speech, on the soul. To employ this influence in the proper manner, women must be morally ordered. "What an awesome hidden power this is within us... but we don't realize it, or don't use it, or use it in a manner that is not for the common good" (119).

What is especially of interest here is Nasif's linkage of this feminine power with the Arab–Islamic cultural heritage. In the speech under discussion, Nasif draws evidence for this power from traditional poetry, citing lines like the following: "We are men melted by lovely eyes, though we melt steel; / We are champions in bloody battle, but are in peace the slaves of beautiful maidens" (119). She also recounts lore of pre-Islamic and early Islamic women of high-status on whose account wars were fought, or who counseled their sons to war for the sake of truth. Nasif thus fuses the image of femininity as chaotic desire with the image of high-status women under the control of virtue in an effort to create a new image of *affective* moral-ordering that repositions femininity within the self. Although this strategy is not in the long run viable, since the two images do not add up to the third, it is an initial step in the transformation of traditional feminine representations.

An article written by Nasif entitled "The Arab Woman Yesterday and Today," addressing an incident that took place in Italian-occupied Libya,[45] illustrates the catalyzing effect of Arab women upon men in a more dramatic manner. A Libyan woman, taken prisoner by the Italians, was rescued by the men of an Arab clan with great loss of life. Nasif's article ecstatically celebrates this heroic instance of self-sacrifice and glory with great bombast. She writes, addressing the rescued woman, "for your sake they penetrated the thickening smoke of cannon raining its downpour upon them, missiles falling upon their heads like burning stone. Hellfire itself would not have averted them from you, O mistress of women, O revivifier of high ambition from its grave, O awakener of living feeling" (290). Nasif pairs the Libyan lady's call to her rescuers, with its contempt for her Italian captors, with the defiant poetic utterance of an ancient Arab woman violated by her captors, whence the title of the article. Nasif goes on to say,

> she called them to arise, and caused them to arise. This is the hidden electricity of women: they weep, and make rivers of blood flow; they laugh and fill the world with gold. They are the spirit of the world, and men the bodies. The body manifests force, but the soul is the secret of inspiration. Women are the intention, men the act. After this can they aggrandise themselves and say that men are more important than women, and women lower than men? (291)

Nasif is rather explicit here in indicating the position of femininity within the individual and national self. We see clearly how the woman, by actuating the capacity for self-sacrifice, signifies this capacity, and becomes its object. The Libyan lady calls up this capacity not because of her tribal or aristocratic status, but simply in her native nobility as an Arab woman. She is inherently chaste, instinctively contemptuous of the Italian "boys." The men who gave their lives to rescue her did so with zeal, unlike the Americans and Europeans on the Titanic who made way for the women only at gunpoint. The significance of the Libyan incident for Nasif is that it reveals that the restoration of women to the tragic-heroic status that they once enjoyed in the Arab-Islamic past is the prerequisite for overthrowing colonialism and restoring national glory. The effect of her representation is the transformation of the tribal-aristocratic honor embodied in the ancient Arab woman into the private moral function of the contemporary Arab bourgeois woman. This moral function, immanent to national agency and publicity as soul is to body and intention to act, makes the bourgeois woman the metaphor of nationality.

The tragic-heroic Arab–Islamic ethos depicted here infuses Nasif's general program for reordering domestic life into a private sphere that is publicly oriented. She lays out her conception of women's freedom and autonomy, for example, as the freedom granted to women by Islam, which is to be restored by allowing women to attend public prayers as they did in earlier times: "I mean the true freedom of life, the freedom of the self from the bonds of enslavement, the freedom to dispose of one's wealth, the freedom of proper treatment or relinquishment in marriage, the freedom of opinion" (160).[46] Like other reformers of the time, Nasif defines the nature of womanhood in humanity, as opposed to mere biological femininity (131). On this basis, women are entitled to education and to "equality with men in value and respect" (132). Though Nasif regards women's familial role as the social function for which they are most necessary, she opposes those who claim that women were not created for work outside the home or intellectual pursuits. "Would that I knew what decree to this effect has issued from God and whence is their certainty without divine authority" (75). In promoting bourgeois norms of domesticity, her primary concern in her speeches to women, Nasif invokes the excellences of Western women, in the manner of Amin, but at the same time warns against Western excesses. For the most part, Nasif decries to Egyptian women their own ignorance, superstition, slovenliness, laziness, incompetent child-rearing, frivolity, mismanagement of time and money, and general lack of care and concern in their household duties.[47] But she also criticizes upper-class women for their blind and frivolous adoption of Western practices.[48] And she sees grave danger for Egyptian society in the marriage of Egyptians to Europeans, and especially in the marriage of Egyptian women to European men.[49] Nevertheless, Nasif is equally critical of Egyptian men in their treatment of and attitudes toward women. The problem for her is not simply the backwardness of women, but the egoism of men that prevents them from responding to the moral influence of women, and the effect of this egoism on the women capable of uplifting society. It is in this area that Nasif develops her depiction of femininity much further than a reformer like Qasim Amin.

Nasif pioneers in her writings the representation of a private, publicly oriented feminine subjectivity that is tragic and serious in character. This subjectivity is anchored in the heroic ethos of Arabic eloquence and in the discourse of tyranny and enslavement. It exhibits the morally ordered nature of femininity and establishes the human and social injustice of the oppression of women. Like other reformers, Nasif describes social dysfunction in terms of tyranny (*istibdad*) of men and enslavement (*isti'bad*) of women, linking this with the current political situation. "How can our men with such tyranny hope for the reform of the nation and the upbringing of its youths in love of independence and constitutional government!" (241–242). In fictional letters and narrative vignettes, in her own public correspondence with the writer Mayy Ziyada, and in her published articles as a whole, Nasif creates a voice of women who suffer and denounce men's oppression. In a letter received "in the post of imagination" a woman whose husband has forsaken her for her sister tells of this dual betrayal and the loss of her children in a grave, forbearing tone interspersed with lines of classical poetry. The author of another letter, which Nasif tells us that she found lying in the street, tells of her intent to leave her husband, whom she married blindly in the customary way at the behest of her family. "I never felt passion" before marriage, she relates, "not because of cold-heartedness or other-worldliness," but in wariness of betrayal, heart-break and shame (285). "I stored up that great power (that is, love) in my breast and did not expend an iota of it, cherishing the hope that I would one day grant it to a worthy husband and spare myself the evil into which lovers fall" (286). Her love was squandered, however, on her ill-chosen mate, who showed her no affection and betrayed her with another woman. The letter-writer's love stored up at the expense of passion is precisely the feminine moral order that is dissipated by the oppressive marital regime and male indifference of contemporary Egypt. And her mode of self-expression embodies this social and human injustice in her personal suffering.

Similarly, Nasif's own mode of expression is to be seen not merely as a means of communication, but as a public display of the moral order of Egyptian womanhood. Like her fictional letter writers, she represents the "cultivated Egyptian woman" (*al-misriya al-mutahaddira*) in her views, her sentiments, and her style. In a letter to Mayy Ziyada, she speaks of the pain that she "drags like weights of iron," explaining that it is not of the familiar varieties that afflict most people. "I have a heart that nearly melts in sympathy for those who deserve mercy and those who do not deserve it. This is the cause of my suffering and the well-spring of my pain. My heart breaks for the state of this corrupt society" (318). In another letter, she says of men the following:

> Quite a marvel is this creature of strange proclivities called 'man'. I believe that he is generous and brave and has a sensitive heart, but I suspect (and some of suspicion is sin) that he is egoistic before all else. My view is that his egoism alone is the origin of his vices. He usurps woman's rights and enslaves her not because he hates her or wishes her evil, but to use her for his amusement, though he loves her. And he dies for her sake, not because he loves her, but to use her for his amusement. In all of this he is vast in cunning, powerful in persuasion. He convinces her and she believes him, yet he is false! (330–331)

The woman, on the other hand, is "always truthful and sincere even when she is mistaken. She loves in order to be consumed in love" like the silkworm that expends itself in producing its silk for the general public and unlike the man who "loves in order to live in enjoyment of love" (331). Nasif, in this complaint to Mayy Ziyada, expresses her depiction of feminine self-sacrifice and male egoism in a morally authoritative rhetorical register associated with those capable of self-sacrifice. She captures in this register the prophetic standpoint of the classical writers and poets who denounced the disorder of their age. Yet she does so in a manner that is not defiant and condemnatory, but forbearing and sympathetic. Her ethos is not that of a heroic virtue that transcends the existing order, but the transformation of this into a virtue of affect that is trapped within the constraints of the existing order. The publicly oriented feminine subjectivity that she creates, bearing the insignia of its Arab–Islamic lineage, cannot be seen as a spontaneous subjective expression, even though Nasif herself suffered all the marital injustices she decries. For this subjectivity is fashioned from the displacement of the discourse of tyranny and enslavement into the private sphere, into the voice of the woman whose affective capacities are to give rise to social order, but are prevented from doing so by male affective repression. In this way, Nasif presents in her public expression an ideal of feminine moral order capable of engendering and standing for nationality that takes form in its struggle against the male egoism incapable of recognizing it.

For Qasim Amin, the liberation of women is the liberation of humanity, and the institution of female concealment, the manifestation of male egoism, is the site of its repression. Nasif, however, creates a voice from within the humanity that is struggling for liberation. This self-expression of what is depicted as society's repressed *immanent* order constitutes literary subjectivity. It is the point of origin of the realistic novel and related forms of subjective representation. In Nasif's writings, it takes an incipient, tentative, limited form but is nevertheless a key element in her creation of a public femininity rooted in privateness. Nasif thereby depicts a feminine agency that is already constituted, but repressed, in contrast to Amin, for whom feminine agency will come into existence and reorder society as soon as women are granted autonomy.

Nasif's description of the relation of women to men as that of soul to body and intention to action asserts the immanence of feminine agency to the national agency of men. In so doing, it establishes the immanence of privacy to publicity, bringing into being the public–private circuit of the national social order. The transformation of the meaning of femininity, the refashioning of the image of chaotic desire into the catalyst of the negation of desire, enables femininity to stand as a metaphor for the nation. Yet the cost of this elevation in representational status is the preservation of the linkage of femininity to desire. For femininity, as the origin of public order, remains rooted in the desire from which it causes this order to arise. Nasif's description shows that women are the nation *in potentia*; they are the aesthetic image of the order that is to be realized by men. Woman and man form a single being, which does not consist of two complementary halves, as Nasif's own discourse of the complementarity of feminine and masculine characteristics would have it, but a being in which the female is comprised within the male as the male's motivating impulse. The nominal gendered separation of roles within the self frees the masculine to represent the purely moral realm of national agency. Such masculinity stands in contrast to that depicted in al-Barudi's heroic lord, who kept his desire always on display so that he could master it at will. The world of privacy, however, comes about through the desacralizing of chaotic desire, its reduction to mere lust, its exclusion from morally ordered affect. And it is precisely the bourgeois woman who is in charge of effecting this exclusion through her unique capacity to ensure that innate human emotions and impulses always immediately turn into moral affect.

Therefore, Nasif's identification of femininity with the immanent order of the private sphere implies the continued subordination of women, but in a new way. Insofar as this immanence is definitive of femininity, women may be confined to it and to their role within the private sphere. Yet at the same time, the status of women as the origin of public order causes them to exceed the private sphere, just as does privacy itself. The definitive public orientation of women's private role links women directly to the public sphere. Reformers like Amin and Nasif enhance this linkage by making the qualification for moral ordering in the home equivalent to the qualification for the enaction of moral order in public. This linkage is enhanced on another level by its role in the self-publicization of bourgeois class status. The private sphere on this basis may serve as the point of departure for movement toward the nongendered assimilation of women into the public order. The establishment of public–private social order thereby calls into being a hegemonic struggle over the nature of this order that centers on women's role in it. The depiction of women's agency and the kind of moral order to which it gives rise determines the nature of public, national order, and at the same time, the extent to which women can take part in enacting this order.

Chapter 5

Fiction, Hegemony, and Aesthetic Citizenship

I have argued in previous chapters that the emergence of nationality, in which the nation is conceived as a self-ordering morally autonomous community, is intimately connected with the emergence of a new way of understanding the nature of order within individuals and how this order comes about. Individuals came to be seen as inherently disposed to attain a level of order within themselves that naturally and spontaneously gives rise to collective order. The idea that order arises immanently within individuals means that the innate feelings, dispositions, and powers of individuals somehow attain moral integration without requiring that it be perpetually imposed upon them. This raises the problem of how feelings and desires based on the senses and oriented toward pleasure and self-preservation come to restrain themselves so as to give rise to an individual agency that can be incorporated into collective agency. If these feelings and desires are understood as inherently chaotic, this kind of self-ordering cannot come about. The development of moral philosophy and general ideas about the self in Britain, France, and Germany during the eighteenth and early nineteenth centuries, and an analogous development in early twentieth-century Egypt, show a transformation in how the innate feelings and desires of the self were understood. Older terms like "the passions" were displaced by terms like "emotions," "affects," and "sentiments," which are not coextensive with the terms that they replaced and imply a different conception of the self.[1] The idea that innate sentiments can be moral in nature and may even be regarded as responsible for morality was promoted not only by philosophers like Hume, but played a central role in the early development of the realist novel. The belief that only emotions can motivate action, and so must be cultivated as attachments to noble values, came to be a common assumption. One of the chief outcomes of this development was the emergence of ideas that identified the uplifting of innate human feelings and sensations into morality as an aesthetic process. The capacity to perceive, imagine, and take pleasure in the beautiful and the sublime came to be regarded in a wide range of discourses as central to the formation of morally ordered citizens. Such ideas reached mature articulation in thinkers like Shelley, Kant, and Schiller and became a staple of social thinking in many domains throughout the nineteenth century and well into the twentieth century. These aesthetic ideas were important not only in making the expression of "personality" and "individuality" a condition of social integration, but in investing the objective, historically specific features of the nation, through the feelings they were thought to awaken, with moral universality.

I will argue in this chapter that the aesthetic dimension of citizenship—the dependence of the citizen's moral order on elevated, authentically human feelings arising from innate impulses—is the central linkage between nationality and realist fiction. The immanent conception of moral order, and specifically its aesthetic dimension, constitutes the realist novel and is the domain that novels develop and manipulate. Such novels depict in their characters the formation of moral dispositions from the inner impulses and social attributes that the novels assign to these characters. In doing so, these novels intimate their specific versions of the nature of innate desire and its moral consummation in the capacity for self-sacrifice, which is obstructed or prevented in a society that is depicted as disordered. In this way, realist novels represent the social divisions and antagonisms of their contemporary societies as specific forms of social disorder that arise from and perpetuate specific forms of moral disorder within individuals. The horizon of order and community is the fusion of the psychic with the social, the union of individual desires in a collective social will. The more dysfunctional is the present, however, the more is it the case that such fusion can come about only in a negative manner, a union of disorder, that consists in corruption, exploitation, and dissipation.

Such representations of the psychic origin of social reality are hegemonic in the sense that they implicitly claim the authority to show the nature of moral authenticity and the social orientation that belongs to it. The modern normative framework in which the private is the origin of the public becomes for the realist novel a literary device through which a seemingly authentic picture of contemporary society is generated out of a metaphysics of the self. The authority for this fictional hegemony is not based on a principle of human and social order, in the manner of social and political ideologies. It is based, rather, in the depiction of an innate human aesthetic and spiritual impulse to order and perfection in a narrative form which is itself aesthetic, and which thereby implicitly lays claim to the same nature as the innate humanity that it depicts. The realist novel therefore, in creating a depiction of immanent moral order as it arises (or is prevented from arising) within the self, is the complement of programs of social order, which claim to be the social expression of the inner order of the human self. At the same time, however, the autonomy of the aesthetic realm from morality, despite the necessity of the aesthetic realm for morality, creates an opposition between fiction and ideology. It is this tension between the aesthetic and the moral that novels exploit to generate their characters and social worlds.

This relation between the aesthetic and the moral arises from a fundamental contradiction in the immanent conception of moral order of nationality and modern normativity. In this immanent conception, the collective body continually produces from itself an ever increasing level of order that perpetually transforms society and the world toward an ultimate horizon of total perfection and order. The continual growth of order, in other words, is the corollary of the continual immanent production of order. Yet this continual production must have some origin, some inexhaustible reservoir from which to be produced, and this origin must therefore in some way be outside of order. It is in its identification as this origin that the modern notion of the aesthetic has been constituted. Love of beauty, held to be intrinsic to the human self, was posited as the pathway to morality. Nevertheless, as will be seen below, it is purely in its form that the beautiful object was thought to intimate the ultimate fusion of desire and moral order, without thereby creating any moral constraint. In this conception, independence from actual moral constraint is intrinsic to beauty and just what enables its moral function. Love of beauty, or any other purportedly innate desire posited as the origin of immanent order, cannot but have some kind of liminal relation to order itself, which gives this origin an aura of freedom and transgression. To be represented, this origin must be given the form of an impulse or practice that appears to be transgressive but turns out to be the authentically human impetus of social renewal and emancipation. A novel, therefore, that sets up this liminal position in a way that it chooses in order to depict social relations in a manner that it chooses, instantiates and exploits for its own purposes the contradiction that makes nationality possible. And in doing so, such novels sustain the normative framework of nationality by continually providing new transgressive forms for its liminal foundation as existing forms come to be fully normalized and lose their transgressive aura.

In the following discussion, I begin by contrasting the perspective on fiction, hegemony, and nationality that I am taking here with other approaches to the topic. I then examine the nature of the aesthetic dimension of citizenship and the importance of this conception in Egyptian political discourse from the 1920s to the 1950s. The chapter ends with an analysis of a seminal Egyptian novel, *Return of the Spirit* by Tawfiq al-Hakim, published in 1933. This novel demonstrates the linkage between romantic, ethnic nationalism, and the subordination of the moral to the aesthetic within the self.

Imagined Communities and National Allegories

My argument is that the fusion of the psychic and the social, the private and the public, on the basis of how feeling and impulse are depicted as giving rise to moral order, is the strategy by which realist novels instantiate the moral framework of nationality to produce their own accounts of social order and disorder. To clarify this perspective further, I will contrast it with two influential positions on the relationship between fiction and nationality, those of Benedict Anderson and Frederic Jameson. Anderson's comments on the significance of the novel as a form of representation in *Imagined Communities* center on the role of the novel in developing the means to imagine an immensely large and yet singular and interconnected society. He indicates two main contributions: the novel's pictorial surveying of the geographical space of the nation, showing the uniformity and interconnectness of its various locales, and thus imparting to the reader an impression of the nation as a geographical whole; and the novel's embodiment of "homogeneous, empty time," which makes the nation possible as a temporal entity, through the central function in the novel of "simultaneity," creating within readers the capacity to form a sense of the ever-present multitude of fellow citizens and their concurrent activity all across the nation. Anderson's focus here lies on the formation of the cognitive elements, in terms of content as well as capacities, required for imagining one's membership in a social group so large that it cannot be directly experienced as a whole. It can be seen that these cognitive claims regarding the contribution of novels to nationality are speculative in nature. There is no way to prove how or to what extent novels have enabled readers to form a coherent image of their nation's geography. Nor is there any way to show that at some point in the past, before the rise of novels, people were unable to imagine simultaneity or homogeneous empty time. It is on the other hand readily demonstrable that many novels depict their characters as members of a society that ought to be a moral community, and which thereby makes moral demands on these characters that constitute their identity. Anderson, however, does not address this issue.

In an essay entitled "Anderson and the Novel," Jonathan Culler evokes the moral dimension of nationality in an instructive manner in the course of his attempt to clarify Anderson's argument. Culler affirms Anderson's focus on the cognitive role of the novel in enabling its readers to imagine a nation by presenting "the space of a community"—not a particular national community per se, but what national communities look like from the inside.[2] Culler thereby insists upon a "distinction between the novel as a condition of possibility of imagining the nation and the novel as a force in shaping or legitimating the nation".[3] The latter, in Culler's view, is not a necessary or crucial dimension of the novel's relationship to nationality. As Culler puts it,

> If we try to argue that the novel, through its representations of nationhood, made the nation, we will find ourselves on shaky ground, but if we argue that the novel was a condition of possibility for imagining something like a nation, for imagining a community that could be opposed to another, as friend to foe, and thus a condition of possibility of a community organized around a political distinction between friend and enemy, then we are on less dubious ground.[4]

Culler's argument is that the novel can enable readers to imagine a kind of community—a nation—without reference to the legitimacy of this community, or in other words, without investing this community with any moral relationship to the novel's readers. Yet, in defining this community in terms of Carl Schmitt's friend-enemy opposition, Culler centrally implicates the moral structure of nationality. For according to Schmitt, the nation, the carrier of "one's own way of life," is the only kind of social group whose existence must be preserved and defended at all costs.[5] The nation alone has friends and enemies; it alone may demand the taking and surrendering of life for its self-preservation. Despite Schmitt's insistence that the nation's existence in this character is a fact as self-evident to its members as their own personal existence, it is obvious that the nation is not a natural, quasibiological being. Rather, its existence as a morally binding entity is a normative ideal, always articulated in competing forms, and in need of winning people's assent in order to command their allegiance. If the novel offers its readers, as Culler argues, "the possibility of adhering to a community, as an insider," a community it presents to them as a nation, it can only do so by representing a community constituted by the moral integration of its members.

The position taken by Fredric Jameson, his argument that "all third-world texts...are to be read as *national allegories*" directly addresses the novel's integration of the psychic and social.[6] Instead of seeing this integration as a representational strategy, however, Jameson sees it as the expression of an objective historical condition—resulting not only in ambiguity as to the nature and basis of this "allegory," but in a failure to grasp its hegemonic implications. According to Jameson, third-world novels appear primitive and alien to Western readers because of a "radical structural difference between the dynamics of third-world culture and those of the first-world cultural tradition in which we ourselves have been formed."[7] This difference is that whereas in the capitalist first-world, the psychic and the political are experienced as distinct, autonomous domains, the third-world, in its earlier stage of economic development, has not yet defused the two. First-world sensibility arises from an individuated, reified consciousness, while in the third-world a *gemeinschaft* collective immersion remains. Third-world novels cannot be about an individual's distinctive psyche, because psychic autonomy is not yet experienced there; rather, "psychology, or more specifically, libidinal investment, is to be read in primarily political and social terms."[8] The purpose of third-world novels is therefore collective in nature—it is to effect a "cultural revolution" aimed at eradicating "subalternity," consisting in "the feelings of mental inferiority and habits of subservience and obedience, which necessarily and structurally develop in situations of domination—most dramatically in the experience of colonized peoples."[9] In other words, the third-world novel seeks to emancipate a collective psyche rather than to depict individual subjectivity. Jameson does not consider that this collective psyche may be a literary device employed for varying purposes rather than the manifestation of social reality.

What then is allegory, and why the nation, which is a rather particular form of collective existence? Allegory refers to the necessarily political meaning of apparently libidinal phenomena, due to the objective state of social development, but as a literary mechanism Jameson leaves it with little specification. We may be initially inclined to take the term in a conventional sense: "the story of the private individual destiny is always an allegory of the embattled situation of the public third-world culture and society."[10] One might infer from this statement that allegory is a direct transfer of the character's attributes and circumstances to the nation as a whole. Jameson, however, dismisses such an inference, asserting that "the allegorical spirit is profoundly discontinuous, a matter of breaks and heterogeneities, of the multiple polysemia of the dream rather than the homogenous representation of the symbol."[11] It is not clear what kind of literary mechanism this characterization amounts to as Jameson does not further elaborate. At bottom, Jameson simply claims that the historical stage of third-world societies is one in which the libidinal always signifies the political, rather than examining how it is possible for novels to effect this connection and to what ends they do so. Moreover, there is no explanation for why it should be the nation that is signified by the emotional investments of fictional characters and not some other form of the political. Jameson's argument can only be based on an underlying assumption that there is an actual, objective relation between nations and the psyches of their citizens. No explanation of what the nation is such that it should have this connection is offered.

Nevertheless, the idea of national allegory contains a fundamental insight, namely, the linkage between private and public, libidinal and social, apparent in many realist novels, and the importance in this linkage of nationality. To naturalize this linkage by attributing it to social actuality, however, is to take "realism" too literally. The joining of private and public is as artistically contrived as any other central relation one finds in literary works, and contrived differently, with different purposes and implications, in different novels. For it is inaccurate to suggest that the public–private division had not yet come into being in the "third-world culture" that gave rise to realist novels. In the Egyptian context, the public–private division had very much become a public norm by the time that novels began to proliferate.[12] It is precisely the modern ideal of the private as the origin of public order that makes realist novels possible. For the representational strategy of these novels lies in positing a division between private and public, a condition of alienation, that lies at the heart of the disorder of the present and can only be overcome when individuals are able to form within themselves the moral disposition that realizes their humanity.

Beauty and the Nation

Realist novels are linked to nationality through their depiction of the immanent nature of moral order within individuals and in the collective body. This depiction is an artistic technique that makes moral dispositions appear to arise naturally from subjective feelings and inclinations. The process by which innate feelings and inclinations rise into the state of moral order has frequently been conceived as aesthetic in nature. The idea that social integration and self-sacrifice require noble sentiments like patriotism, love of freedom and justice, and so forth, and that these noble sentiments can be best cultivated by means of stories, poetry, music, and other arts, has had wide currency. The general sense that "refined" or "spiritual" emotions and sentiments have some kind of aesthetic quality or impetus has become pervasive. What I am calling the aesthetic dimension of citizenship is the necessity in the ideal of nationality that there be some process by which subjective feelings and impulses come to be constituted in such a way that the expression of individuality will be at the same time participation in a moral order. We can examine how this works as an aesthetic process by considering the account provided by the German writer Friedrich Schiller in his treatise *On the Aesthetic Education of Man*, published in 1795.[13]

Schiller's aim in this work is to establish the fundamental role played by art and the perception of beauty in bringing human beings from the state of passive sense perception and subjugation to nature to the state of rational moral autonomy. The problem, as he sees it, is that modern individuals are alienated from the laws that govern them and only accede to them through compulsion. The reason is that the exigencies of modern society and its complex division of labor cause a fragmentation of people's mental capacities. They are reduced to specific functions and cannot develop their mental powers in a total and harmonious fashion. As a result, they are incapable of realizing moral rationality and instead remain confined to the dictates of material needs and bodily passions. Society is populated not with citizens but with savages and voluptuaries motivated by self-interest alone.[14] How then are such individuals to unify their wills with the lawgiving state, which Schiller calls the representative of the "pure ideal man" that is within all of us? Schiller argues that this is precisely what cultivation of the aesthetic capacity to perceive beauty brings about. In aesthetic perception, the sensual and rational powers are simultaneously activated in a manner that synthesizes and liberates them from both physical and rational constraints. Through the perception of form the senses and emotions, which had been merely passive responses to stimuli, are drawn into order. At the same time, rationality is freed in aesthetic form from abstract laws and concepts that are alienated from the material world to unite with materiality and sensuality. In this state of freedom and indeterminacy, the capacity for the actual union of feeling and reason, motivated moral action, is born.[15] Thus, Schiller says, "the inevitable effect of the Beautiful is freedom from the passions" (106). In this way, we are liberated from subjugation to nature and physical necessity. "Man is superior to every terror of Nature so long as he knows how to give form to it, and to turn it into his object" (121). The work of art, which mirrors the human being in capturing the infinitude of form in finite material, lifts feeling out of passive sensual response into moral universality, the power to give laws to nature. This is why "it is through Beauty that we arrive at Freedom," including political freedom, the highest work of art (25, 27).

Schiller's philosophical account of how developed aesthetic capacities are necessary for moral autonomy and citizenship gives us only one way in which this necessity has been invoked. Nevertheless, we see here how the aesthetic capacity, as the origin of moral order, stands in a liminal relation to this order, and how beauty, the object of this capacity, unites all the oppositions that cleave everyday human existence: matter and spirit, emotion and reason, desire and moral law, passivity and agency, and necessity and freedom. In early twentieth-century Egypt, and especially from the 1920s, similar conceptions of the moral function of the aesthetic and its relation to nationality became prevalent in public discourses. These went along with the appearance of a new vocabulary for the naming of the innate feelings and impulses of the self. Qasim Amin's reference to the mental faculty he calls "*wijdan*," meaning the conscience or innate moral sensibility, has been discussed in the previous chapter. This concept became centrally important to writers of the following generation. Terms like '*awatif* (affects or sentiments), *irada* (will), *ghara'iz* (instincts), *al-mathal al-'ali* (moral ideal), became standard in moral and psychological discussions. This can be seen, for instance, in Ahmad Amin's *Kitab al-Akhlaq* (*Book of Moral Traits*, 1924), which acquired a textbook status on this topic. Amin's work, which draws heavily on European moral theorists, displays an immanent conception of moral order throughout. "All people... have an innate predilection towards honor, truth, honesty, and the other virtues," Amin holds.[16] "Human beings act on instinct and rationality together and it is not possible to separate the two. Instinct determines the goal and rationality finds the means to attain that goal."[17] Instinct, however, cannot become the virtues towards which it is predisposed without the proper cultivation. "The more a society progresses, the more egoism and altruism within it incline toward union and the formation of a single element. In the view of a person in a developed society egoism and altruism do not conflict."[18]

Numerous writers of the period identified this cultivation of the spirit with art and the perception of beauty, and in doing so posited the aesthetic realm as the innate human origin of individual and national moral order. We may consider here the particularly influential and ambitious formulation provided by the Egyptian writer and liberal politician Muhammad Husayn Haykal (1888–1956) in his work *Thawrat al-Adab* (*The Rebellion of Literature*, 1933).[19] In this work, Haykal argues that literature and art are the primary manifestations of the innate human force striving for ultimate perfection. "Freedom of the pen is the highest manifestation of human freedom in its highest form" (17). For this reason, literature and art are central to the progression of human civilization. "Human civilization is a perpetual revolution whose manifestation is literature and art" (10). Literature is revolutionary because the human spirit is subject to the repression of tyrants, who are motivated by base, egoistic instincts to suppress the desire for freedom. Literary writing, however, expresses "the human force that connects human beings to the high forces of being, and elevates them above the level of animals wherein reside the unstable material forces that men of violence and tyranny depend upon" (17–18). Haykal expresses here the repressive hypothesis—the idea that the innate human impulse towards order and fulfillment has been repressed throughout history by tyranny and corruption. Since literature is the direct expression of this impulse, it is inherently oppositional and emancipatory.

The problem in Egypt, however, according to Haykal, is that there is a dearth of fictional literature, which is the kind that is needed in modern society (rather than the classicizing poetry that remained preeminent through the 1920s). The reason for this, he argues, is "our failure to train the emotions properly, even though this proper training is what secures for the emotions the capacity to enjoy life in the most beautiful, noble and enlightened manner" (84). The absence of refined emotions among the Egyptians explains their inferiority to the English in performing acts of charity and other altruistic deeds. For "the weakness of emotional cultivation among us now is such that it leaves all of our emotions weak and egoistic, incapable of rising but barely above the level of the instincts." As a result, "love among us is still close to sexual instinct." Egyptians are nearly incapable of experiencing what Haykal calls "love in its noble, human sense of complete participation in embodying life as force, beauty and light, love as an elevated, human sentiment whose basis is denial of the ego and elevation of the self to the world of goodness, beauty and truth" (87). As can be seen, Egyptians are morally and nationally inferior to the English precisely because of the deficit among them of cultivated, refined sentiment, the sentiment that produces and appreciates works of art and that makes self-sacrifice possible. The remedy for this condition, Haykal suggests, is to awaken these elevated moral sentiments by turning to national history and the national homeland. The peasant who worships the national beauty of the Egyptian countryside is present within all Egyptians. Art that springs from this source "impels people to work for the increase of this beauty. That is because it makes life more beloved to them and calls them to increase its beauty and to assist nature in bringing out its charm and radiance" (119). In this way, Haykal links objective features of the national community with the aesthetic process that gives rise to moral universality, a linkage that is developed in the same manner by the novel *Return of the Spirit*, discussed below.

Haykal's exposition of the nature of literary expression sketches a metaphysics of human history as the evolution of "life" toward its ultimate realization. This view of history shows up in different forms in many major writers of the period. Civilization, as Haykal puts it, "is the impulses of life towards the ideal that the community desires to attain. It is, moreover, the human community's picturing of its connection to existence in its entirety, a connection related to the past and penetrating into the depths of the future" (217). Civilization, then, the "perpetual revolution" of human history, is the enactment of the "elevated, human sentiment" that is aesthetic in nature and awakened by beauty.

As evidence of the currency of this aesthetic basis of human order across the political spectrum, consider the views advanced by the Egyptian socialist and promoter of psychoanalysis and science, Salama Musa (1887–1958), in his book *The Art of Love and Life* (1953?).[20] Musa argues that fear, greed, and violence degrade sexual, marital, and other private relations in Egyptian society and that this results from Egypt being a "competitive society" instead of a socialist "cooperative society." Instinct, being natural, is intrinsically exorbitant; the competitive society, instead of subordinating and harnessing instinct, encourages it to dissipate continuously in hierarchical aspirations and divisive resentments (14). The jealousy and fear of the future that govern Egyptian social relations "derive from a psychological configuration (*nizam nafsi*) that arises from the economic basis of the society that we live in" (17). This applies most dramatically to the rapacious instinctual gratification of sexual relations in Egyptian society.[21] For "sexual pleasure in its essence and in its style is the point of crystallization of our social orientation and our social morality..." (85), and "our social order replicates its patterns in our sexual order" (86). The cooperative society, however, is based on and fosters the intrinsically human disposition of love, which is seen most vividly in art, culture, and attraction to natural beauty, and which subordinates and sublimates instinct into the service of a higher social purpose.[22] "This love is what makes a human being human" (76). Instinct thus becomes order at every level, including personal habit-formation and domestic life. "The democratic home is the basis of a democratic society" (129). Musa sums up the uplifting of instinct into order in the following manner: "Psychic energy cannot tolerate suppression and confinement and for this reason through some thing, a thing we believe to be good, a channel is opened up for us into which this energy can proceed." If this energy is confined, the result is "neurosis" or "psychosis" (197). When this energy is channeled into struggle for humanity and society, the result is personal happiness and social cooperation.

Opposing ideological programs could be founded on the same aesthetic basis. The famed Islamist intellectual, Sayyid Qutb (1906–1966), who began his writing career as a literary critic, developed an Islamist metaphysics of history closely resembling that of Haykal in structure. Qutb bases this in his own version of the repressive hypothesis, consisting in the claim that humanity has been repressed through the division of the material and spiritual that occurs in all non-Islamic societies. According to Qutb, human beings have suffered in past civilizations and in the present world an "alienation of the innate sensibility (*wijdan*)," resulting from the disjuncture between the inner desires and aspirations of human beings, that is, the spiritual realm, and the material conditions in which they must live, which are governed by physical necessity, instinct, impulse, and egoism.[23] The effect of Islam, however, is precisely the eradication of this division between inner ideals and material reality. "Islam unifies the needs of the body and the desires of the spirit in an order, and secures emancipation of the innate sensibility in interior feeling and in exterior reality" (37). Islam orders society and our lives in such a way that our sensual responses and impulses are automatically morally ordered. For "life is a unity made up of material and spiritual powers that can never be separated without dysfunction and disturbance, and the human being is a unity made up of desires aspiring to the heavens and impulses clinging to the earth, which cannot be separated" (26). These claims show that Qutb is asserting that Islam brings about the same kind of unity that others attributed to works of art.

Qutb's distinctive innovation is his doctrine that to attain inner emancipation and moral order, human beings must first renounce any claim to autonomy.[24] The artist-creator of the universe, as well as of the innate sensibility of human beings and the social laws that conform to it, must be accepted as the only autonomous being. Any human attempt to impose form on human society, that is, to create its laws and its system of order, is subject to the egoistic, material desires of human beings. To allow human beings to create laws is to allow tyranny. Therefore, the acceptance that laws come only from God liberates humanity from all forms of tyrannical repression of innate humanity, be they political, social, economic, or bodily. For this reason, Islamic law is the social form of freedom that corresponds to human beings' inner desire for freedom. Thus, "Islam is the eternal dream of humanity, embodied in a reality lived out on earth" (29). This dream is the progression of life toward ultimate fulfillment. "The purpose of Islam is to impel life towards renewal, growth and development, and to impel human energies towards creativity, release, and elevation" (279). In this way, Qutb comprises within his Islamist vision the immanence of moral order within human beings, as well as within history, but only by stripping humanity of any actual moral agency. Only within the singular "national" community that enacts God's laws does moral order and the liberation of humanity come about. The relationship between God and man that Qutb creates on the basis of the immanence of order is of a different nature than the relationship based on the externalization of order that is found in premodern Islamic thought. It is as if Qutb has adopted his principle of divinity from Feuerbach's theory of why belief in God exists—that those whose innate human capacity is repressed by injustice project this capacity as an external deity that they will unite with after death.

The purpose of the foregoing discussion has been to show that the fusion of the psychic and the social, the private and the public, that constitutes the ideal of nationality requires a process by which innate feelings and dispositions are elevated into moral order without losing their particularity. This union of the universal and the particular is often conceived as aesthetic in nature. Such a union underlies notions that "personality" and "individuality" participate in a higher collective order and that the particular defining features of the nation contain moral universality. Any ideology or program of social ordering that claims to give rise to an autonomous collective agency depends, implicitly or explicitly, on some claim or assumption regarding how desire and feeling bring about their own ordering. The aesthetic dimension of citizenship, in other words, is indispensable to nationality.

Beauty, Love, and National Identity

The discourses considered above posit a source of humanity within the self, such as the innate sensibility, that transmutes impulses into elevated sentiments. These discourses, however, merely make external, descriptive assertions about this human interiority that associate it with particular values and content. Realist novels, on the other hand, create depictions of this interiority by narrating the formation of moral dispositions. The manner in which a novel contrives the moral dispositions of its characters to arise determines what kind of linkage there is between the private and the public. In other words, the nature of public order, or of its failure, is seen in the process of moral formation. This is so because the authentic, human moral disposition is the basis of collective integration. The center of all of this, then, is how desire and emotion are contrived to turn into the capacity for self-sacrifice.

For this to take place, emotional investment must be shown to negate itself as an egoistic desire for pleasure and to turn into pleasure in the kind of self-sacrifice that constitutes moral order and thus humanity. In a sense, the affection turns into its own renunciation, but the new form it takes is depicted as what was its inner truth all along. A key manner in which novels create this representation is through the aesthetic nature of love. Emotional attachment to beauty is depicted as desire for the condition of perfection, in which lies the total release of emotion and gratification of desire. But at the same time, this perfection is order, which involves constraint and thus self-sacrifice, the fundamental human capacity. Love therefore has the potential to subsume its egoistic dimension in self-sacrifice for the sake of humanity. The nature of love and self-sacrifice and the mechanism by which love becomes moral motivation take widely differing forms with widely differing implications in different novels. The different social contents and orientations that can be invested in these elements may link novels to social and political ideologies. But what separates the novel from ideology is the novel's depiction of the source of moral order, the inner humanity that stands in a liminal relation to order. By definition, this interiority that continually renews society, that generates history as a perpetual revolution, cannot be captured within any definitive framework. Love of beauty can only engender morality so long as it remains in itself dangerous and independent of moral constraint.

My argument, then, is that the psychic and social integration effected in novels is a representational strategy that depicts the destiny of individuals and their private lives as incorporation into a national ideal. This kind of representation is hegemonic because it sets up the moral basis in the private sphere for justifications of social order or reordering. On this basis, novels acquire the capacity to invest everyday life with national historical significance. Or to put it another way, novels bring national history into the structure and disposition of the personal desires of ordinary people. The key novelistic form in this regard is the *Bildungsroman*, which narrates an individual's coming of age, integration into adult society, transition from naïve, childish indeterminacy to the composure and completion of maturity. Any literary form or social ritual that encapsulates the process of incorporation into the social order lays out the origin and nature of this social order. In the realist *Bildungsroman*, according to M.M. Bakhtin, "the image of the emerging man begins to surmount its private nature (within certain limits, of course) and enters into a completely new, *spatial* sphere of historical existence." The character represented as coming of age

> emerges *along with the world* and he reflects the historical emergence of the world itself. He is no longer within an epoch, but on the border between two epochs, at the transition point from one to the other. This transition is accomplished in him and through him. He is forced to become a new, unprecedented type of human being. What is happening here is precisely the emergence of a new man. The organizing force held by the future is therefore extremely great here—and this is not, of course, the private biographical future, but the historical future. It is as though the very *foundations* of the world are changing, and man must change along with them.[25]

The world that Bakhtin speaks of here is the character's own world, the social body into which he emerges. The possibility of this mutual *historical* emergence, the transformation of private, biographical time into the time of national history, lies in the creation of a correlation between the disposition of desire on the private level and the "epochs" of national history. In other words, in the kind of *Bildungsroman* that follows the classical form, in which the character's maturation and social integration are successful, the dawning epoch of national history is a new society generated from a new mode of properly ordering desire to achieve the self-integration of adulthood. In variant forms of the *Bildungsroman*, in which, in one way or another, the character's emergence is unsuccessful or deviant, the necessity of a new society is implied by the particular manner in which the present fails. In either case, the structure of the social order has its origin in the individual moral process.[26]

We may consider in this regard Tawfiq al-Hakim's novel *'Awdat al-Ruh* (*Return of the Spirit*, 1933), a key early instance of the realist novel in Arabic, as well as of the *Bildungsroman*, and the first Arabic novel of this type explicitly to merge its depiction of everyday private life into the evolution of national history.[27] The novel, written in the late 1920s, is likewise a major document of the pharaonic nationalism promoted by a number of leading Egyptian writers during that decade. Moreover, the novel's Romanticism further aligns it with many of these same writers, who called for literary forms that would directly express inner feeling and experience as well as contemporary social life, an authentically "Egyptian literature" emancipated from the externality of classical Arabic genres. The manner in which *Return of the Spirit* sets up the immanence of moral order and invests it with ethnic content demonstrates the linkage to moral universality that gives meaning to romantic nationalism. The nature of this linkage underlies the form of politics arising from the novel's romantic nationalism—a politics of communal eruption—and enables an understanding of how this politics is related to the politics of perpetual moral struggle examined in the following chapter.

The central element in *Return of the Spirit* is the reversion to primordial desire, which constitutes the self, the relation between private and public, and the nature of Egyptian identity and collective agency. Love of beauty, which is always natural beauty, effects an automatic immersion in and unity with nature. Unlike the kind of aestheticism seen in Schiller, in which the disinterested, rational element in artistic beauty is central to its moral function, for *Return of the Spirit*, the formal perfection of natural beauty is inherently moral and gives rise to emotional attachment to self-sacrifice without any need for rationality. This is made possible by the novel's exclusion of matter and instinct from nature. Hence, the reversion to primordial desire takes the form of a liberation from bodily and other external determinations and union with the life force underlying nature, which enables self-sacrifice in social communion, giving rise to the nation as the artistic, civilizational expression of the natural life force. The bifurcation of nature into matter, on the one hand, and spirit, which is authentic nature, is the central paradox that sustains the novel. Somehow, egoistic, bodily instinct turns into noble, spiritual feeling, while being its opposite. The moral process, the relation between private and public, and the nature of Egyptian identity are contained in the bridging of this antithesis. The figure that encodes this antithesis and guarantees its traversal is the modern Egyptian woman, who is thereby consigned to the threshold of moral order.

Return of the Spirit, set some time shortly before the anticolonial demonstrations and riots known as the 1919 Revolution, recounts the story of Muhsin, a secondary school student, who has come to Cairo for his schooling and lives with his three uncles, his aunt, and a servant from their village in a cramped apartment. Muhsin is the son and future heir of a Bey who owns a large plantation in the countryside. Muhsin's uncles and aunt, the Bey's half-siblings, do not share his social status and typify nonelite social classes. In the neighboring building lives the beautiful and elegant Saniya, two years older than Muhsin and not yet married, but secluded from male society as was the custom. Muhsin, having caught a glimpse of Saniya, has fallen desperately in love with her, and due to his youth, is allowed to give her singing lessons in exchange for piano lessons. Muhsin's two younger uncles themselves become smitten with Saniya, which exacerbates household tensions. Saniya, however, is interested only in the manly and aristocratic downstairs neighbor, Mustafa Bey, who has also fallen in love with her. Muhsin and his uncles, ennobled by their love and loss of Saniya, establish a new and elevated communion with each other centered on Muhsin's funereal grief. But the sudden advent of Sa'd Zaghlul's banishment by the British and the subsequent demonstrations enable Muhsin's household communion to embrace the nation:

> All that was in his heart of cruelly disappointed love turned into burning patriotic emotion. And all the feelings of the sacrifice he was ready to make for the sake of the one worshipped by his heart turned into bold feelings of sacrifice for the sake of the one worshipped by his homeland. And this is what happened to Abduh and Salim to a lesser degree.[28]

In the meantime, Saniya agrees to marry Mustafa only after artfully inducing him to embrace his destiny as a captain of national industry.

The novel establishes that Muhsin's love for Saniya is a reversion to primordial desire by identifying his condition with that of the Egyptian peasantry. While visiting his parents in the countryside, Muhsin witnesses a scene that reveals to him the true meaning of his love. In his solitary wanderings, he comes upon a peasant hovel, in which he sees through open doors an infant and a calf both suckling at the udders of a cow while the others are away in the fields. Muhsin becomes aware at an emotional level of the communion with nature lived daily by Egyptian peasants, and which is shared by all human beings at the beginning of life, but slowly lost by city-dwellers as they grow up. He is able to apprehend this vision because "feeling (*ihsas*) is the knowledge of angels, and reasoning (*al-mantiq al-'aqli*) is the knowledge of human beings." Muhsin perceives that as a person grows up,

> humanness increases, and angelhood diminishes. In place of the feeling of a general unity between him and other beings comes the feeling of wants and desires that make him contemptuous of all that is other... Therefore he is abandoned by the light of angels manifested in purity, innocence, the feeling of unity, and the spirit of social communion, which is replaced by the blindness of the man, manifested in passions, lusts, the feeling of egoism and individualism. The sense of unity of existence is the sense of God. Thus angels and children are closer to God than is the grown man! (2:31–32)

In the model of the self given here, the condition of primordial desire, unification with the life force underlying nature, is itself the moral condition. The sense of this condition, authentic emotion, is corrupted by the desires of the body and of the empirical self in general. Reason is regarded here as nothing more than the calculative capacity of the empirical self, the means by which egoistic desires pursue their satisfaction. This model of the self is very much akin to the externalization of premodern conceptions of the self, in the sense that there is an antithesis between divine order and worldly passions. The difference, however, is that here, primordial desire and not rational constraint is identified with divine order. This is so because the novel disassociates "passions," "lusts," the instinctual and bodily, in short, all violent and chaotic forces, from the primordial energy underlying existence. The novel depicts this underlying energy as consisting in only the beauty of nature, which is in turn identified with what we deem to be morally beneficial. In other words, moral order proceeds from aesthetic order. Self-sacrifice, the angelic state, is not imposed by external constraint, but is the highest pleasure of human existence.

The ancient Egyptian peasants dwelled in this state, and this was the key to the social organization and solidarity, the communal self-sacrifice, that led to their monumental achievements. Muhsin viscerally apprehends the connection between what he witnessed and the animistic religion of ancient Egypt. "The feeling of absorption in existence, that is, the sense of absorption in God. This is the feeling of that suckling child and calf! This is the feeling of angels, and it is also the feeling of that ancient Egyptian people!" (2:33) And the Egyptian peasants now living have not altered in any way since ancient times; they are the same people in the same primordial condition.

> Don't the peasants of Egypt even now glorify animals in their hearts, feeling no aversion to living with animals in the same domicile, and sleeping with them in the same room? Is it not so that the Egypt of angels with its pure heart has not left Egypt? And that it has inherited—over the passing of generations—the feeling of union without knowing it?" (2:33)

Egyptian peasants are very close to nature—they are one with it—which does not signify savagery, but the highest spiritual and social advancement. It gives rise to their unlimited capacity to undergo suffering for the good of the community, as Muhsin witnesses in a few everyday rural dramas, and disposes them to worship whatever embodies their sense of communion. "Can there be found in this world a solidarity as beautiful as theirs, or a feeling of unity like theirs?" (2:36) In this way, the novel casts the Egyptian peasantry as the moral substrate of the nation.

The national, civilizational superiority of Egypt that results is explained by a French archeologist, who attributes authentic civilization to the "hidden treasure" of the heart rather than to the cold intellect championed by Europeans. "All we have done—we European upstarts—is to steal from those ancient peoples the surface symbol, without the hidden treasure. Bring a European and open his heart and you will find it empty and forlorn!" (2:55) Europeans cannot imagine "the emotions that made this entire people into a single individual" (2:59). What are these momentous emotions? "The feeling of joy in communal pain...the smiling sufferance of horrors for the sake of a common cause...the feeling of faith in the worshipped one and sacrifice...and unity in pain without complaint...this is their power!" (2:61) These are the emotions behind the glory of pharaonic Egypt and the building of the pyramids. "This people, at one time in history, became a single human body, finding pleasure in pain in a common path: Khufu, the embodiment of the worshipped one and the symbol of the goal" (2:62). The Egyptian peasants now singing as they toil in the fields outside the house retain this "spirit of the temple." Indeed, "what a marvelous industrial people they will be tomorrow!" (2:61) The French sage concludes by announcing that to reach once again the heights of the pyramids the Egyptian people needs only a suitable object of worship— "the man who will embody its emotions and hopes and be the symbol of its goal" (2:64). The Egyptian peasantry's primordial unity with nature, and thus with existence as a whole, enables them to be and act as a single moral agent. Self sacrifice, the definitive moral act, is automatic for them to the degree that they enjoy pain in the cause of unity.

Love transports the lover to the same condition of unity enjoyed by the peasants. Muhsin resolves that his vocation will be "to express what is in the heart of the entire nation" (1:129). And in an impromptu peroration, he identifies "love of beauty" as "love of the heart" (1:132). The heart that experiences love of beauty is thus one with the heart of the nation and the heart that is the "hidden treasure" of the peasants. This is why Muhsin asks himself whether he can sacrifice for his worshipped one in the way that he has seen the peasants sacrifice. Love for Saniya brings about similar, though lesser effects in his uncles. Abduh "feels an extraordinary energy in all of his body calling him to speech, to movement, to enthusiasm" (1:205). Even Salim, who starts off with lust, eventually reaches a more elevated plane. Although the feelings aroused by Saniya initially have the effect of driving Muhsin and each of his uncles apart, their disappointment over her loss and the power of Muhsin's profound grief draw them into a sense of shared suffering. "It was as if the great heart of Muhsin contained enough sacred fire to fill the heart of Salim and to complete what lacked in the heart of Abduh" (2:190). She becomes for them "a symbolic name (*ism ma'nawi*) that signified only the worshipped one for whose sake they suffered common pain" (2:191). This communal grief turns into patriotic fervor and sacrifice with the eruption of the 1919 Revolution. In this way, Saniya's charms have drawn the three of them back into the primordial unity in which Egyptian national identity lies.

Saniya's powers of moral transformation derive not simply from her beauty, but from her ability to display and withhold herself to greatest effect, and ultimately, from her ability to contain and manage her sexuality. The effects of Saniya's beauty are made possible by her "contrived modesty, perhaps the finest magic by which the Egyptian woman is distinguished!" (1:141) Consider the effects of her beauty on Mustafa: a five-second glimpse of her makes "a new world" suddenly open up before his eyes, makes him perceive within himself a "nobility," "beauty," and "purity," of which he was never before aware, and transforms him into a "new man" who repudiates his former self (2:138–139, 167). The narrator informs us that the wealthy and titled Mustafa "is nothing but a young man lacking in ambition (*himma*); his nature is not corrupt, nor is he of low morals" (2:129). In other words, Mustafa is devoid of the social virtue that enables one to undertake self-sacrifice for the benefit of society. We learn that Mustafa has become an idler because he and his friends missed out in their youth on the transformative experience that creates an inner zeal to aspire to high aims.

> In those golden years the heart should experience its first and last effervescence, revealing to the self in the light of that fire the powers and treasures that are concealed in it, but alas... How can youth illumine the heart without knowing woman!... the woman with a heart... with a soul... she who inspires great deeds... not the whore whom they saw every Friday night for 20 piastres!

This effervescence is love, the love of beauty, which leads the self back into primal unity. Thus, Mustafa's friends could not be moved by natural beauty due to their "souls that had been poisoned and deadened by the exhalations of prostitutes full of the germs of base matter" (2:126). Matter is the substrate of "humanness," the contagion of women who fail to withhold themselves. An angelic woman like Saniya displays her beauty, but by virtue of her "heart" and "soul," withholds herself in a manner that awakens within men their sublime powers and spurs them to self-sacrifice.

Saniya ultimately demonstrates her abilities by inducing Mustafa to give up his plan to sell the factory he has inherited to a Greek comprador and instead take it over himself with ambitious intent. Yet if Saniya has brought Mustafa and the others into the realm of angels, this does not mean that she herself is included there. She does not participate in the primal unity into which she brings the men who fall for her. To be sure, Saniya has a virtue of her own that is critical to her effects. "Suddenly her conscience called out to her that truth: 'Virtue for a woman is not that she never love; rather, virtue is that she love sublimely a man of sublime heart and character'!" (2:164) Yet this feminine virtue is not moral in nature. For as the narrator tells us, "a woman happy in love is egoistic to the point of savagery!" (2:210) Feminine virtue then, which is feminine love, is not the kind of love that men experience, but is a savage egoism, humanness rather than angelhood. This means that even the ideal woman cannot enter into social integration. She enables men to turn private feeling into public virtue, but she herself cannot inhabit the public realm. In this way, Saniya is reduced to the status of an aesthetic object, even though she is the only one who appears to exert moral effort. And it is this apparently moral but actually instinctual effort that creates the linkage between matter and spirit, egoism and morality, by which men become moral effortlessly.

The figure of Saniya, therefore, serves as a conduit to primordial desire and Egyptian identity in a manner that separates the liminal origin of moral order from the spiritual masculine self while at the same time allowing the possession of this origin.[29] The transgressive appearance of the intermingling of the unmarried sexes that drives the narrative is subsumed in the spiritual national agency for which it is necessary. The budding artist Muhsin can be the high-priest of national communion only because his relation to Saniya is purely aesthetic in nature—his youth precludes any sexual prospects and he in any case recoils from her sexuality (2:208). The social order—subordination of the popular masses under aristocratic leadership supported by the *efendiya*—is justified by the superior aesthetic sensitivity of the land-owning classes, who are thereby one with nature like the peasants, but who are at the same time capable of expressing this unity in the form of high civilization. The sociality and self-sacrifice of the peasants, arising from their unity with nature, is the underlying identity of all human beings. Egyptians are closer to human identity than others (especially Arabs and Turks)[30] because all Egyptians were peasants not so long ago, and require only the proper object of worship to awaken their peasant hearts.

This object of worship transforms Egyptians into a collective agent with a single will and a single pleasure in self-sacrifice. The novel shows how this takes place by culminating its narrative with the 1919 Revolution. It depicts this revolution as arising from "the new blazing emotion" felt by "all classes of the people" that "exploded in all of their hearts in the same instant, because all of them are children of Egypt and have a single heart" (2:242). This blazing emotion of patriotic fervor is identical to the love of beauty kindled by Saniya and to the unifying emotion induced by art (1:172). The total emotional release occasioned by love/worship, the outpouring of primordial desire, is at the same time the highest moral condition, and finds its expression as art, civilization, and progress. The common feeling of Egyptians therefore can never be wrong. It is inherently moral and universal, and cannot be judged by any standard but itself.

This reduction of the moral to the aesthetic and investment of the aesthetic with what is purported to be the definitive feature of Egyptian identity results in a politics of communal eruption that elides all social divisions and excludes any form of politics associated with them. Class differences and social hierarchy are shown to be subsumed in communal identity. The singular political phenomenon in the novel—the 1919 Revolution—is depicted as a kind of Dionysian exuberance of emotion in primal unity.[31] This politics has no actual content other than the primal unity of which it is the expression. The ostensible political aim of the 1919 Revolution—liberation from British rule—is scarcely mentioned, much less the diverse political motives involved. The actual struggles and grievances that give rise to such action are excluded from what is properly political. The public sphere is constituted by the expression of communal identity, rather than by communal self-ordering, which is the process of attaining this identity.

And the aesthetic nature of communal, moral, human identity reinstates the legitimacy of the ruling aristocracy, which shows its entitlement to spiritual and political national leadership in the superior love of beauty of the two protagonist characters.[32]

It can be seen that there is a gap between the novel's ideology of Egyptian peasant identity and the aesthetic process by which it generates humanity and moral universality. The novel cannot display in its narrative how Egyptian peasant lineage links the characters' love of beauty to the mass actions of the 1919 Revolution. This linkage can only remain at the level of assertions made by the narrator and the French orientalist sage. The gap between the novel and the ideology it seeks to promote is the gap that necessarily lies between the aesthetic dimension of citizenship and ideologies of identity and order. For the liminal realm of humanity required by these ideologies and displayed in novels is by definition incompatible with a principle of order and identity. It can give rise to moral order only by constituting the threshold of moral order. *Return of the Spirit* short-circuits this location by making moral order arise from it automatically, or in other words, by making moral order an epiphenomenon of the love of beauty. Anyone who loves beauty is by definition moral. To create an actual moral orientation for itself, therefore, the novel resorts to an external, asserted association of Egyptian peasanthood and national eruption with romantic love. In the novel examined in the next chapter, the *Trilogy*, this latter association is reworked in a manner that much more deeply exploits the aesthetic dimension of citizenship.

Chapter 6

Excess, Rebellion, and Revolution: Egyptian Modernity in the *Trilogy*

The *Trilogy* of Nagib Mahfuz, which stands at the end of his series of realist novels set in Cairo that began to appear in 1945, morally configures everyday Egyptian life in a manner that encompasses the political development of Egypt from 1917 to 1944.[1] In doing so, it projects a revolutionary politics of hegemonic struggle whose horizon is a humanist, rather than a nationalist, realization of national unity and agency. The Egyptian nation is not the goal of humanity but the form in which Egyptians may attain humanity, which lies in the moral maturity of modernity. The *Trilogy* distances modernity from the West by making it the necessary outcome of the internal moral development of Egyptian society. This development begins with a static and traditional psychic and social order whose collapse results in dissolution and tyranny. From its standpoint within this comprehensive crisis, the novel generates an authentic moral disposition that promises to be the basis of a dynamic, unceasing social transformation. This manner of representing Egyptian society is distinctive in that it creates a trajectory of national development with great internal coherence that plays out on the level of everyday individual experience. On a deeper level, the novel's oppositional vision of modernity, in which humanity is liberated through the progressive elimination of social inequality, stands in stark contrast to the socially affirmative aesthetic nationalism put forth in *Return of the Spirit*. Nevertheless, analysis of the *Trilogy* reveals that its progressive political orientation and its construction of a revolutionary modernity remain rooted in the spiritual/material opposition that underlies aesthetic citizenship..

The *Trilogy* differs markedly from *Return of the Spirit* in many formal respects—its narrational neutrality, quotidian verisimilitude, somber atmosphere, pervasive irony, and lack of any explicit "message." Moreover, the *Trilogy* is not organized through the resolution of overarching plot structures, but through the contrasting depictions of its successive generations. Indeed, the *Trilogy* is regarded as the culmination of realist technique in the Arabic novel, fully instantiating what Erich Auerbach calls "tragic seriousness." These features of realist technique, however, are grounded in a deeper difference between the two novels. The *Trilogy* anchors nationality in the process of attaining to communal unity rather than in the spontaneous expression of an underlying, preexisting unity. Regression to the underlying, life energy in which human beings are unified with each other and with nature does not bring about morality and agency in the *Trilogy*. In *Return of the Spirit*, love of beauty automatically frees the lover from worldly attachments and enables self-sacrifice. Self-sacrifice in the *Trilogy*, however, is not the automatic result of an achieved state, but a continuing painful moral exertion, a sustained self-negation of desire, that brings little in the way of pleasure or bliss. The union of desire and order is a human historical destiny that cannot be attained by individuals. The moral process itself takes over centrality here, and the final state at which it aims is a regulative ideal rather than a present reality, a historical rather than biographical horizon of fulfillment.

The *Trilogy* transfers the logic of self-fulfillment to history as a whole, wherein the achievements of individual selves are mere moments. This transfer takes the form of a vitalist historical metaphysics evoked in fleeting instances of the narrative. Primordial desire is designated "the surge of life" (*wathbat al-haya*) and its internal impulse toward an ultimate, total self-realization is called "the will of life" (*iradat al-haya*).[2] The will of life can only be realized through the progressive ordering of the excessive surge of life, that is, through the moral process and the action that expresses it. The relationship between the surge of life and the will of life, desire and order, governs the social development depicted in the *Trilogy*. The static, patriarchal society of the past is constituted by the exclusion of primordial desire from the social order by way of traditional religion, status hierarchy, and social restrictions. The patriarch enjoys a circumscribed and contradictory state of self-completion that requires the repression of social dependents. With the collapse of this order, primordial desire enters society, but cannot be mastered by its members, who have lost the protective barriers of the past. Their desire is dissipated in egoism while exploitation and tyranny prevail. Thus, the tragic nature of individual human life has both an existential and a social dimension. The impossibility of bliss and completion in modern life is the tragic condition of human existence for all. But the widespread failure of human beings to engage in their innate capacity of enacting the will of life through self-sacrifice is the tragedy that results from social disorder. This gap between the surge of life and the will of life, or primordial desire and moral agency, underlies the world of Mahfuz's realist novels and generates their narratives.

The model of the self operative here is constituted by excess and rebellion. Desire exceeds the forms of life available to individuals, causing them to rebel against their forms of life. In the traditional order, excess is partly accommodated, and otherwise contained and repressed. Open rebellion is foreclosed by the accepted legitimacy of the order. In the phase of social dissolution, however, rebellion takes the form of directing desire into objects that seem to promise total egoistic fulfillment. This is because society is not ordered so as to impel individuals toward moral action, but instead offers diverse patterns of dissipation as well as a specious ideal of fulfillment in the rapacious aristocracy. Yet the social order is not shown as determining the patterns of psychic investment of the characters. In Mahfuz's realist writing, the characters represent the social order. It is in their dispositions of desire that we see this order. Therefore they are condemned to enact, according to their various psychic profiles, the forms of dissipation that characterize a dysfunctional society. On the other hand, the characters committed to transforming the social order, who play always secondary or minor roles, are psychologically opaque, in the sense that there is no window into how their moral disposition came about, and why their psychic development differed from that of other characters, even those in the same family. The gap between the surge of life and will of life thereby subsists in the relationship between the psychologized, egoistic characters, and the psychology-free moral agents.

In other words, in the world of the *Trilogy* and Mahfuz's other realist novels, there is little emphasis on the mechanism by which the ordering of desire, the accession to morality, comes about. Characters are either of one type or the other. The *Trilogy* therefore does not follow the paradigm of the classical *Bildungsroman* in which the hero experiences a rite of passage by which he attains to maturity and social integration.[3] Instead, psychic immaturity is generalized to society as a whole as a pathological condition of arrested development. The central characters of the realist novels, aside from the patriarch of the past, either achieve social incorporation in a false, morally inverted manner, or remain isolated, passive figures. The mechanism for ordering desire is not to be found at the individual level, but at the social level. Social revolution is the form that rebellion must take in order to eliminate the psychic illness that pervades society and to enable thereby the unhindered maturation and social integration of individuals. This is why the categorical failure of marriage in existing social life to serve as the means of fulfillment and integration is the narrative axis in all of the realist novels, and the nexus of public and private dysfunction.

In its portrayal of psychic and social disorder, the *Trilogy* lays out the moral logic underlying any historically progressivist politics of hegemonic struggle. This logic is constituted by the perpetual exclusion of primordial desire from full habitation of the forms of social life, or in other words, the historical succession of repressive social orders. The motive force of history is the transformation of repressed desire into the power to transform society. Instead of enclosing this moral process within an objective principle of historical progress, as is often the case in political ideologies, the *Trilogy* thematizes this process itself. The disposition of desire that gives rise to moral action is "faith"—identification with society and humanity in a manner beyond any specific content, which is at bottom faith in the human capacity for agency. Scientific advancement, though a key value in the *Trilogy*, is intimated to be by itself insufficient for the advancement of humanity. Experiences of regression to primordial desire—romantic love and patriotic fervor—are in the *Trilogy* short-lived escapes from everyday life, incapable of providing a basis for social integration. They are not forms in which primordial desire is realized, but temporary freedom from existential constraint. In this way, however, the exclusion and repression of primordial desire contains the necessity of its eventual expression as communal and indeed human oneness. It can be seen then that the forms taken by the political in *Return of the Spirit* and the *Trilogy* are opposing polarities of the same moral logic, giving rise to antithetical consequences.

The *Trilogy* recounts the story of the family of al-Sayyid Ahmad Abd al-Jawad, a prosperous merchant in old Cairo, over three generations. It consists of *Bayn al-Qasrayn* (1956), set in the years 1917–1919; *Qasr al-Shawq* (1957), set in 1924–1927; and *al-Sukkariya* (1957), set in 1935–1944. All three titles are names of localities in the medieval part of Cairo. The first book is dominated by the personality of Sayyid Ahmad himself, who presides as a severe, despotic, unapproachable patriarch at home, while enjoying a reputation for honor, generosity, and charm in his neighborhood and social circles. Though he is sincere in worship and pious in demeanor, he spends his evenings in drunken revelry with his friends and adulterous liaisons with female singers (*'awalim*) and other available women. His meek and illiterate wife, Amina, and two daughters, the plain, industrious, and sharp-tongued Khadija, and the beautiful and indolent Aisha, both of marriageable age, devote their lives to domestic activity, since they are not permitted to leave the house. The eldest son, Yasin, born of a short-lived previous marriage, resembles his father in looks and passions, but is devoid of resolve and self-control. With only a primary level education, he has recently begun his career as a petty bureaucrat. The second son, Fahmi, is a sober and studious law student. The youngest child, Kamal, is a mischievous but outstanding primary school student. The action revolves around the rise and fall of the furtive hopes and desires of the family members before the unquestionable will of the father, whom they worshipfully love and of whom they are mortally terrified in equal measure. Nevertheless, the dreams of the sisters are fulfilled when they are wed to the Shawkat brothers, idling petty aristocrats of a family close to Sayyid Ahmad. Yasin is also wed, after a blundering sexual indiscretion provokes his father to impose this remedy, but then divorced, after further incontinence. The ardent Fahmi, rebuffed by his father in his desire to be engaged to the girl next door, assuages his disappointment with patriotism, throwing himself into the 1919 Revolution. The revolution, with its daily demonstrations and violent confrontations with British troops, alters the daily life of the family, and subjects Sayyid Ahmad himself to indignities, not least of which is the unprecedented disobedience of Fahmi, who abjectly defies his command to shun dangerous activities. Joy and relief on the successful conclusion of the revolution, however, will be snatched away from the family, for Fahmi, taking part in an approved, celebratory parade, is killed when British soldiers unaccountably open fire.

The shadow of Fahmi's loss hangs heavily in the second book, which opens five years later and centers on Kamal, now graduating from secondary school and about to enter the Teachers' College, as well as on Sayyid Ahmad, whose social preeminence and mastery have begun to decline with age, and Yasin, who continues his concupiscent follies through a second marriage and into a third. The daughters both have children and remain in constant contact with their father's household, while their own is roiled by Khadija's clashes with her mother-in-law. Amina, still bereaved, has been granted freedom to visit her daughters and beloved places of worship. The dominant narrative thread is the development of Kamal—his worshiping adoration of Aida, the haughty, French-reared sister of his wealthy best friend; his shattering disillusionment upon her marriage; his loss of religious faith due to his reading in philosophy and science; his turn to alcohol and prostitutes to soften the rigors of the intellectual quest for truth upon which he embarks. The trajectories of Sayyid Ahmad and Yasin are intertwined by their unwitting trade-offs of mistresses, which culminate in Yasin's marriage to his former lover, a lute player, just after she had nearly ensnared Sayyid Ahmad into taking her as a second wife. Thereafter, Sayyid Ahmad succumbs to severe illness brought on by high blood pressure, from which he recovers, but which ends his glorious days of virility and excess. The book closes with news of Saʻd Zaghlul's death, as well as of the imminent death of Aisha's husband and two sons from cholera.

In the bleak third book, Kamal continues to be the center of attention. Set in his career as a primary school teacher, Kamal has become an embittered intellectual who has been rewarded with nothing but benumbing doubt by his continuing philosophical inquiries. We follow his descent into ever deeper despair, punctuated by periodic eruptions of longing for Aida. His ambivalence toward marriage culminates when he falls in love with Aida's younger sister, whom he meets by chance, but cannot bring himself to propose to her. His own sister Aisha, now withered by grief, has long since moved back to their father's house with her gorgeous but frail daughter Na'ima, who herself soon dies in childbirth, leaving Aisha with nothing left to live for. Sayyid Ahmad, upon retiring and selling his shop, steadily declines in health and spends his last months bedridden. Amina, now also elderly, frequents mosques and tombs and tends to her husband and daughter. Khadija's two sons, Abd al-Mun'im and Ahmad, enter and complete university. The former adheres to Islamism and goes into law while the latter adopts Marxism and works as an editor at a leftist journal. Yasin's son from his first marriage, Ridwan, stunningly attractive and secretly homosexual, also pursues law, and through his activism in the Wafd party enters a liaison with a cabinet-level politician, which opens to him the gates of advancement and influence. The dim political situation continues to deteriorate, despite the conditional independence treaty won by the Wafd from the British in 1936, as the Wafd splinters, political corruption and malaise deepen, and the advent of the war exacerbates misery. As the novel ends, Abd al-Mun'im and Ahmad languish in prison for their political activism and Amina lies on her deathbed. There is, however, some hope that Kamal, stimulated by his nephew Ahmad, may yet emerge from his long-standing crisis.

These broad outlines of the *Trilogy* indicate that although the appearance of rising political ideologies within the family itself portends the emergence of a new society, the focus of the novel lies rather on the psychosocial dynamics of the dismal present. It will be seen on deeper examination that the dispositions of desire of the primary characters are in each case rooted in the dynamic of excess and rebellion, and moreover, take their character in relation to the disposition of desire that gives rise to moral agency. Egoistic desire in the *Trilogy* and in the other realist novels goes far beyond its representation in the discourse of tyranny and enslavement, where it is limited to a set of motifs depicting enslavement to the preservation and gratification of the body. The realist novels acquire their tragic character by crafting enslavement into psychic destinies that originate in the human condition and take form from social relations. The specific dispositions of desire are not only depicted from the inside, and thus sympathetically, but in a manner that intimates the distinctive moral structure of the world in which they operate. The achieved moral condition is now a horizon to be dimly perceived within the moral failure of the present, rather than a habitable external perspective from which to judge the present.

The presence, therefore, of psychoanalytic motifs in Mahfuz's realist novels, alongside conventional character-motifs prevalent in nineteenth century realist novels, should not be taken as an autonomous focus on the workings of the psyche, but in terms of the metaphysical and social significance of such motifs within the world of the novels. The nature and function of psychic profiles in these novels grows out of the general interest in psychology and psychoanalysis that had been keenly in evidence among Egyptian intellectuals since the 1920s.[4] The tenor of Mahfuz's realism bears most resemblance to the ideas of Salama Musa (1889–1958), who sought to link Freudian psychopathology to social conditions. Musa, a preeminent Egyptian writer of the twentieth century, was an advocate of socialism and scientific thought and an intellectual mentor to Mahfuz, who based on him a minor character in the *Trilogy*.[5] A brief consideration of Musa's views reveals and clarifies their relation to Mahfuz's novels.

In his book *Fann al-Haya wa al-Hubb* (*The Art of Life and Love*, 1947), Musa presents an account of the psychic and social nature of love founded on the idea that the "psychic configuration" (*nizam nafsi*) of individuals corresponds to the economic configuration, either cooperative or competitive, of their society.[6] Musa's account aims at establishing the same kind of psychic and social fusion apparent in Mahfuz's realism, and likewise designates the constellation of sexuality, love, and marriage as the site in which the condition of society reveals itself. Musa's pronouncement that "our social order replicates its patterns in our sexual order" could be taken as a motto for Mahfuz's writing, in which it applies however in both directions.[7] Musa's outlook, however, differs from the world of Mahfuz's realism in that Musa attributes psychic dysfunction directly to the competitive basis of the social order and does not bother to delve deeply into the nature of the psyche that he lays out. He is content with an unresolved duality of the instinctual in which sexuality is controlled and sublimated by the maternal love instinct in cooperative societies but runs unchecked in competitive ones. Nevertheless, Musa's method of discovering the truth of the social order within the psychosexual order finds its apotheosis in the realist fiction of Mahfuz.

The primary characters in Mahfuz's novels are driven by a utopian impulse to achieve a condition of perfection and bliss that is denied them by the constraints of everyday life. They seek full release of the psychic energy, the surge of life, whose repression they suffer. Rebellion against these conditions defines two fundamental character types—those characters who aggrandize themselves, scorn or disregard others, and seek to overcome constraint through social domination, and those who, beset by a sense of lack and inadequacy, fear the social world, and seek to escape constraint by surrendering themselves to romantic love and spiritual contemplation. The former attempt to subordinate the world to their selves, while the latter take refuge in another world, "the sky," where spiritual bliss can be enjoyed. These are the archetypal forms of egoism, both inversions of the moral disposition that engenders self-sacrifice. The self-aggrandizing form reaches a villainous pitch in deprived characters motivated by *ressentiment*, who cast off all moral values and social ties for the sake of power and pleasure.[8] In the *Trilogy*, such figures are more subdued in their presence and less explicitly malevolent than in Mahfuz's earlier novels. In any case, it is important to note that characters of this type are not impelled by sexuality per se, but subordinate their sexual lusts to a broader desire for domination.[9] Characters wholly in the thrall of irresistible sexual impulses, like Yasin in the *Trilogy*, are usually depicted as victims of their upbringing and circumstances who have little control over their actions.[10] There is also a class of inert, complacent characters who have little purpose or ambition beyond the needs of everyday domestic life. Their psychic energy is too feeble to exceed their form of life and they are often described by others as "domesticated animals."[11] Of the nonegoistic characters, there are mothers, like Amina in the *Trilogy*, who sacrifice their own desires almost completely for the sake of their families, which however renders them incapable of identifying with the greater good of society. Finally, there are the revolutionaries, socialist, or Islamist, who subordinate all personal desires to faith in a moral principle by which they are subsumed into their humanity.

The Logic of the Traditional Order

In contrast to the recurrent character types in Mahfuz's realism, the patriarch of the *Trilogy*, Sayyid Ahmad, appears to enjoy a state of completion and self-fulfillment that defies the condition of constraint and limitation suffered by all others. As has been generally noted, Sayyid Ahmad stands in the novel for a social order that belongs to the past. He is stereotypical of traditional society in his appearance, piety, occupation, and mode of authority, but with an ironic twist—his nightly revelries, his indulgence in forbidden pleasures, and his enjoyment of social esteem and adulation nonetheless, seem to turn the stereotype on its head. If the *Trilogy* maps a transition from a traditional, in some sense timeless social order, to the emergence of a new order—and this is intimated in the very title of its first book, originally the title of the whole, "between the two palaces"— then the disposition of desire exhibited by Sayyid Ahmad is indicative of the nature of that traditional order, the fixed point from which historical development begins. Indeed, the progress of time in the novel, as is often expressed by its characters, may be seen as a steady decline from the fullness of the past, an inexorable fragmentation of an original unity. The family idyll—despite its ironic undercurrent—that the narration establishes by its initial anchoring in the patterns of daily life, is subsequently shattered repeatedly by grievous events. Sayyid Ahmad, around whom this ironic idyll revolves, enjoys a degree of social mastery and internal integration never to be matched by his descendants. His sons, modernized members of the *efendi* class who belong to a diffuse social environment in which they languish without status or weight, seem to be mere fragments of his towering personality and are conscious of falling short against his standard. Their psychic dysfunction and the social dysfunction of their age are to be understood in relation to the psychic equilibrium of the father.

In Sayyid Ahmad, perhaps the most celebrated literary character in modern Arabic literature, Mahfuz inscribes the dialectic of excess and rebellion as a static yet contradictory state of equilibrium whose destruction gives rise to modern history. The central feature of this equilibrium is the absence of repression within the psyche of Sayyid Ahmad, which he sustains through the exercise of repression over his family. This equilibrium is made possible, moreover, by the structural division in Sayyid Ahmad's social world that allows for a perfect balance between adherence to norms that engender order, and controlled violation of these norms for the sake of pleasure.[12] Traditional religious faith protects and legitimizes the order as a whole by directing the most powerful and therefore dangerous form of desire, love, to God, the external origin of the order. This is the exclusion of primordial desire from the social order.

Much previous discussion of Sayyid Ahmad has centered on his shocking capacity to reconcile sincere religious conviction with flagrant impieties, attributed by the narrator to Sayyid Ahmad's belief in the triviality of his misdeeds, his faith in God's forgiveness, and above all, his lack of inclination to self-examination.[13] More important than Sayyid Ahmad's consistency of belief and action, however, is the psychic consistency of his behavior. In the world of the *Trilogy*, conventional marriage and domestic life, the private sphere, cannot satisfy or contain the desires of individuals with strong vital impulses. This pertains not only to sexuality, but to the quest for fulfillment as a whole. For Sayyid Ahmad and his cronies, the convivial society of estimable men, with ready access to wine, women, and song, defines the realm of self-realization. This is especially so for a man like Sayyid Ahmad, who sparkles in such company. "Often he felt that the role he played during his nightly gatherings was of such importance as to be the sought-for hope of life" (331–332). Family life, however, is in no way associated in itself with gratification or pleasure. Rather, it is the realm of discipline that makes social integration possible. On the one hand, Sayyid Ahmad's family is an extension of his person whose control and subordination assure his social reputation and status. On the other hand, the future happiness and success of Sayyid Ahmad's children can only be secured, he believes, by means of a severe discipline that will prepare them to occupy and retain respectable positions in society. For this reason, he deliberately affects a façade of harshness and severity that requires suppression of his actual feelings. The narration emphasizes Sayyid Ahmad's love for his family and willingness to sacrifice for them.[14] The home therefore becomes a domain of repression and self-control for the father, though only contingently, and absolutely so for his family.

By virtue of this social division, the patriarch is able to enjoy a condition of inner completeness denied to those who are mere extensions of his being. The nature of Sayyid Ahmad's psychic equilibrium reveals the fundamental opposition within psychic energy, or the life force, on which the *Trilogy* is centered. Sayyid Ahmad can be the man that he is because "he succeeded in conciliating between the 'animal' devoted to pleasure and the 'human being' aspiring to high principles in a manner that combined them into a harmonious unity in which neither side dominated the other and each effortlessly enjoyed its own independent life." As a result, his psyche is characterized by "a unity free of any sense of either guilt or repression" (438). It is necessary, then, to understand what is meant by pleasure and what is meant by high principles. The occasion for these remarks of the narrator is Sayyid Ahmad's polite refusal of the advances of the desirable wife of his bedridden neighbor. For "he would not consent to deviate from his principles of sanctifying the honor of others in general, and that of his friends and neighbors in particular." Indeed, Sayyid Ahmad's degree of respectfulness regarding social relations is "ideal"—he wants to preserve his status and likes to be well-regarded by others. This makes it clear that "high principles," identified as what is "human," consist in the curbing of one's self for the sake of social order and solidarity. Pleasure, then, may be understood as antithetical to principles—the unraveling of one's self, the release of its "animal" passions. Uninhibited pleasure would necessarily result in the undoing of social solidarity. Sayyid Ahmad's pleasure, therefore, is kept within strict boundaries. He makes sure "to fear God in his play as he did in serious matters." His self-dissolution is confined to the violation of those limits upon the self that need apply absolutely only to women, children, and the socially inferior, that is, limits whose violation does not impair, indeed often enhances, the social solidarity of high-status males. The harmonious union of the animal and the human lies in the reciprocal relationship between the realm of pleasure and that of principles—the subjection of pleasure to principles ensures the maintenance of social status, which in turn confers the right to enjoyment of pleasure.

The liminality of emotional release can therefore never be complete for Sayyid Ahmad; he enjoys much pleasure, but never bliss. He is closed off from the full force of the surge of life, which would wreck the internal equilibrium he has earned through self-mastery. This can be seen in his immunity to romantic love. Although "he took lust to its most elevated physical level," a woman to him is but a "tantalizing dish" that can be readily replaced with another when necessary. "He did not know true love, which would have been capable of either enthralling him to a powerful attachment unmoved by principles, or putting him in a difficult emotional-moral crisis of unavoidable pain" (375, 438). In other words, "true love" is too extreme an emotional investment to be contained within Sayyid Ahmad's closed psychosocial system. Unlike pleasure, true love, by definition as we see here, cannot be governed by principles, because it is the full surrender to primordial desire, rather than a partial, structured release. Only forms of love that are investments within the closed circuit itself can be sustained, else they must be given up, like his attachment to his first wife, Yasin's mother, who would not yield to his strict regime.

The only form of full release available to Sayyid Ahmad is his faith in God, which is characterized by "fertile, pure love," and which absorbs vital, instinctual energy in the same manner as his pleasures, without generating conflict (347, 348). Sayyid Ahmad surrenders himself, by inner necessity, to the God who has made his life possible by anchoring the social order in which he can be who he is. This love, or faith, is the directing of the dangerous desire or life force that would destabilize the closed order to a destination outside the order. And this destination, God, is the life force itself objectified and separated from social existence. Sayyid Ahmad's worship, therefore, is the investment of desire, or life energy, back into life itself as the transcendent origin of the psychosocial order. The investment of desire into God, i.e., back into itself, is the self-negation that takes this desire out of the psychosocial order in a manner that sustains the order. Faith anchors the closed system in a point external to it, in the mysterious power responsible for its existence and legitimacy. In other words, worship of a transcendent God makes the social system a closed, static order by placing the dynamic, unconfinable force of life that is responsible for the system outside of it. Faith in God is the only "true love," unfettered by principles, that the static order allows, because it is precisely the love of the source of this order's principles. It is a love that affirms the restrictions one must place on one's desire, so it is in other words, virtue.

Such is the nature of traditional religious faith in Mahfuz's realism, so long as it retains its social dimension. It is on this basis that Sayyid Ahmad affirms the social order and his position within it, complete within himself and without aspirations to greater wealth or higher social position. His state of inner completeness is sustainable so long as he retains his personal powers and the social structure remains intact, for the emotional investments of his dependents, their love, fear, and adulation of him, incorporate them as well into his circuit. In this way, Sayyid Ahmad embodies a traditional psychosocial order with an internally legitimate, closed character, that can persist timelessly if free of external disturbance. To represent things in this manner, the *Trilogy* makes Sayyid Ahmad a perfect instantiation of the necessary social values, so extreme in his application of them that many institutions of his society as it is historically known must be excluded from depiction, and others, like wedding celebrations, are anathema to him, due to their mingling of the domestic and the pleasurable. Moreover, the domestic sphere must be depicted as almost completely isolated from external society, such that the only social life enjoyed by the family members takes place among themselves when the father is absent, and their only external social links are those motivated by plot requirements. The author contrives that the family has but a single relative, Amina's mother, whose sole function is to provide Amina refuge when she is temporarily expelled from the household. Such social isolation of the domestic sphere is necessary so as to subordinate it entirely to the figure of the father, and determine its character according to the rigid social division for which he stands.

Love, Patriotism, and Primordial Desire

Sayyid Ahmad's internal harmony and completion are dependent on his personal powers, his social mastery and mastery of himself, and must break down with the inevitable process of his own physical decline, not to mention the grievous shocks that fate has in store for him. At the same time, however, his social order as a whole breaks down due to the dissolution of its boundaries. It is clear from the outset that Sayyid Ahmad's sons are to have a different social destiny from that of their father. This is due not only to their differences from him in personality and education, but to the different social environment into which they, as bourgeois professionals, are to assimilate. With the disappearance of Sayyid Ahmad's close-knit, locally centered, autonomous social world and its "sought-for hope of life," the instinctual love for the God who instituted this world disappears as well. Traditional religion becomes a set of disembodied superstitions that no longer sustain a psychosocial order and can no longer motivate principled action. The result is that order disappears as primordial desire floods the social body unrestrained. The traditional form of self-completion is no longer possible, and the new generation clings to fragments of the old order instead of facing the prospect of mastering desire without a state of completion and gratification. This is the state of social crisis, the present of Mahfuz's realist novels, whose internal structure, in terms of the dispositions of desire its victims exhibit, sets up the authentic moral orientation that will transform society.

The nature of the social crisis is depicted in Sayyid Ahmad's sons, who have no access to his patriarchal mode of fulfillment. The result is that the repression of daily life defines their experience. Without any concrete sphere in which to live a life governed by principles, they succumb to extreme emotional investments like love and patriotism, or else desultory dissipation in bodily desires. Yasin, for example, sets his hopes on a life of sexual bliss in marriage. With great chagrin, however, he finds his interest in his wife flagging after a mere three weeks, and domestic life soon reverts to the intolerable confinement that it formerly had been. Having inadvertently discovered his father's secret lifestyle, he longs to emulate it. But the moral framework that makes this lifestyle possible is out of his reach. Not only does he lack his father's strength of will and personal authority, but lacks in connection his father's faith and social integration. His own religious beliefs have no restraining effect on him, and his society is limited to the company of other lonely drinkers at bars. He is doomed, therefore, to a life of marital discord, repeated divorce, and surreptitious visits to brothels, not to mention a stagnant, barren career as a petty bureaucrat. It is not Yasin, however, but his younger brother Kamal who most deeply lives out the psychosocial impasse engendered by the demise of the old social order.

The *Trilogy* represents in Kamal the deficit that lies at the center of the Egyptian present. This deficit is, obversely, the basis of the moral disposition capable of founding a new order that is neither static nor hierarchical. In contrast to *Return of the Spirit*, moral, human existence in the *Trilogy* emerges only when authentic self-sacrifice *constitutes* emotional investment. Naked desire, untransformed by a process of self-sacrifice, can have no sustainable outcome and no form of realization. Kamal's doomed attachment to Aida, his failure to emerge from it intact, his passivity, social isolation, and debilitating doubt reveal the nature of the powerful forces that have been released into the social body and which are no longer to be managed within a static equilibrium. His plight subverts any vision of an aesthetic nationalism consisting in spontaneous communal unity arising from love of beauty, for it indicates that love of beauty by itself is incompatible with moral struggle. Love of beauty, therefore, does not automatically bring self-sacrifice and nationality into being. Indeed, the outcome of love of beauty in itself is betrayal of nationality. Herein lies the tragedy of the demise of the traditional order. There is no more any prospect of psychic equilibrium through the exclusion of primordial desire, nor any possibility of fulfillment in surrender to primordial desire. The only path, short of absolute self-negation in mystical asceticism, is perpetual self-sacrifice in and for humanity without prospect of fully realizing one's own desire. The failure to adopt this course and to accept the forlorn reality of modern existence signifies the persistence of immaturity, arrested psychosocial development, whose outcome is the disorder and dissipation of Kamal's society.

Kamal's character belongs to a specific type in Mahfuz's realism that can be understood more clearly in light of two precursors from earlier novels. The first is Ahmad Akif in *Khan al-Khalili* (1945), an unmarried petty bureaucrat nearing middle age, whose ambitions have been frustrated and who seeks solace and self-esteem through study of medieval Islamic learning. The narrator attributes his social passivity and failure to marry to his early upbringing, his father's severity, and his mother's excessive devotion. "He was brought up in fear and coddling, fearing his father, people, and the world, and taking refuge from this fear in the shadow of his affectionate mother, who did for him what he should have done for himself."[15] Ahmad Akif falls in love with a beautiful young girl who lives in his building, but unable to take any action, fantasizes a devastating German bombing raid that leaves no survivors aside from himself and the girl. Ahmad Akif's egoism (despite his guilty conscience) and passivity arise from an ingrained wish that the unapproachable world should be made to fit his desires, just as his mother used to make it do when he was a child, even if this entails the destruction of society.

Of this same type is Kamil, the protagonist of *al-Sarab* (*The Mirage*, 1948), an explicitly oedipal character who shares further parallels with Kamal. Both are ironically named, "*kāmil*" having the meaning "perfect, complete," and "*kamāl*" the meaning "perfection, completion." Kamil is an attractive but pathologically shy and sexually dysfunctional young man who failed to complete his schooling before his early twenties. He is the son of a savage, alcoholic Turkish aristocrat who divorced his mother. Kamil grew up in complete dependence upon his mother, to the point that he did not sleep in his own bed until well into adulthood. He had virtually no contact with the outside world, aside from school, which was to him a form of torture. He suffers from a sexual syndrome described by Freud, in that he is euphorically attracted to feminine beauty and purity, like that of his mother, but is sexually aroused only by females whom he finds repulsive.[16]

After falling in love with a beautiful young woman whom he sees daily at his tram stop, he overcomes his shyness for the first time and succeeds in winning her hand in marriage. Though he is ecstatically in love with her, he finds himself irremediably impotent in her presence, setting the stage for the tragic outcome of the novel.

What is of interest here is not so much the oedipal syndrome suffered by Kamil in itself, but the meaning that is associated with its elements—his love and the bifurcation of his desire. We see here a pathological version of the same bifurcation between love of beauty and sexuality that is found in *Return of the Spirit*. When Kamil first sets eyes on his beloved, he experiences a new form of bliss that promises to rescue him from his life as a lowly, friendless bureaucrat whose only outlet is guilty masturbation in the dead of night. "My self told me that beyond this dry, cramped, fettered life is a life that is soft, expansive and free."[17] He discovers his "heart" for the first time and resolves to devote himself to the pleasure it holds in store for him by way of his beloved. "I realized that she is my joy and bliss and that she is my spirit and my life, and that the world without her countenance is not worth a grain of sand!" (38). Kamil has found, through her beauty, access to the well-springs of life within himself, life in its primordial purity. For this reason, he envisions happiness as self-dissolution. "I was seized by a heated, sincere desire for happiness which had no meaning for my self but that I dissolve into her and she dissolve into me" (44). But because the bliss of immersion in her beauty is purely spiritual in nature, a release from necessity to a sense of unbounded freedom, his body dies in its presence. He tells us that when he lay beside his wife, "my soul filled with life as never before, but my body remained cold and stiff with no pulse or life, as if my soul took over every drop of my life. I was intoxicated by a spiritual, radiant, euphoric, heavenly ecstasy" (96). This situation, however, is untenable, not only in his failure as a husband, but because his body comes back to life whenever euphoria subsides. As a result, he reverts to masturbation, and eventually finds full sexual release in a woman who fits the form of his cravings. "I felt in my depths a desire for this woman not less than my desire to live. Indeed it was life itself and honor, manhood, confidence and happiness" (131). He is thus riven between the two poles of his inner life force, and can give up neither, yet dismisses the notion that his beatific wife ("I worship her," 99) could be subject to the same "animal feeling" and "savage lust" that he cannot escape. His pathological condition and wretched failure, which indirectly lead to the death of his wife and mother, thereby embody the contradiction inherent in human worldly existence.

Like Ahmad Akif, Kamil is plagued by the wishful residuum of his mother's ordering of the world for him. He has "never emerged from the narrow circle of his self" into the "joys," "virtues" and "meanings" of social fellowship. "Perhaps I would not have been satisfied but for the world to empty itself of its cares to devote its life to my happiness, and since it could not do that I rejected it out of impotence and fear and became its enemy" (47). We see more fully in Kamil, therefore, the form of egoism that he instantiates. His repudiation of the unmotherly social world and attachment to the self-enclosed happiness formerly provided by his mother, at her own expense, causes him to cling to this state of completion in the form of a spiritual bliss signified by the perfection of beauty. Such bliss is precisely the ephemeral negation of the world and its web of necessity, and of the self insofar as it is bound up in the world. Even as the novel, which is narrated as Kamil's personal confession, comes to an end, Kamil continues in his ensnarement, now between a longing for spiritual, ascetic renunciation of the world (*tasawwuf*), and the reappearance of his mistress. Here the fundamental contradiction in human existence appears fully as the opposition between love/spirituality and bodily gratification.[18] We see in Kamil then that romantic love of beauty does not lead to morality and self-sacrifice, because it is nothing more than the wish for a maternal world that sacrifices itself for one's every desire, and is thus the betrayal of morality.

With the character Kamal in the *Trilogy*, this orientation finds its fullest development. Kamal differs from his predecessor in key respects, and is on the whole a more subtle and complex instantiation of his character type, as are most characters in the *Trilogy*. Unlike the benighted Kamil, Kamal is an intellectual, and suffers not from paralyzing shyness, but from a moderate lack of social self-confidence due to his appearance, his large nose and protruding forehead. Oedipal motifs are present in the depiction of his childhood—he has a strong attachment to his mother, felt resentment toward his father in early childhood when he was no longer allowed to sleep with his mother, and like his brothers, is enamored of his beautiful sister Aisha.[19] These motifs, however, are subdued, and do not take an explicitly abnormal or pathological cast. The development of Kamal centers on the repetition of extreme emotional investment and disillusionment, and is evident from his boyhood in the first book of the *Trilogy* to the closing chapters of the novel. Kamal's character develops only in terms of the content of these investments; the pattern of his being is set from the beginning. Kamal's character, particularly in his relationship to his nephew Ahmad Shawkat, serves as the linkage between the inherent contradiction in human existence, the deficit at the heart of the social present, and the revolutionary struggle that is to redeem both. Through his character the aesthetic, aristocratic hegemonic order of *Return of the Spirit* is decisively repudiated.

Like the other characters of his type, Kamal responds to the severity of his father and the affection of his mother, which is not, however, depicted as coddling, and to the frustrations and constraints of everyday life in general, by preoccupation with a spiritual realm made up of religion, beauty, and fantasy. As a boy, he finds pleasure not only in whatever mischief he can get away with between home and school, but in teaching new parts of the Quran he learns to his mother, especially those involving angels and the *jinn*. The nearby mosque of the Islamic hero al-Husayn inspires the deepest religious passion and veneration in Kamal and signifies to him "the splendor of dreams" as will his future beloved Aida. He weeps over the stories of Husayn's martyrdom and imagines his head, entombed in the mosque, to be eternally radiant and impervious to decay. Kamal is captivated by the fantastic adventure stories his brother reads, and finds much diversion in the world of the garden and the chickens his mother keeps on the roof. He is much taken with the beauty of his sister Aisha, and that of a girl also blond and blue-eyed pictured on a tobacco shop advertisement, reclining with a cigarette in a plush room before a scene of the Nile visible through her window. He imagines joining the girl in her luxurious lifestyle, boating on the Nile, and gazing into her eyes. Kamal's disregard of the impropriety of this alluring smoker[20] acquires deeper significance in his befriending of the blond blue-eyed British soldiers who encamp in front of Sayyid Ahmad's house when the 1919 Revolution begins. "How beautiful they are! I've never seen anyone more beautiful than they...As though they were all Aisha" (527). Though he is accused of betraying the Egyptian cause, Kamal insists that "they are much more beautiful than Sa'd Zaghlul" (528).[21] Kamal disassociates the elements of his spiritual world from bodily impurity, and is disturbed though fascinated when they overlap. For example, he is unable to accept any connection between his sister's pregnancy and the revolting birthing of a cat that he once witnessed, believing that the human and the animal "are further apart than is the earth from the sky." He is desperately curious to observe Aisha's delivery, unaware of how outlandish is his expectation to do so (564). This kind of childish naïveté, seemingly excessive in a boy of eleven, persists in Kamal into adulthood, lending his character a marked immaturity.

Kamal's spiritual world, indeed his very being, finds its culmination in his absolute, anguish-ridden emotional attachment to Aida, which takes up the second book and persists in its after-effects to the end of the third. Kamal's relationship with Aida is parallel to Muhsin's relationship with Saniya in *Return of the Spirit*. Above all, both relationships consist in regression to primordial desire through love of beauty. The contrast in the meaning with which these relationships are invested, therefore, lies at the center of the contrasting moral visions of the two novels. Kamal's beloved Aida is the elder sister of his schoolmate and closest friend Husayn Shaddad. Their father Shaddad Bey is a grand cotton merchant who works to advance his social ambition by cultivating ties with the royal family and men of state. There is thus a deep class divide between Kamal and his popular social world and the aristocratic world of the Shaddad mansion. Like Saniya, Aida is beautiful, sophisticated and westernized. Due to her partial upbringing in Paris, she is not inhibited from engaging in brief interactions with her brother and his friends when they come to the Shaddad home on Friday afternoons. As the second book of the *Trilogy* begins, Kamal, just graduating from secondary school, has already been madly in love for the past two years.

Kamal's love has the form of self-annihilation in the overwhelming emotion that engulfs him in Aida's presence. He experiences this as transport to a realm that he calls "the sky." When she first addressed him by name the melody of her voice "settled deep inside to sing perpetually with an unheard voice that entranced your heart in a heavenly happiness known to none but you." He was possessed as a prophet receiving revelation, "as if a voice from heaven had chosen you and uttered your name." In his love, he exults in "an ascent above life and living things," for "a bridge spread over with roses of happiness connects you with the heavens" (590). In Aida's presence "he found that every thought throbbing within his self was directed towards the sky." Her presence "robbed him of perception, time, space, people and his self, and it was as if he had become a disembodied spirit floating in space towards its worshipped one" (664). When she is before him, his awareness is of a purely spiritual nature, "like an enchanting melody in the audition of which we dissolve completely"; perceptual memory of her appearance comes to him only afterwards, in moments of semiconsciousness (665). Aida is therefore experienced by Kamal not as a material creature of this world, but as a heavenly, divine being, who occupies his prayers as the angelic face of his quest for spiritual purity (592). Aida is "an angel on a brief excursion to this world" and can be called a "woman" only for want of the true name of her order (603). It is impossible to associate physical animality with her. Kamal suffers anxiety even in considering that she must eat, until he finds that she does so in a most elegant manner (685).

Aida embodies and calls forth the inner force of life that is above and beyond the life of this world. Her dark-haired and dark-complexioned beauty derives not from "lines and forms and colors" like that of Aisha and her daughter, but is "an overwhelming tremor of the heart, a soul full of life, a rapture in whose ether the spirit swims until it embraces the heavens" (601). The melodious beauty of Aida's voice "calls to the sky" (670). The idea of marriage to Aida or sexual relations with her is unthinkable. Kamal tells his neighborhood friend, who has proposed an encounter with two loose neighborhood girls, "I consider lust a contemptible instinct... Perhaps it was created in us to inspire us with the feeling of resistance and sublimation in order that it should become worthy of rising to the level of true humanity. I must be either a human being or an animal." When asked whether this applies to marriage as well, Kamal replies, "Those who love truly never marry." Realizing the outlandishness of this, he says, "Those who love what is above life never marry, that's what I meant" (620). True love as experienced by Kamal is precisely love that soars above quotidian life, love that has no social outcome, and this is what he identifies as humanity. Kamal articulates the nature of this condition most fully at a later stage, when crushed by the loss of both Aida and his religious faith, he discovers the euphoria of intoxication, which he finds to be precisely what he experienced when Aida once called his name: "Wine is the spirit of love when its lining of pain is removed" (772). For in intoxication "the suppressed surge of life (*wathbat al-haya*) is released as it was *the first time* in absolute freedom and pure ecstasy. It is the natural feeling of the surge of life when it is freed from the body's coil, society's shackles, memories of history, and fears of the future" (771).[22]

This passage is the key to the psychic nature of Kamal's character and the metaphysical foundation of the *Trilogy*. The identification of love with drunkenness affirms that love is the release of primordial desire, but at the same time establishes the amoral and escapist nature of this release. The aesthetic perfection whose image Aida offers, the self-contained yet unlimited order of the romantic symbol, embodies a condition that is no longer bound by any material exigency, in which moral constraint has become unnecessary and meaningless. It is a glimpse and a sense of the infinite, of absolute release and gratification. But this image and this sense can have no correlate in actual existence, where all being and all action are subject to exigency. In actual life, order comes only at the expense of moral constraint. One cannot be or do anything outside the medium of bodily, social, biographical, and psychological determinations. In the *Trilogy*, then, the state of psychic self-completion can be experienced only as a wholly absorbing, self-enclosed condition of euphoria that has no issue beyond itself. In this condition, all action is paralyzed and all connection with the world is suspended.

In the case of Kamal's relationship to Aida, the amoral character of Aida's attraction is bound up in the class division that separates them. Kamal worships Aida's beauty, and since her aristocratic elegance is an integral determinant of this beauty, it comes into the purview of his worship. The adolescent Kamal, a strict Muslim and ardent patriot, suspends his values when it comes to Aida. She is "neither completed by virtues nor diminished by vices. Flaws appear in her pearly crown as ornaments that enthrall you." He takes no offense at Aida's disregard of social proprieties.

"Does it lower her in your eyes that she defies social norms? No, it lowers these norms that she defies them" (590). The social and religious improprieties of the Shaddads and their circle stem from their lack of any identification with the Egyptian people. Aida prefers speaking French to Arabic, and Husayn plans to live in France. Husayn and his friends regard common Egyptians and their leader, Zaghlul, as beneath them, and support the aristocratic politicians whom Kamal and his folk know as "the traitors." Husayn explains his disdain for Zaghlul and Egyptian commoners by saying, "I love beauty and despise ugliness, and it is unfortunate that beauty is rarely found among the people" (682). This exaltation of pleasure in beauty above any other value is behind Husayn's wish to devote his life to "tourism of the mind and body" in Europe rather than to any productive vocation. In this way, the Shaddads are depicted as an elite class foreign to Egyptians in their manners and sympathies, bearing a meaning opposed both to patriotism and moral constraint. Kamal is nevertheless dazzled by the Shaddad family's elegance and grace in all things, and reveres them as "angels" and "gods." In attaching his heart to them, despite its equally fervent attachment to Sa'd Zaghlul, Kamal reenacts his childhood political betrayal in a more blatantly self-contradictory manner.

The inner meaning of Kamal's love is pain. Not only is its bliss untranslatable into any actual form, but Aida herself must betray it in that she cannot correspond to her impossible image. Love springs from the deficit in Kamal's being whose restitution seems to lie in Aida. "She is above love so long as love is a deficiency that can only be perfected through the beloved" (669). Kamal, however, is not perfected through the beloved, but made to see himself as intrinsically imperfect. "You are the same one who at times, alone with yourself, is overcome by a painful, ill sensitivity over the number of your flaws and you count them mercilessly in your small being and your humble world and your human failings." Kamal tries to live with the notion that the purpose of his love is "to love her ... there is nothing beyond it" (590). Yet even in the happiest days of his love, Kamal is afflicted by "the sickness of a heart that worships in perplexity and knows not what it seeks from its devotion!" (667). He seeks solace in "spiritual drugs," like nature, science, art, and worship, finding that his joy in contemplating Aida always brings melancholy in its wake. This melancholy turns to excruciating pain, however, when Aida terminates her occasional interactions with Husayn's friends. Pain becomes a part of his being, "as though it were an original organ of his body or an essential force in his soul, or it had been a severe illness that had become a chronic and settled one after its violent spasms had subsided" (714). The announcement of Aida's engagement definitively establishes what had been implicit all along: "Aida and pain are two words with the same meaning. You must love pain and celebrate defeat from this day onward" (722). Kamal's anguish results not simply from his bereavement of Aida's presence, but from Aida's fall from the sky to the earth, from angelhood to human animality, by entering marriage. "Pain! Not for losing the beloved, for indeed you never aspired to possess her, but for her descent from the heights of her sky, her wallowing in the muck after an expansive life above the clouds... because she consented to have her cheek kissed and her blood shed! And her body to be degraded. How severe are my anguish and my pain!" (752).

Yet Aida's marriage is a decisive moment of rupture only in a symbolic sense; it dramatizes the existential contradiction that governs Kamal's life, but he has always lived this contradiction and will continue to relive it. His process of disillusionment perpetually renews itself, and indeed, is the state of his being. Thus, on hearing later of Aida's pregnancy, and imagining her subject to the same physical processes experienced by ordinary females like his sisters, who now take the place of the cat, the pain he feels is undiminished by his previous disillusionments with Aida's angelhood (767). And so it happens ten years later in the third book, when Kamal hears of the bankruptcy and suicide of Shaddad Bey, who thereby lives up to his name.[23] Once more, Kamal is "disciplined by this family with the lesson of fallen gods" (835). In other words, he lives the fall of Aida all of his life, in every instance in which what he has taken to be the "sky" turns out to be bound up in the earth. He never moves from the naïve fantasy world of childhood to the reality of adulthood, but perpetually lives the disintegration of this world. Yet in the structure of the novel, Kamal's dreams are more than mere childish delusions. The fact that Aida is a sexual being, that she has the typical aspirations of a haughty upper class girl, that she has mocked Kamal's appearance and used him to prod her splendid aristocratic suitor into action, all of this is the tragedy of human existence.

Kamal's rebellion against his plight, his response to the loss of Aida and the failure of love, consists in nothing more than enmity toward the conditions of actual life and the quest to find a way to abide in "the sky." Kamal believes that the heroic absoluteness of his love must be redeemed, and "he will not abandon his long-held dream to win his worshipped one in the sky, in the sky where there are no artificial distinctions and no outsize heads and noses, in the sky Aida will be mine alone by virtue of the laws of the sky" (698). On Aida's wedding night, "he was engulfed by the feeling that he was the victim of an outrageous transgression conspired by destiny and the law of inheritance and class structure and Aida and Hasan Salim [the groom] and an obscure hidden power he did not want to name." He harbors an "eternal rancor" toward the "iniquitous powers" that have "cast him out of the circle of human happiness." He resolves to lead a life of war and struggle, although he does not know against whom he will fight or in what way (750). This rebellion, however, is directed against the conditions that frustrated his love, rather than against this love itself, for "it was not an illusion nor the echo of an illusion, it was the life of life, and if circumstances can take control of the body what power can reach the soul?" (755). Soon after, in the deepest throes of his loss, the eighteen-year-old Kamal relinquishes his faith in religion (though not in God) after reading Darwin. He develops a secular outlook whose values are science, philosophy, and humanity, and whose goal is truth. Yet Kamal has not altered in this way the underlying disposition of his desire. "What if I had to choose between Aida and the life of ideals? But Aida always appears before my eyes behind my ideals" (767). Kamal expresses the nature of his ideal most clearly in the conclusion he draws from the relationship that he discovers between intoxication and love.

> This captivating ecstasy is the secret of life and its highest goal... How can we make life a perpetual euphoria like the euphoria of wine without resorting to wine? We won't find the answer in struggle or building or war or striving, because all of these are means and not ends. Happiness will not be realized until we finish with exploiting all means in order to live a purely intellectual, spiritual life undisturbed by anything else. This is the happiness of which wine has given us the model (772).

The means of life—the activities devoted to survival in the material world—are not for Kamal life's inner meaning and purpose. Life's purpose is the freeing of its inner force, as seen in the condition of love and intoxication, and which Kamal now identifies with the intellectual quest for truth. Life is liberated within us, in other words, when we renounce the world and contemplate the nature of life. Self-dissolution in a state of freedom outside of all exigency remains the self-contained end of existence that Kamal seeks. He has gone no further than what he once said, in his heart, to Aida: "Here is my life which I shall devote to knowing you; can there be desire for any knowledge beyond that?" (603). In the treatises of Western metaphysicians, Kamal will continue his search for the spiritual liberation that eluded him in his love for Aida. As the years pass, however, he finds that the "sterile riddles" of Western philosophy provide no answers, and fail to console him of his hopeless love.[24] A school teacher by day and a philosopher by night, Kamal will continue to live the falling of the sky that has always been his fate.

The social dimension of Kamal's internal contradictions, his metaphysical illness, his failure to achieve adulthood, lies in his anguished ambivalence toward marriage. In the *Trilogy*, marriage is the fundamental site of moral and social order. Kamal's plight reveals that with the demise of the traditional order, marriage has lost its former psychosocial basis and turned into a symptom of social dysfunction. As has been noted, the young Kamal rejects marriage as "the earth of contracts and sweat," and in response to the question of whether he will ever marry, declares (inwardly), "either the sky or nothing!" (750). He retains this attitude in adulthood, though in an increasingly bitter and despairing manner. "He directed his gaze upwards and believed that marriage would force him to lower it... Nothing remained in him with regard to women other than a lust to be satisfied... He was beset by a strange feeling that the day he married would seal his doom" (824). He wrestles painfully with the opposition between his celestial aspirations and his material dissipation without success. "There is no place in his life that is free of contradiction and thus of anxiety. Because of that, how much his heart yearns for the realization of a harmonious unity characterized by completion and happiness, but where is this unity?" (826). Though he divides his energies between intellectual inquiry and weekend drinking and whoring, in a manner reminiscent of his father's balancing of the "human" and the "animal," he is, in contrast to his father's harmonious unity, psychically riven. "And I, in intense perplexity, perpetually waver between the blaze of instinct and the breeze of renunciation (*tasawwuf*)!" (863). Kamal's "pernicious illness," his unshakeable yearning for the sky, takes the form of this perplexity (*hayra*), or "loss of faith in everything," which leaves him trapped between the two poles of desire and paralyzes him from action. His doubt is not simply a cognitive doubt over the truth of the philosophical doctrines he studies, but the absence of psychological investment in a moral principle that would enable him to contain and transform his primordial yearning into will. As Kamal's friend declares to him, "Faith is will not knowledge" (883).

Kamal cannot marry, then, because "marriage is a kind of faith" (824). Love, "that unfathomable pain that incinerates the self until it sees in the light of its holy fire marvels of the secrets of life, then leaves behind it nothing but debris," forecloses marriage rather than laying its foundation (863). Love is escape from material constraint, from instinct and subsistence, doomed though it may be, while marriage is precisely the edifice of these constraints. Kamal can only wistfully envisage an impossible marriage that would complete his self by uniting love and lust.

> Should it be granted to me one day to find them both in a single human being I will achieve the peace that I seek. For that reason, life will continue to appear to me as elements that are not in harmony. I seek "marriage" in public as well as private life, and I don't know which is the basis of the other, but I am certain that I am miserable in spite of my lifestyle which affords me my share of the pleasures of thought and the pleasures of the body, like a speeding train that does not know whence it came or whither it is going. Lust is a beautiful, tyrannical woman who is very soon overthrown by

disgust, and the heart cries out in painful despair seeking eternal happiness, in vain. Therefore complaint does not cease, and life is a great fraud (864)

This is not a genuine hope to find the right girl someday, but rather the proclamation that the only marriage worth imagining is the one that cannot exist, the one that would fuse the spiritual and the material, which are in Kamal's world necessarily mutually exclusive. The identification of "public marriage," meaning the espousal of a philosophical doctrine, a faith, with "private marriage," is the crux of Kamal's personal crisis and the crisis of his society. As the means of realizing personal self-completion and bliss by fusing the poles of human desire, marriage is an impossibility *tout court*. Marriage must be, rather, the incarnation of the moral principle by which primordial desire on the personal level is negated and transformed into psychosocial order. In the world of the *Trilogy*, the social function and institutional integrity of marriage are incompatible with aspirations of personal happiness. Marriage requires the sacrifice of both lust and love, and resignation to the daily struggle for subsistence. Sayyid Ahmad thrived in it only as a god-fearing patriarch in control of its complementary coexistence with his extramarital life of pleasure. Others are content in it because they are "socialized animals" who have no aspirations beyond daily subsistence. With the passage of the traditional order, its floodgates burst by primordial desire, the "human" foundations of marriage have been swept away.

The inundation of primordial desire takes the form not only of love, but of patriotism. "Perhaps patriotism, like love, is one of those forces that we submit to even when we have no faith in them" (827). Patriotism, like love, is an absolute emotional investment that knows no restraint. It is a transport out of everyday existence into the same sky found in love. This is revealed most clearly in the depiction of Fahmi, Kamal's older brother, in the first book. Fahmi's trajectory is parallel to that of Muhsin in *Return of the Spirit*, in that Fahmi moves from disappointed love to patriotic participation in the 1919 Revolution. Fahmi's story, however, is ironic in character and outcome, thereby instantiating the altered meaning of patriotism in the *Trilogy*. Fahmi's feelings for Maryam—a simple, middle class neighbor, also two years his senior—although they do not reach the extreme limit seen in Kamal, nevertheless constitute "an emotion that knew no bounds," a romantic love that brings him deep disappointment and anxiety when he is barred from becoming engaged to Maryam before finishing his law degree. At the same time, Fahmi is politically engaged and possessed of fervent patriotic sympathies, which offer him an outlet from the stifling atmosphere of his home. "Talk of patriotism" transports him to an "enchanted world" full of "life and enthusiasm." For amidst the "lassitude and apathy" of his home, "the flame of anguish would ignite in his breast, and he would seek any kind of outlet from its oppression that would allow him to ascend to the sky" (489). The otherworldly and self-contained nature of patriotic feeling is further evident when Fahmi throws himself into revolutionary agitation. In the "pure, elevated life" of the demonstrations, "life had lost its value as a means entirely, and had soared in value as an end until it encompassed the sky and the earth." Ordinary, bodily life becomes worthless in its contrast to the full release, in patriotic action, of the desire that is normally suppressed and fragmented. "His suppressed emotions, his love, enthusiasm, ambition, idealism, and dreams were astray and scattered, until the voice of Sa'd rang out" (505). In other words, patriotic action engenders the euphoria of the unification and total release of desire, just as does love.

In contrast to love, however, this effect occurs not merely on the individual level, but as an immersion in the collective emotional release of the community as a whole. Sa'd Zaghlul's demand for independence incites popular response because it "stirred deep repressed passions like a new medicine" that promises to cure the people's "inveterate illness" (491). When the revolution erupts, Fahmi feels the same release from "grief and anguish" at Sa'd's exile that his nation as a whole experiences. "There could not but have been an explosion that unbound the chest of the homeland and his own chest like an earthquake that releases the accumulated vapors within the earth" (504). We see this same effect much later in the mature Kamal, who though he is an agnostic, learned skeptic, still participates, despite himself, in patriotic rallies. "His presence in this crowded throng releases within the depths of his self drowned in solitude a new person throbbing with life and enthusiasm." In such events, "the suppressed powers of the self...are set free." As a result, "his life is renewed, his instincts erupt, his loneliness dissipates, and he is reconnected with the people so that he participates in their life and embraces their hopes and agonies." Even Kamal feels that he is capable of martyrdom in this condition, though he is perplexed by his feelings (826–827). In contrast to Fahmi and Kamal, Sayyid Ahmad, despite his genuine patriotic sympathies that move him to donate generously to the cause, draws the line at any sacrifice that would affect his way of life. His patriotic emotion is like that of his love-life: it is strictly bounded so as not to vitiate his social and internal equilibrium.[25]

Like love, then, patriotism is an access of life force that intoxicates those who suffer repression and lack. It is a rebellion, in this case a collective rebellion. Its unbridled collective emotion is therefore a threat to Sayyid Ahmad's harmonious order. His social standing becomes meaningless when a lowly seminary student creates a dangerous and humiliating situation for the Sayyid and his sons at Friday prayers by accusing Yasin of being a collaborator. Moreover, Fahmi, despite immense guilt and shame, openly disobeys his enraged and astonished father for the first time when he is unable to swear that he will quit his revolutionary activities. Fahmi "worshipped [his father] as much as he feared him," making his action tantamount to a rebellion against fully recognized divine authority. It therefore brings about in him an intractable internal conflict, for rebellion against the political repression that he hates has necessitated rebellion against the patriarchal repression to which he submits. Like love, patriotism is an enmity toward the oppressive conditions of life, an escape into the freedom of emotional release, but its enmity is focused on the political oppressor. Fahmi "was impelled by the noblest of emotions and the most abominable ones, love of his nation on the one hand and the desire to slaughter and massacre on the other" (522). This "nation" then is all but empty of content, as it is the image of total release in contrast to the repression of everyday life. Fahmi's patriotic fantasies involve personal heroism and glory, rather than any social vision of an independent Egypt, and "are always crowned with the image of Maryam." Immersion in collective emotion, then, remains a morally unbounded impulse to personal bliss.

This is seen in the ironic character of Fahmi's trajectory and of the 1919 Revolution itself. The central ironic element is the betrayal of Maryam, who is seen surreptitiously smiling at a British soldier from a back window of her house. Fahmi's mother and siblings are stupefied by this brazen immodesty, and Fahmi is beside himself with grief and disbelief. Considering that Maryam occupies the same position with respect to him that Saniya occupied for Muhsin, it is a shocking act indeed. For it casts an ironic pall on the meaning of both love and the patriotism that arises from it. Beauty can no longer be regarded as morally or politically pure. The bliss attained through love of beauty cannot be the ultimate state of completion and virtue. The subsumption of moral order in aesthetic order becomes an illusion. Therefore the equivalent euphoria of patriotic emotion is likewise called into question. The irony of Fahmi's narrative culminates in the nature of his martyrdom. Despite his heroic daydreams, Fahmi has never actually put his life on the line in the demonstrations, but has always fled when violent confrontation erupted. His attachment to ordinary life is strong enough to reassert itself when guns begin to fire. As he marches in the peaceful, approved parade, held to celebrate Sa'd Zaghlul's release, Fahmi feels guilty about this, and envies the glorious wounded heroes, but is at bottom glad to have made it through alive. His "martyrdom" in this demonstration, as the victim of random, unexpected British fire, is therefore deeply ironic, in that he is not intentionally risking his life, nor has he done so in the past. Whereas Muhsin completed his narrative as a (lightly) wounded hero morally worthy of martyrdom,

Fahmi dies an inadvertent martyr with full honors. This does not cancel his heroism, but puts it under question, as his nephew will put patriotism itself under question many years later. Moreover, the fact that the British continue to shoot Egyptians with impunity, even in their victory celebration, shows the hollowness of this victory. Fahmi's narrative then, parallel to Muhsin's in form, subverts it in meaning. It is befitting that Fahmi's final perception before his death is "nothing but the sky, calm, smiling, exuding peace" (575).[26]

The association of beauty and moral betrayal runs deep in the *Trilogy* and can be seen in the character and fate of the novel's beautiful women. Aisha's character is revealed when she is caught by her sister smiling from the window at a police officer. The officer's marriage proposal thereafter is rejected by Sayyid Ahmad, who of course knows nothing of Aisha's transgression. Aisha's eventual fate is the death of her husband and children. This same officer, nearly thirty years later, jails Aisha's nephews. Maryam allows Fahmi to observe her unveiled on the roof while she gathers laundry. He, smitten, ignores this worrying immodesty, only to be later betrayed by it. She, after two failed marriages, the second to Yasin, is last seen, in the third book, as a prostitute serving British soldiers. Aida, having mocked and used Kamal and publicized his declaration of love to her, wins herself a glamorous life as a diplomat's wife in the capitals of Europe. During World War II, she divorces her husband when he has an affair and returns to Egypt. Due to her family's fall into poverty, she becomes the junior wife of an older, high-ranking bureaucrat, and dies soon after of pneumonia. Thus falls to earth for evermore the worshipped angel. Two other women, Yasin's mother and Maryam's mother, both promiscuous, also die of sudden illnesses after marrying beneath their status. This pageant of death and degradation testifies that in the *Trilogy* beauty is the most damning of curses. The only beautiful woman to escape a wretched fate, though not of course substantial misery, is Amina, Sayyid Ahmad's wife. She, however, devoted completely to service and obedience, is depicted as entirely oblivious of her beauty and sexuality. In no instance is she shown to accord these aspects of her being any thought or base upon them any action. She has morally neutralized her sexuality, which is apparently the condition for avoidance of perdition.[27]

Political Struggle and the New Moral Order

The demise of the old order, the crumbling of its barriers—traditional religion and patriarchy—against primordial desire, means that there is no longer any external, preconstituted framework to protect individuals from their inner forces. It means that individuals are now abandoned, naked refugees who must fashion their own, internal process of moral transformation, their own "faith," in order to rescue themselves from anguish and futility. "Perhaps we are mistaken to search in this world for its meaning when it is our primary task to create this meaning..." (914). There is no more any prospect of a static equilibrium, a balancing of principle and pleasure, humanity and animality, on the basis of a repressive, yet legitimate, social order. All individuals are now confronted with their true humanity, which lies in grappling with and mastering the full force of their desire. The struggle to transform animality into humanity becomes the law of every dimension of life, for there are no longer any zones of safety in which partial regression remains partial and poses no threat to psychosocial order. There remains, however, a key, and indeed constitutive, disjuncture in the *Trilogy* between desire and morality, seen in the absence in its representation of the mechanism by which the moral transformation of desire takes place. This absence enables the *Trilogy* to have it both ways, to join psychic or social illness and moral fault, present tragedy and future optimism, existential deficit and hegemonic order.

This can be seen in the novel's depiction of Abd al-Mun'im and Ahmad Shawkat, Khadija's sons, the grandsons of Sayyid Ahmad. These characters, one an Islamist and the other a Marxist, demonstrate the moral disposition that brings about political struggle and makes social transformation possible. We are not permitted to see into these characters, however, in the same manner that we are in the case of the novel's other primary figures. We do not learn why or how they have taken up their respective ideological orientations, as they enter the action already set on their paths as teenagers. Nor do we find out what in their upbringing has enabled them to escape the moral disorder that is general in their society. Let us take the example of Ahmad, who is more sympathetically and extensively portrayed than his brother. Ahmad undergoes an experience similar to that of Kamal, in that he falls in love with an elegant aristocratic beauty with haughty airs and Turkish features whom he meets at university. Despite his leftist convictions, he is able to suppress his qualms about appealing to his own family's status in seeking her favor. "So where are his principles? He felt somewhat ashamed. The heart and its passions do not know principles. People fall in love and marry outside the circle of their principles and without regard to them... Far be it from populist principles to interfere with aristocratic love!" (887). These thoughts are revealed to us in order to show his surrender to the unprincipled force of love and the moral betrayal that it entails. Ahmad, however, unlike Kamal, is set on marriage, indicating that his surrender is not so complete as was his uncle's. Though crushed by his beloved's rejection of his marriage proposal, due to his lack of riches, he is able immediately to turn his woe at her loveless materialism into indignation with their "dysfunctional society" (901). Ahmad turns his private rebellion against the repression of his desire into sympathy for the repression suffered by his society as a whole. This is the lifting of innate disposition into noble moral affect that other characters in the novel, most notably Kamal, fail to achieve. Ahmad's subsequent "year of agony during which he wrestled with disappointed love and overcame it" is dispatched in a single sentence, while Kamal's endless enthrallment requires two volumes.

Ahmad's decisive contrast with Kamal lies not only in his transformation of failed desire into love of humanity, but in his eventual marriage, which is the only one in the novel that conjoins love and principle and thereby incarnates a new psychosocial order. Chastened by aristocratic love, Ahmad later falls for a rather different kind of woman—his supervising editor at the leftist journal that he joins, a woman of a poor family four years his senior, lacking in aristocratic beauty, but possessed of the character of "a man of strong will and discipline" (910). The fundamental nature of Ahmad's feelings toward this zealous Marxist, who refuses to discuss love because it "means joy, comfort and aversion to imprisonment," is moral rather than aesthetic in nature. "I worship her when she says, 'I suffered poverty for a long time'. This frank statement elevates her above all other women and mixes her with my soul..." (937). Moreover, it is made clear that this love is not the definitive force in Ahmad's psyche. "He indeed loves her, but he does not embark on his struggle in the name of love... He has faith in the principle and he is in love with her, and he can forgo neither this nor that." We are not privy, however, to the underlying nature of this love—its relation to "the surge of life" and to sexual instinct. There is certainly no promise here either of escape from material contingency or of permanent sexual gratification, and therefore a tremendous psychic renunciation has taken place. Yet the nature of the psychic investment that constitutes this form of love is left obscure. It is as if marriage, as a human and productive relationship, is the disciplined form that pleasure is to take in the new order.

Not only does Ahmad enact the moral disposition underlying faith in principle, but he is able to articulate it in a manner that culminates the novel's development. In one of the final episodes of the *Trilogy*, Ahmad and his brother are arrested and jailed for their political activism. Entering the wretched cell, peopled by common criminals as well as political activists, Ahmad comes to a clear apprehension of his situation.

> A common human stance unites us despite the difference of our beliefs in this dank, dark place... Why don't you concern yourself with your private

affairs, this is what the police chief asked me, when I have a beloved wife and comfortable livelihood. The truth is that a human being may be happy in being a husband or employee or father or son but he is fated to suffer or to die in that he is a human being...What impels me on this dangerous, splendid path? It is the human being hidden within me, the human being aware of itself and conscious of its general historical human situation. The distinction of the human being from other creatures is that it may freely, contentedly, fate itself to die. (966)

As always, self-sacrifice is the quintessentially moral act, definitive of human being, arising from the fundamental human condition of excess and rebellion, which is instantiated in the petty thug or drunkard just as much as in the political agitator. In this latter emphasis, however, comes to light the tension in the *Trilogy* between identification of humanity with the human condition per se, and identification of it with the form of rebellion against this condition that realizes its inner meaning, that advances life toward the ultimate liberation of primordial desire, and that is thereby obligatory upon all human beings. Ahmad tells Kamal that "life is work, marriage and general human obligation... General human obligation is perpetual revolution, which is unceasing work for the realization of the will of life, embodied in its development towards the ideal" (969). It is no accident that this "call to faith," as Kamal describes it, is issued from a prison. For imprisonment is the novel's emblem for the unity of the existential condition of humanity with the sociopolitical condition of the Egyptian people. Hegemonic political struggle necessarily reveals this unity in its naked reality, because this struggle embodies both the human condition and the inner moral meaning of this condition. Liberation from private discontent cannot be pursued on the private level, but only on the level of common humanity, of the species as a whole.

In this lies the moral advancement of modernity to a higher level of existence, the dawning of a new epoch in human development. Ahmad's formulation indicates that the will or agency of an individual exists through subsumption in the will of life, the struggle for human liberation, which takes the form of perpetual revolution. Self-sacrifice can no longer be limited to the finite maintenance of a local, static economy, but is now the law of life as a whole, the full engagement and transformation of primordial desire on a universal social level. This means that social transformation is to become an unceasing collective project that will proceed without the security of a fixed, protective framework of social order. The disposition of desire that Ahmad articulates has therefore no pregiven ideological content. For this reason, his Islamist brother agrees to his formulation wholeheartedly. It is a moral obligation that, as Kamal's friend puts it, admits of "the full range of contradictions" (969). Indeed, the novel's pairing of the two brothers with opposing ideologies and parallel activist trajectories, despite its more sympathetic portrayal of Ahmad, indicates the primacy of the moral disposition itself over its actual content. The novel objectifies and relativizes Ahmad's Marxism by refusing structurally to position it as superior to its Islamist "brother," despite intimations to this effect. In this way, the *Trilogy* promotes ideological content, the views of its more sympathetically depicted characters, without inscribing any positive ideological doctrine into its moral orientation.

This can be seen in the manner in which the novel connects socialism with authentic humanity. Mahfuz himself characterized the *Trilogy* by the "crystallization of socialism within it as the goal of our development and cure for the ills of our society."[28] This socialism, however, has no content beyond the elimination of social inequality, that most odious, no longer legitimate remnant of the traditional order. There is no attempt to define socialism as a specific social configuration that gives rise to order and agency in a specific manner. The novel pointedly abjures definitive ideological demonstrations of this variety. Rather, the necessity of eliminating hierarchy is worked into moral authenticity through the association of the ruling class with the egoistic values of amoral aestheticism, self-aggrandizement, exploitation, and devotion to pleasure. This is seen not only in "aristocratic love," but even more vividly in the contrast between Ahmad's marriage to a working class woman and his cousin Ridwan's homosexual liaison with a grand politician. The bourgeois-popular alliance is morally progressive and oriented toward social struggle, while the bourgeois-aristocratic alliance is sexually deviant and prostitutional, issuing in the reproduction of social and political corruption. Ahmad's marriage is society's hope for the future, while Ridwan's relationship encapsulates the current order. Socialism is simply the movement to overturn this exploitative and repressive order, to establish the common human desire for liberation as the basis for social cohesion. Even Islamists are said in the novel to espouse socialism, though in an unscientific, mythological manner.[29] Socialism, then, takes meaning in the narrative as the social expression of the novel's authentic disposition of desire, a struggle *against* inequality, rather than one *for* a program for ideally reconfiguring society.

The oppositional thrust of the novel is enabled by the gap between Ahmad's moral maturity and Kamal's failure to achieve this maturity. This gap is not simply an idiosyncrasy of Kamal that we can dismiss once we have seen Ahmad, but is a structural necessity of the novel's representation. Kamal is the character whose desires and motivations are made transparent, while much in Ahmad is left obscure. The critic Ghali Shukri has gone so far as to suggest that Ahmad should not be considered an independent figure, but a projection of what Kamal aspires to be.[30]

This view is untenable, since Ahmad has an objective and effectual presence in the narrative, but derives from the sense that if Ahmad has attained moral maturity, marriage, and social purpose, why can Kamal not do so?[31] Though some hope that he may achieve these is offered on the novel's final page, the narrative is centered on his failure to do so, his continued enthrallment to his "chronic illness." The novel in effect splits the trajectory of the development from childhood to maturity between Kamal and Ahmad, with the result that these are two separate states lacking in a mechanism of transformation. While conventional narratives are structured precisely by such a mechanism, the *Trilogy* is structured by its absence. We are to agree with Kamal when at the novel's close, he condemns his "egoism," brands himself "a traitor," and attributes his anguish to his betrayal of his humanity (969). Yet we are to identify with him nonetheless.[32]

The nature of the mechanism of moral transformation in a *Bildungsroman* determines the moral status of the society that is represented. The more dangerous and difficult the trial the hero must undergo, the more threatened or disordered is his society. In every case, the hero is symbolically and perhaps actually saving and refounding the social order. The extreme situation of the absence of such a mechanism is a key feature of the realist *Bildungsroman* and its strategy of social critique. This absence means, in effect, that there is no social order. Society must be founded anew on a different basis from before. In this way, the *Trilogy* represents society as a whole in a liminal condition, between two ordered states, with the result that its characters are condemned to a state of terminal liminality.

In other words, the gap between desire and morality, childhood and maturity, on the level of individuals, is a representational strategy that enables the novel to cast the present as a self-enclosed period of psychosocial crisis. Whereas the reader is confronted with the choice of being Kamal or Ahmad, the characters have no apparent means of transforming themselves. Were Kamal provided a preset course of maturation to follow, he would no longer be tragic and could not embody the social crisis. Society is in crisis precisely because its members are trapped in moral deficiency. Anyone who has a clear way out and does not take it cannot draw sympathy. Yet the presence of Ahmad and Abd al-Mun'im shows that society itself, if not the lost victims of its crisis, has the means of transformation. How these figures can come about must be left obscure, else it will be too easy to blame the others for not being like them. The effect of this gap between the morally ordered characters and the others is that the process of moral transformation is transferred from the individual biographical level to the level of social evolution. Society's stages of development consist of the types of individuals who embody these stages. Thus, those who show us its disordered phase are sacrificed by the novel to their function of representing this phase.

The representational significance of the absence of a moral mechanism is that it enables the novel to avoid specifying what moral transformation actually consists in. Faith in humanity, in contrast to love of beauty, for example, is not a spontaneous propulsion into morality, because it is already a moral condition. Nor is it a way of ordering society that automatically orders the members of society. How does one acquire this faith? How does one choose one of its many varieties? Such questions, posed by Kamal at the novel's close, display the intentional indeterminacy of the moral orientation the novel generates. Faith in humanity, at bottom, is worship of and love for the human capacity for self-sacrifice, which is the only means by which desire can ever reach realization. It is the direct reinvestment of desire into itself as its own negation. This form of faith and love does not exclude desire from the social order by way of its objectification in God, but directly converts it into self-sacrifice wholly within social existence. In this way, the novel enacts its strategy of appearing to isolate the essence of human being, of human agency, as a naked self-negation that is beyond symbolization in an object or person and beyond formulation as a principle of ordering society.

Despite the human universality of the novel's ideal of liberation and fulfillment, the orientation of individuals toward this ideal can only take place through nationality. What is at stake here is not the destiny of humanity as a whole, but the subsumption of Egyptian society into humanity. And this can take place only by means of the realization of collective unity and agency on the level of the Egyptian nation. The novel is organized on two levels, that of the existential deficit of the human condition, and that of the "illness" specific to Egyptian society that prevents its members from redeeming this deficit. While ill individuals may have no access to a mechanism of moral transformation, Egyptian society as a collective unit does have such a mechanism: the revolution that will eliminate oppressive foreign/aristocratic rule and order Egyptian society so that it is oriented toward the human ideal. Indeed, action toward this end is the decisive criterion of order and agency in individuals. In other words, an Egyptian may realize his or her humanity, that is, respond authentically to the human condition, only by engaging in political struggle for colonial liberation and social reform. This is the meaning of "perpetual revolution" and "work towards the realization of the will of life." In this way, faith in humanity redeems the blind communal fervor of patriotism as its disciplined, authentically directed form. Nationality is here distinct from nationalism, in that the human ideal does not lie in an objective characteristic of the

Egyptian people to which spontaneous expression must be given. Rather, the human ideal, despite its universality, can only be approached through the subsumption of Egypt as a collective unit within it. There is no path to liberation nor any state of ultimate self-completion and harmonious unity on the purely individual level. These aspirations must be negated in the form of national political struggle so that they can be realized on the level of humanity.

There is nothing out of the ordinary in contriving things so that nationality is the key to humanity. What is especially noteworthy about the *Trilogy* is that it fuses nationality with a liberatory narrative of modernity by way of depicting the internal moral development of Egyptian society. It creates a form of Egyptian national history that has an unprecedented level of coherence and necessity, fashioned from the intimate elements of quotidian existence. The modern potential for both liberation and tragedy arises according to a necessary logic out of the collapse of a traditional economy of desire. What gives rise to modernity, as a moral condition, is not imitation of the West, but authentic human reaction to the forces within Egyptian life that impede human liberation. Disjoining modern liberation from the West in this manner enables the novel to cast progressive elements of political and social equality that are ordinarily associated with Western modernity into alliance with anticolonial struggle. The latter, a dominant value in Egyptian society at the time, is ineffectual in the novel unless it goes along with struggle against class hierarchy, patriarchy, religious persecution, and objectification of women.[33] For the Egyptian people are "in need of recurrent revolutions to serve as inoculation against malignant illnesses, and in truth tyranny (*istibdad*) is their endemic illness" (827)—that is, tyranny in its multiple forms. The maturity of Egyptian society, its modernity, will consist in the progressive liberation from these tyrannies.

Revolution (*thawra*), therefore, on both the political and the psychosocial levels, is the moral disposition that the novel generates out of its depiction of the opposition between spiritual bliss and bodily gratification that constitutes human desire. On the political level, the novel projects a decisive revolutionary moment of communal oneness in which "the people [will] become a single mass of will" (953), resulting in the reordering of society on a human basis. The psychosocial level, however, dictates that this human basis cannot be a static, sutured order, like that of the past, but must be a continual progressive movement, a "perpetual revolution," toward ultimate human liberation. For the full force of primordial desire can never again be excluded from the social order. Attaining the maturity of modernity means precisely the inescapable necessity of attempting to master and direct the energy of life on one's own, without the protection of repressive orders or egoistic withdrawal into mother surrogates, and this is rebellion because it is the struggle to rid actual existence of all the obstacles to life's full expression.[34] The meaning of politics, therefore, in the disordered present, is fomenting the inaugural revolution of perpetual revolution. The moment of collective agency to which politics aspires is not the decisive expression of an eternal, underlying communal oneness, but the point of departure of an everlasting process of attaining to unity. In other words, the novel makes it possible to call for will, unity, and agency on the national political level while pushing these to a distant horizon on the social and individual level. It gets to promise the blissful moment of transcendent completion without relinquishing the moral imperative of forever striving for this moment.

In this way, the novel presents its orientation as oppositional rather than affirmative of the existing order. It depicts an incipient process of continual liberation through self-sacrifice that will not impose a fixed order. This process will be liminal, like the disordered present, though not an issueless state of chaos, but an unbounded movement forward. This continuous liberation of modernity, however, is nothing more than the obverse of the organic national totality depicted in *Return of the Spirit*. The progressive *liberation* of innate human desire through struggle against inequality, as part of a wider struggle to subdue the world's antihuman constraints, is not at bottom different from the *expression* of innate human desire through transforming the world in accordance with it. The process of self-realization gives rise to the same kind of action as the state of self-realization. The only difference is that one is the immanent unfolding of the absolute, while the other is an absolute point that spreads until it encompasses all. The political implications of these obverse moral logics can diverge considerably, as can be seen in the relationship between the *Trilogy* and *Return of the Spirit*. Yet they both proceed from the representation of an innate human desire for self-realization that exceeds the body, material contingency, society, the empirical ego, space, and time. In both cases, desire is conceived of as anterior to and distinct from actual existence. And in both cases, the manner in which desire will proceed to express or liberate itself is determined by the form in which it may successfully infuse actual existence. This is the form from which hegemonic ordering proceeds.

Therefore, the process of liberation is in each of its successive moments equivalent to the expression of communal unity. This is what makes "provisional" hegemonic formations, like that of the political revolution projected in the *Trilogy*, possible. It, in fact, makes every step in the process of liberation possible. Framing the release of innate human desire according to one moral logic or the other enables the difference between an oppositional and an affirmative orientation, but they are fundamentally the same logic. The counterhegemonic depiction of modernity as the progressive elimination of inequality and other constraints, perpetual transformation with no fixed order, is founded on its own internal order of progression, even when it declines to name this order. In the *Trilogy*, this can be seen in the austere renunciation required to escape egoism and moral condemnation. Moreover, it already inheres in the configuration of present society. All those who dissipate their desire from "below," who belong to the "people," including petty criminals, prostitutes, and the like, are cast as misdirected rebels against the human condition, victims of the corrupt order. Whereas all those who dissipate their desire from "above," or in their quest to get there, are cast as participants in the corrupt order. The former may be incorporated into the liberatory movement, and are at the least sympathetic figures, while the latter are the enemy. The *Trilogy*, however, does not attempt to represent the new form of order that it prefigures. It remains rooted in the social crisis of the present, preoccupied with the tragedy of the individuals who are lost to it. From this perspective, society's movement from the cocoon of the traditional order to a state of maturity is one of sorrow and misery, despite the promise of a commensurate redemption to be enjoyed by society as a unit but of no avail to the victims of its crisis.

If the egoistic characters of the *Trilogy* have no apparent means of transforming themselves, this does not impair the ideal of social integration operative in the novel. For fictional hegemony aims at incorporating the reader into its normative framework, and the representation of characters is merely a means toward this end. The novel's moral function is indicated in the novel by Kamal's friend, a fiction writer, who says in advocacy of his vocation, "Science gathers human beings in the light of its thoughts, and art gathers them in an elevated, human affect. Both develop humanity and impel it towards a better future" (861). The nature of this affect is not further specified, but is presumably the emotional identification with the human condition that we see in Ahmad. Another indication of the novel's moral function is provided in Ahmad's reflection on his family's prejudices: "The bourgeoisie is full of complexes. It needs an expert psychoanalyst to cure it of its illnesses, an analyst who has the power of history itself!" (924). It seems evident that the bourgeoisie has found its psychoanalyst in the *Trilogy* itself. The novel cannot have this function, however, without contriving to represent the Egyptian nation as a moral being whose psychic center lies in the bourgeoisie. The quotidian verisimilitude of its depiction of three generations of a middle-class Egyptian family conceals a logic of psychosocial development with politically oppositional implications. The novel's realism draws its readers into accepting its world as their own and thereby defining themselves in relation to the authentic moral disposition that orders this world. This does not mean that the novel's success is to be gauged by how many of its readers become political activists. The novel's hegemonic function lies rather in the relation it establishes between the private experience that it depicts and its ideal of national integration.

In the *Trilogy*, love continues to stand at the threshold of moral order, yet in a dangerous and equivocal manner. The bliss, release, and freedom experienced in the love of beauty offer a taste of the perfection and order sought by the surge of life. But this perfection and order cannot be realized in beauty because there is no actual liberation from the material constraints of actual existence. The result of this perception of beauty is therefore pain, caused by the intense longing for a release that is impossible. That the surge of life invests itself in this total manner in beauty, however, shows that its ultimate aim, the will of life, can only be perfection, order, and liberation from material constraint. Since the necessity and contingency of material existence cannot be escaped, the only way that perfection and liberation can be realized is through the imposition of order on material existence. This is the meaning of perfection and liberation, because there is no "sky," only an earth that must be made into the sky. Their meaning, in other words, is the moral process, self-ordering, which is at the same time the ordering of material existence. Love of beauty, therefore, can only realize itself as love of the human capacity to be ordered and to create order. Human beings must turn their love of beauty into love of the human capacity for self-sacrifice. This is love of humanity, since the capacity for self-sacrifice is what constitutes humanity. Desire, the surge of life, must direct itself to its own negation as excess so that order may result. Whatever this may actually mean, it is in practice a difficult process. In the *Trilogy*, there is no mechanism that induces people to turn the surge of life into the will of life. "Faith" in a principle—another way of saying love of self-sacrifice—already presupposes the moral leap. This gap between the egoism of the raw love of beauty and the humanity of adherence to principles is seemingly traversed by revolutionary struggle. The transgressive and liminal nature of this struggle seems to subsume the innate impulse of excess and rebellion into self-ordering action. Revolutionary struggle appears to combine freedom and order. It seems to resolve the problem of how will and agency are born from innate impulse. The problem, however, is that will is already required in order to renounce beauty for revolution. If it were not, the characters of the *Trilogy* could not exist. Humanity in the *Trilogy*, and indeed in any theory of modernity based on the repressive hypothesis, is located in this gap between unlimited desire and the possibility of its expression. Eliminating the gap by creating a mechanism that naturally leads to self-sacrifice would eliminate morality by making it automatic, and eliminate as well human history as the progressive liberation of humanity. In the aesthetic foundation of citizenship, humanity is either a mystical property of internal contradiction, or is elided in its reduction to nature. These are the two polarities that constitute nationality as a moral ideal.

Epilogue

If the line of inquiry pursued in this book is cogent, it shows that investigating the nature of modernity and modern norms requires tracing their emergence in non-Western as well as Western societies. If these norms could gain public dominance in a wide range of societies, it must be asked: What were the conditions that made this possible in different social and normative contexts? Addressing this question enables us to move beyond teleological notions of the intrinsic "Westernness" of modernity by finding out at what level modern normativity could be articulated to existing norms outside the West. Seeing how modern concepts were formed through the modification of preexisting concepts in a variety of contexts reveals much more about modernity than the assumption that it is simply a natural and inevitable development of "Western" culture. Moreover, investigating the rise of modern normativity outside of the West brings out features of modernity that may be latent or obscure in Western historical development but which may have played important roles. The Middle Eastern context, in which the transition to modern normative concepts occurred in a relatively brief span of time, provides instances of rapid and striking conceptual shifts that may help to shed light on similar, less apparent developments in Europe. Uncovering the non-Western "prehistories" of modern norms enables us to escape the tenacious assumption that Western modernity is radically other to non-Western premodernity, and that anything that diverges from what is speculatively designated as the Western paradigm must be an intractable persistence of "otherness" or a failed imitation of authentic modernity.

I have aimed in this book to sketch a genealogy of modern moral and social ideals over the course of the late nineteenth and early twentieth centuries in the Middle East and particularly in Egypt. I have argued that to understand the nature and logic of modern normative concepts, it is necessary to trace their emergence from preexisting norms and to focus on what it means, in both cases, for individuals and societies to be ordered. This approach has led me to raise questions that are not often addressed directly in many current methods of approaching normative transformation. Such methods tend to posit an underlying historical logic, such as rationalization, or the expansion of capital or governmental power, that produces within individuals and the public sphere the values and aspirations necessary for the continued advancement of the underlying historical logic. This way of looking at things, however, cannot account for how a putative logic of social development can efface existing concepts and values and produce the concepts and values it requires directly out of itself. Nor can it account for the multiplicity of ideologies and normative debates in the public sphere, except by classifying them as either upholding or reacting against the logic of modernity.

Investigating the public discourses of the colonial period, their conceptions of order, their strategies for claiming social authority, leads, I have argued, to different conclusions. Focusing on the appeal to nationality of social reformers shows that they invoked the ideal of a morally integrated self-ordering communal body to justify the social reorganization that they called for. They blamed the failure of society to attain this ideal on the egoism and moral enslavement of their compatriots and set forth the social arrangements that they claimed would bring about order on individual and communal levels. The self-ordering, autonomous community that they envisioned relied on a relationship between individual and communal order that was different from what had obtained in previously existing social ideals. It came increasingly to be seen that order should arise immanently within all individuals, thus resulting in their union as a single body possessed of will and agency. It is on this basis that far-reaching transformations of society were called for and legitimized. If we take this new relationship between individual and communal order as a key element in modern normativity, it becomes clear that liberalism is not the only political ideology that can be regarded as modern. Whereas liberal reformers like Qasim Amin argued that rational autonomy is the key to self-sacrificing citizens and social integration, radical Islamists like Sayyid Qutb held that only adherence to Islamic law could effect this result. While an Egyptian nationalist like Tawfiq al-Hakim depicted peasant heritage as the origin of personal self-completion and national glory, an Arab nationalist like Sati' al-Husri saw these to lie in the social communion enabled by a common language. Although these writers each gave the ideal of an autonomous, morally integrated national community a different content, this ideal formed the shared terrain on which they engaged in public debate with competing ideologies. And it served as the basis on which they made hegemonic claims regarding how society should be ordered, what institutions should govern social life, and who should command social leadership.

The central element in these depictions of the integrated communal body lay in what it means to be a morally ordered human being, and specifically, how individuals realize their humanity by attaining this status. It is here that the inner nature of the transformation of virtue into nationality most clearly reveals itself. What I have called the ideal of virtue, as articulated in a number of moral and political discourses of the Islamic intellectual tradition, depicts order as the restraint imposed upon chaotic desires by an externalized element, whether within the self or within society as a whole. Modern normativity, however, has tended progressively to diminish the role of such an externalized element and to envision the emergence of order as a natural, immanent process rather than as an imposition of restraint. This immanent conception of order does not resolve the inherent contradiction of the ideal of virtue, but reconfigures it in a manner that creates a new cultural dynamic. Order is conceived as emerging from an innate desire that is the origin of humanity, freedom, and progress. The cultural forms and discourses that seek to represent the nature of humanity for their own purposes depict particular forms of desire as the wellspring of authentic humanity. To do this, they must depict an innate desire that in its original state is outside of order—apparently transgressive and dangerous—only to then reveal that it is actually the impetus of human morality. A cultural dynamic emerges in which every form of desire that is successfully depicted in this way soon loses its transgressive and dangerous cultural meaning and can no longer represent innate desire. Humanity is always seen as a force that has been repressed, but which once it has overcome this repression, will bring about order, progress, and fulfillment.

The transition from virtue to nationality, from an externalizing to an immanent conception of the self, entailed the emergence of a new understanding of what it is to be human. This new notion of humanity was not based on a sudden reevaluation of the moral capacity and status of the human individual. It derived rather, at least in part, if not in large part, from an increasing emphasis on the self-ordering and moral autonomy of the communal body as a whole. Burgeoning professional and bureaucratic classes of increasing public influence but without a specific form of public status benefited from this way of representing society and the advancing centralization of the social order encouraged it. The new notion of humanity thus arose in tandem with a new conception of social integration and communal agency—nationality. What it means to be human was defined by different claims about what it is in human beings that enables them to integrate with each other as a single unit. This is seen on many levels, and particularly in the transformation of the moral status of femininity, which was seen as playing a central role in the private formation of citizens.

Understanding the nature of humanity on the basis of an envisioned communal integration has been in evidence across the political spectrum. Whereas leftist ideologies tend to make the nation a mere stepping stone to a wider human solidarity, rightist ideologies insist on the nation's separateness by morally valorizing "objective" distinctions, even when they affirm a human solidarity of autonomous nations. Yet the coming to order of the nation is still fundamental, as has been seen, for leftist intellectuals like Antonio Gramsci, Salama Musa, and Nagib Mahfuz. For these writers, the particularities of a people's historical character, and the form of disorder that subjects it to tyranny and repression, determine its unique path to the attainment of universality. This common underlying structure of humanity and community that forms the basis for the hegemonic claims made by a multiplicity of competing ideologies means that these ideologies can never escape each other. As long as the same moral ideal and normative logic are in effect, subtle manipulations of the internal structure of nationality are all that separate opposing political positions. At the same time, slippages among ideological positions and combinations of their doctrines are frequent and inevitable. Liberal and leftist critiques of nationalism, for instance, have failed to address the reliance of liberal and leftist ideologies on nationality. Such reliance ensures the kinship and mutual permeability of all discourses that draw on nationality. Any one of them is inconceivable without the others.

On the view presented in this book, modernity has multiple non-Western histories. The starting point of these histories, from the perspective of the present, is the cultural and social elements and conditions that made a transition to modern norms possible in a given place. These histories of modernity are not discontinuous, in the sense of a radical break between modernity and premodernity. But they are nonteleological. The elements and conditions that made transformation possible were not destined to result in modernity. They may not have even been much connected with each other. The supervention of other elements, events, or catalysts, however, brought them together in a new way and initiated a new course of development. Only retrospectively can the histories of those original elements and conditions be regarded as part of the history of modernity. If we see this type of process as a regular feature of the movement of history, on different levels, there is no point in characterizing it as a type of discontinuity. Only if we were to regard a culture as a bounded system that unfolds according to its singular internal dynamic would such superventions and transformations constitute discontinuity. We do not regard cultures as bounded systems or discrete entities, however, and we do not regard history as teleological. It stands to reason, then, that the Western history of modernity should be viewed in the same way.

Notes

Introduction

1. Ernest Gellner, *Nations and Nationalism* (Ithaca: Cornell, 1983). Gellner argues that "nationalism is...an effect of industrial social organization" (41) and that "nationalism is, essentially, the general imposition of a high culture on society" (57). "A high culture pervades the whole of society, defines it, and needs to be sustained by the polity. *That* is the secret of nationalism" (18).
2. Ibid., 21–23.
3. "Durkheim taught that in religious worship society adores its own camouflaged image. In a nationalist age, societies worship themselves brazenly and openly, spurning the camouflage." Ibid., 56.
4. Ibid., 133.
5. This discussion is based on Anthony Smith, *National Identity* (Penguin, London, 1991).
6. Ibid., 87–91.
7. Ibid., 162. On the familial nature of ethnicity see also pp. 12–13.
8. See John Breuilly, *Nationalism and the State* (Manchester: Manchester University Press, 1993), 62.
9. Elie Kedourie, *Nationalism* (New York: Frederick A. Praeger, 1961), 110. For his claim that nationalism is concerned only with the self-determination of culturally distinct nations, and has no further political content, see pp. 80–90.
10. Kedourie argues that "nationalism and liberalism far from being twins are really antagonistic principles" (p. 109), and insists that English and Wilsonian references to nationality are merely "Whiggism" which has no relation to nationalism (130–133).
11. Benedict Anderson, *Imagined Communities* (London: Verso, 1991), 143.
12. Ibid., 144.
13. Anderson sees language as a limiting basis of human communion, and therefore regards common language as the basis of the nation: "from the start the nation was conceived in language, not in blood..." (145).
14. This is perhaps why the prominent theorist of the nation, Anthony Smith, says that "[t]he quest for the national self and the individual's relationship to it remains the most baffling element in the nationalist project." *National Identity* (London: Penguin, 1991), 17.

15. Antonio Gramsci, *Selections from the Prison Notebooks*, ed. and tr. by Quintin Hoare and Geoffrey Nowell Smith (New York: International Publishers, 1971), 57. In Gramsci's view, however, such hegemony was never achieved by the Italian bourgeoisie, and as a result Italian society had not been progressively transformed and cleansed of its precapitalist elements. This is the problem that he seeks to account for with his notion of "passive revolution."
16. Ibid., 60.
17. Ibid., 129.
18. Ibid., 130.
19. Ibid., 132–133.
20. Ibid., 133.
21. Ibid., 418, whence all of the quotations in this paragraph.
22. Ibid., 360.
23. Ibid., 419.
24. The necessity of instituting some kind of order "creates an unstable balance and a constant tension with the subversive logic of democracy" (189). Laclau and Mouffe do not explain how order is generated; the purely subversive democracy cannot be the source. It seems that in their vision order is a default state that is progressively democritized over time. But at the same time they seem to view liberal democratic societies as subject to endless reconfiguration as each new order is immediately subverted, with this condition as the ultimate norm.
25. Democracy is "only a logic of the elimination of relations of subordination and of inequalities" (188) and contains no "set of proposals for the positive organization of the social" (189). In a traditional hierarchical order there is no real political antagonism because "a system of differences which constructs each social identity as *positivity* not only cannot be antagonistic, but would bring about the ideal conditions for the elimination of all antagonisms—we would be faced with sutured social space, from which every equivalence would be excluded." Only with the supervention of democratic discourse does the possibility of deeming a relation of subordination to be oppressive arise: "there is no relationship of oppression without the presence of a discursive 'exterior' from which the discourse of subordination can be interrupted" (154). In a sutured society this interruption never takes place.
26. See *Neopatriarchy: A Theory of Distorted Change in Arab Society* (New York: Oxford University Press, 1992).
27. The prime instance is Jalal Al-i Ahmad's "occidentotic" or "west-struck" Iranian.
28. Ranajit Guha, *Dominance without Hegemony* (Delhi: Oxford University Press, 1998), 100–101.
29. Ibid., 62.
30. *Nationalist Thought and the Colonial World* (Minnesota: University of Minnesota Press, 1993), 28.
31. Ibid., 28, 41.
32. Ibid., 43–49.
33. Ibid., 51.

34. Ibid., 38.
35. Theodor Adorno and Max Horkheimer, *Dialectic of Enlightenment*, 54–57.
36. Following Adorno and Horkheimer, Chatterjee defines Enlightenment as "an entirely new idea of man's *control* over nature—a progressive and ceaseless process of the appropriation of nature" which "necessarily also becomes a means to the *power* of the Self over the Other. In short, knowledge becomes the means to the domination of the world" (14). Adorno and Horkheimer, however, see Enlightenment rationalism as the continuation of the long-standing moral ideal of control over nature as self-mastery. Chatterjee regards the idea of control over nature as definitively modern and Western.
37. Ibid., 17. C.A. Bayly has critiqued the claim of the purely "derivative" nature of Indian nationalism, citing an indigenous tradition of regional loyalties and discourses of "rational patriotism" (involving ideals of just government) throughout pre-colonial India. He argues that Indian nationalism drew upon normative content from these traditions in its formation, but does not indicate how the native normative ideals connected with imported ones. See *Origins of Nationalism in South Asia* (New Delhi: Oxford University Press, 1998).
38. Chakrabarty's notion of radical "cultural difference," which he argues is elided by historians seeking to provide rational accounts of non-Western histories, appears to be predicated on a false analogy between a "culture" and the Derridean signifier. Derrida attempts to demonstrate that language cannot create the effect of meaning unless the relation of *différance* constitutes its signifiers. World history, however, is not a language or a system of signs, and there is no reason to understand a "culture" as a signifier.
39. Dipesh Chakrabarty, "The Time of History and the Times of Gods," 57.
40. Ibid., 53–55.
41. Dipesh Chakrabarty, *Provincializing Europe: Postcolonial Thought and Historical Difference* (Princeton: Princeton University Press, 2000), 14–15.
42. Timothy Mitchell, *Colonising Egypt* (Berkeley: University of California Press, 1991), 14.
43. Ibid., 33.
44. Ibid., 165.
45. Ibid., 55, 149.

1 Sovereign Virtue and the Emergence of Nationality

1. For the explanations of the necessity of monarchic rule provided by classical Islamic thinkers, see Patricia Crone, *God's Rule: Government in Islam* (New York: Columbia University Press, 2004), 259–284. On the externality of the monarch to the social order, see Aziz al-Azmeh, *Muslim Kingship* (London: I.B. Tauris, 1997), 123.
2. Abu Uthman Amr b. Bahr al-Jahiz, "Min Kitabihi fi al-Nisa'" in *Rasa'il al-Jahiz*, ed. Abd al-Salam Harun, 4 vols. (Cairo: Maktabat al-Khanji, 1964), 3: 150–151.

3. Ali b. Muhammad al-Mawardi, *Adab al-Dunya wa al-Din*, ed. Abdullah Ahmad Abu Zina, 2 vols. (Cairo: Dar al-Sha'b, 1979), 2: 246–247. See also his *Al-Ahkam al-Sultaniya wa al-Wilayat al-Diniya*, ed. Muhammad Fahmi al-Sirjani (Cairo: al-Maktaba al-Tawfiqiya, 1978), 5.
4. Abu al-Abbas Ahmad b. Abd al-Halim b. Taymiya, *Al-Siyasa al-Shar'iya fi Islah al-Ra'i wa al-Ra'iya* (Cairo: Dar al-Faruq, 2008), 28.
5. Abu Hamid Muhammad al-Ghazali, *Ihya' 'Ulum al-Din* (Halab: Dar al-Wa'y, 1998), vol 1, 29.
6. On this conception of order, see Al-Azmeh, *Muslim Kingship: Power and the Sacred in Muslim, Christian and Pagan Politics*, 128–129.
7. This kind of synthesis is seen earlier in the works of the writer Miskawayh (d. 1030), from whom al-Ghazali drew heavily. See Abu Ali Ahmad b. Muhammad Miskawayh, *Tahdhib al-Akhlaq wa Ta'thir al-A'raq*, ed. Hasan Tamim (Beirut: Dar Maktabat al-Hayat, 1980). On al-Ghazali's ethical theory and its place in the history of Islamic ethical theory see Majid Fakhry, *Ethical Theories in Islam* (Leiden: E.J. Brill, 1991).
8. *Mizan al-'Amal*, ed. Sulayman Dunya (Cairo: Dar al-Ma'arif, 1961), 272. References to this text are hereafter cited in the text by page number.
9. For the discussion of the meanings of these terms, see *Ihya'*, 3: 4–6.
10. See *Ihya'*, vol. 4, 365. "Excessive love" (*'ishq*) is here the fullest form of love of God (393). It is not clear how love of God, a state of the rational faculty, is supposed to be related to love experienced by the lower self. Al-Ghazali, Miskawayh, and others, seem to regard sexual love as an affect of the body, although it is love of beauty (*Mizan*, 402). Other types of love, however, those that create social solidarity, are regarded as belonging to the rational self when they are contained properly. Nevertheless, when they are not properly contained and directed they seem to be grouped with sexual love.
11. Al-Ghazali provides an extensive discussion of the virtues in which each one falls between two vices, the impulse unrestrained, and the impulse overly weakened or absent. See *Mizan*, 264–287.
12. There is much scholarship on Ibn Khaldun's political theory. Some of the more influential accounts are: Muhsin Mahdi, *Ibn Khaldun's Philosophy of History: A Study in the Philosophic Foundation of the Science of Culture* (Chicago, IL: University of Chicago Press, 1964); Muhammad Mahmud Rabi', *al-Nazariya al-Siyasiya li-Ibn Khaldun* (Cairo: Dar al-Hana, 1981); Aziz Al-Azmeh, *Ibn Khaldun: An Essay in Reinterpretation* (London: Frank Cass, 1982).
13. For an analysis of the psychological concepts used by Ibn Khaldun, see Jihad Nu'man, *Ibn Khaldun wa 'Ilm al-Nafs* (Juniya, Lebanon: Dar Nu'man, 1982).
14. Abd al-Rahman ibn Muhammad ibn Khaldun al-Hadrami al-Maghribi, *Tarikh Ibn Khaldun*, 7 vols. (Beirut: Dar al-Kutub al-'Ilmiyah, 1992), vol. 1, book 2, section 17. Hereafter referenced in the text by book and section number.
15. See Al-Azmeh, *Ibn Khaldun*, 52–53.

16. Ibn Khaldun allows that there is a kind of rule which is a rule of sheer force, not guided by reason or religion, but he does not explain how this kind of rule comes about or remains in effect (3.25). One instance of this kind of rule is the decayed state of sovereignty that comes about with the decay of group feeling and virtue. Ibn Khaldun also posits two types of rational sovereignty—a kind that pursues the well-being of the polity as a whole, as with the ancient Persian kings, and a kind that pursues the well-being of the rulers, to which the well-being of the ruled is subordinated. This latter, he says, is the rulership of all current kings, Muslim and non-Muslim (3.51).
17. Stefan Sperl, *Mannerism in Arabic Poetry* (Cambridge: Cambridge University Press, 1989), 26.
18. Ibid., 21.
19. On the function of the *qasida* in legitmizing political authority, see Suzanne Stetkevych, *The Poetics of Islamic Legitimacy* (Bloomington: Indiana University Press, 2002).
20. Abd al-Rahman b. Hasan al-Jabarti, *'Aja'ib al-Athar fi al-Tarajim wa al-Akhbar*, ed. Abd al-Rahim Abd al-Rahman Abd al-Rahim, 4 vols. (Cairo: Dar al-Kutub al-Misriya, 1997), vol. 1, 13.
21. Ibid., 14–17.
22. On the nature and significance of this newspaper, see Nikkie Keddie, *Sayyid Jamal al-Din "al-Afghani": A Political Biography* (Berkeley, CA: University of California Press, 1972), 214–228.
23. Jamal al-Din al-Afghani and Muhammad Abduh, *al-'Urwa al-Wuthqa*, ed. Salah al-Din al-Bustani (Cairo: Dar al-'Arab, 1993), 59.
24. The claim that Islamic virtues are designed to create unity and dominance occurs throughout, for example, "Comity and dominance are two strong pillars and bases of the Islamic religion, and two ordained obligations upon whomever clings to it. Anyone who opposes the command of God in what he has made obligatory regarding these two [pillars] suffers the consequence of his wrath in ignominy in this world and punishment in the hereafter" (76). The liberal reformer Adib Ishaq (1856–1885) frequently addressed Egypt as a collective entity in his newspapers during the late 1870s and early 1880s. See for example, Adib Ishaq, *Muntakhabat dimn arba'at ajza'* (Alexandria: Matba'at al-Adab, 1885?), 88.
25. On al-Barudi's role in the rise of modern Arabic poetry, see M.M. Badawi, *A Critical Introduction to Modern Arabic Poetry* (Cambridge: Cambridge University Press, 1975), 16–29, and Salma Jayyusi, *Trends and Movements in Modern Arabic Poetry* (Leiden: Brill, 1977), 1: 37–39. For a biography of al-Barudi, see Ali Muhammad al-Hadidi, *Mahmud Sami al-Barudi: Sha'ir al-nahda* (Cairo: al-Maktaba al-Anglu-Misriya, 1969).
26. On the Urabi revolt see Alexander Schölch, *Egypt for the Egyptians: The Socio-Political Crisis in Egypt 1878–1882* (London: Ithaca Press, 1981), and Juan Cole, *Colonialism and Revolution in the Middle East: Social and Cultural Origins of Egypt's 'Urabi Movement* (Cairo: AUC Press, 1999).
27. Schölch, 331.

28. He and his cabinet resigned in May, 1882.
29. See Schölch, 297.
30. Husayn al-Marsafi, *al-Wasila al-Adabiya li-l-'Ulum al-'Arabiya*, (Cairo: al-Matba'a al-Malikiya, 1289–1292 A.H.), 2: 474.
31. Salma Jayyusi argues that, "liberal thought in the nineteenth century and the relative intellectual freedom were not in contradiction to the basic attitude in the old poetry which, despite the abundance of eulogy, was often free and always proud in spirit. This is why al-Barudi's sort of traditionalism, based on the better examples of Classical poetry, was harmonious and acceptable." *Trends and Movements*, 39.
32. Al-Hadidi, *al-Barudi*, 119.
33. Ibrahim al-Yaziji, *Al-'Iqd: Diwan al-Shaykh Ibrahim al-Yaziji*, ed. Nazir Marun Abbud (Beirut: Dar Marun Abbud, 1983), 25–28. According to the gloss on the poem it was composed in 1883. See also A. A. Duri, *The Historical Formation of the Arab Nation*, tr. Lawrence I. Conrad (London: Croom Helm, 1987), 162, 179 n. 82; Bassam Tibi, *Arab Nationalism: A Critical Inquiry*, tr. Marion Farouk-Sluglett and Peter Sluglett (London: Macmillan, 1981), 78.
34. *Diwan*, 27–28; verses 33–39, 42–43.

2 The Death of the Hero and the Birth of Bourgeois Class Status

1. On the *efendiya*, see especially Lucie Ryzova, "Egyptianizing Modernity through the 'New *Effendiya*' : Social and Cultural Constructions of the Middle Class in Egypt under the Monarchy," in *Re-envisioning Egypt 1919–1952*, ed. Arthur Goldschmidt, Amy J. Johnson, Barak A. Salmoni (New York: American University in Cairo Press, 2005), 124–163, and Israel Gershoni and James P. Jankowski, *Redefining the Egyptian Nation, 1930–1945* (Cambridge: Cambridge University Press, 1995), 7–11. The *efendiya* in Iraq is discussed in Michael Eppel, "The Elite, the Effendiyya, and the Growth of Nationalism and Pan-Arabism in Hashemite Iraq, 1921–1958," *International Journal of Middle East Studies*, 30(2) (May, 1998), 227–250.
2. Much of the recent scholarship on emerging discourses of motherhood and feminine domesticity in the late nineteenth and early twentieth centuries deals with these issues. See, for example, Omnia Shakry, "Schooled Mothers and Structured Play: Child Rearing in Turn-of-the-Century Egypt" in Lila Abu-Lughod ed., *Remaking Women: Feminism and Modernity in the Middle East* (Princeton: Princeton University Press, 1998), 126–170 and Lisa Pollard, *Nurturing the Nation: The Family Politics of Modernizing, Colonizing, and Liberating Egypt, 1805–1923* (Berkeley, CA: University of California Press, 2005).
3. On women's associations in particular, see Beth Baron, *The Women's Awakening in Egypt: Culture, Society, and the Press* (New Haven: Yale University Press, 1994), 168–181.

4. See Ryzova, "Egyptianizing Modernity," who argues that the *efendiya* is not the "middle class as a socioeconomic category" (133), but a "cultural term" (126) defined by the adoption of "markers of modernity" (150). Similarly, Eppel, in "The Elite," argues that in Iraq, "the term *efendiya*...had less to do with economic status and social origins, than with education, culture, style of dress, and Westernized behavior" (231). Both of these researchers, however, in making such a sharp distinction between "*efendiya*" and "middle class," seem to assume that the latter can be defined on a rigidly economic basis.

5. Zachary Lockman has argued that another class category that came to the fore in Egypt during the colonial period, the "working class," should be regarded as discursively as well as economically constituted. He shows the role that the *efendiya* played in helping to create this class category, for hegemonic purposes in the early twentieth century. See Zachary Lockman, "Imagining the Working Class: Culture, Nationalism, and Class Formation in Egypt, 1899–1914," *Poetics Today* 15(2) (1994): 157–190.

6. See S. Somekh, "The Neo-classical Arabic Poets" in *The Cambridge History of Arabic Literature: Modern Arabic Literature* (Cambridge: Cambridge University Press, 1992), 55–63. See also, Yahya Haqqi, "Marathi Shawqi" in *al-Majalla*, 144, Dec. 1968, 62–63. Also, S. Moreh, "The Neoclassical *Qasidah*: Modern Poets and Critics," in *Studies in Modern Arabic Prose and Poetry* (Leiden: E.J.Brill, 1988), 32–56.

7. For a history of the Arabic *marthiya*, as well as a bibliography of secondary sources, see the article "Marthiyah" in *Encyclopedia of Islam*, vol. 6, eds. C.E. Bosworth, E. van Donzel, B. Lewis, and Ch. Pellat (Leiden: Brill, 1986), 602–608. See also Mustafa Shuri, *Shi'r al-Ritha' fi Sadr al-Islam* (Cairo: Dar al-Ma'arif, 1986), and Bushra Khatib, *al-Ritha' fi al-shi'r al-Jahili wa Sadr al-Islam* (Baghdad: Mudiriyat Matba'at al-Idara Mahaliya, 1977). For a discussion of various motifs and themes of the pre-Islamic *marthiya*, see Suzanne Pinckney Stetkevych, *The Mute Immortals Speak: Pre-Islamic Poetry and the Poetics of Ritual*, (Ithaca, NY: Cornell University Press, 1993), part 3.

8. See S. Stetkevych, "Abbasid Panegyric, The Politics and Poetics of Ceremony, al-Mutanabbi's 'Id-poem to Sayf al-Dawlah," in *Tradition and Modernity in Arabic Language and Literature*, ed. J.R. Smart, Curzon, 1996, 119–143, especially 130–135.

9. Ibn Rashiq al-Qayrawani, *Kitab al-'Umdah fi Mahasin al-Shi'r wa Adabihi wa Naqdihi* (Beirut: Dar al-Jil, 1981), 2: 147.

10. The funeral elegy and eulogy have been employed to establish or consolidate collective identities in other contexts as well. For an analysis of the public, political role of funeral orations in ancient Athens, see Nicole Loraux, *The Invention of Athens*, tr. Alan Sheridan (Cambridge: Harvard University Press, 1986).

11. Umar al-Dasuqi, *Fi al-Adab al-Hadith*, (Cairo: Dar al-fikr al-'Arabi, 1964), 2: 69.

12. I.e., the funeral procession and the burial. Since the burial must take place within hours of the death, it is limited in how organized an event it can be.

For information on funeral rites and practices in nineteenth century Egypt, see E.W. Lane, *An Account of the Manners and Customs of the Modern Egyptians* (London: Ward, Lock and Co., 1890), chap. 28.

13. C.f. Shawqi Dayf, *Al-ritha'* (Cairo: Dar al-Ma'arif, 1968), 82.
14. On Ahmad Shawqi's importance as a poet, see Badawi, *A Critical Introduction*, 29–42; Jayyusi, *Trends and Movements*, 46–51.
15. Only the *nasib* section of this and other panegyrics to the Khedive Abbas Hilmi is included in standard editions of the *Shawqiyat*. The poem was published in *al-Shawqiyat*, 2nd. ed. (Cairo: Matba'at al-Islah, 1911), 67–69. Most of the verses cited here were republished in Muhammad Sabri, *al-Shawqiyat al-Majhula*, 2 vols. (Cairo: Dar al-Kutub, 1961), 1: 152–153.
16. See *al-'Umdah*, 2:128–143, for a description of panegyric conventions with respect to the social station of the praised figure. On Isma'il Sabri, see Jayyusi, *Trends and Movements*, 39–42.
17. *Diwan Isma'il Sabri Basha*, ed. Ahmad al-Zayn (Cairo: Lajnat al-ta'lif wa al-tarjamah wa al-nashr, 1938), 54–58.
18. In 1906 villagers in a small village known as Dinshaway were accused in murky circumstances of killing a British soldier. Four were sentenced to death and eight to flogging and jail. Egyptian public opinion was outraged, and the repercussions of the incident in England contributed to the replacement of Lord Cromer as Consul-general the following year. See Jacques Berque, *Egypt: Imperialism and Revolution*, tr. Jean Stewart (London: Faber & Faber, 1972), 236–239. For the literary response to this event, see Mounah A. Khouri, *Poetry and the Making of Modern Egypt* (Leiden: E.J. Brill, 1971), 65 ff.
19. "*Muhannad*" ("wrought of Indian steel") is a standard sword epithet, but here it seems to include a reference to the British and their Indian empire.
20. Sigmund Freud, "Mourning and Melancholia," in *The Standard Edition of the Complete Psychological Works of Sigmund Freud*, ed. and tr. James Strachey (London: Hogarth Press, 1957), 14: 244–245.
21. Freud, *The Ego and the Id*, in *The Standard Edition*, 19: 35–36.
22. This paradigm occurs most often in elegies for ruling figures. The "heir" is usually his own successor, but is sometimes another ruler who can now take his place. In this sort of *marthiya*, the lament for the deceased is followed by a panegyric for his successor. For examples, see al-Farazdaq's elegy for al-Hajjaj b. Yusuf beginning, "*liyabki 'ala -l-hajjaji man kana bakiyan…waqifi*" in *Diwan al-Farazdaq* (Beirut: Dar Sadir, 1966), 2: 5; see also al-Buhturi's elegy for al-Muwaffaq with praise of the Caliph al-Mu'tadid, which begins "*nas'a wa aysaru hadha -ssa'yi yakfina…*" in *Diwan al-Buhturi*, ed. Husayn Kamil al-Sayrafi, 4 vols. (Cairo: Dar al-Ma'arif, 1963), 4: 2188 (no. 821); and see the elegy of Ibn al-Mu'tazz for Abu Ahmad al-Nasir li-din Allah, likewise with praise of al-Mu'tadid, which begins "*la tudriku -l-hajibati illa sarimatun…al-jawamizu*" in *Diwan Ash'ar al-Amir Abi al-Abbas Ibn al-Mu'tazz*, ed. Muhammad Badi' Sharif, 2 vols. (Cairo: Dar al-Ma'arif, 1977), 2: 344 (no. 553). The celebrated Persian elegy by Sa'di for the Abbasid Caliph al-Musta'sim, killed by the Mongols during their invasion of Baghdad, also

follows this pattern, ending with praise for Sa'di's patron Abu Bakr b. Sa'd b. Zangi. This poem can be found in *Kulliyyat-i Sa'di*, ed. Muhammad Ali Furughi (Tehran: Sazman-i Intisharat-i Javidan, 1963) 503. See also p. 501 for another elegy of this variety.

23. Peter M. Sacks, *The English Elegy: Studies in the Genre from Spencer to Yeats* (Baltimore, MD: Johns Hopkins University Press, 1985), 28.
24. For a biography which is itself a eulogy, see Abd al-Rahman al-Rafi'i's *Mustafa Kamil Ba'ith al-Haraka al-Wataniyya* (Cairo: Dar al-Nahda al-Misriya, 1962). For Kamil's political activity and its significance, see Albert Hourani, *Arabic Thought in the Liberal Age 1798–1939* (London: Oxford University Press, 1962), 199–208.
25. See al-Rafi'i, *Mustafa Kamil*, 276–310, where passages from a number of the elegies composed by leading poets are quoted. The poet Hafiz Ibrahim was a close associate of the religious reformer Muhammad Abduh, who was a political adversary of Kamil. The poet Ahmad Shawqi's patron, the Khedive, was at odds with Kamil when the latter died.
26. See Khouri, *Poetry and the making of Modern Egypt*, 168–170 for a translation of passages from this poem. On Mutran see Badawi, *A Critical Introduction*, 68–84, and Jayyusi, *Trends and Movements*, 54–64.
27. Just before his death, Kamil had vigorously defended Islam from the aspersions cast on it by Lord Cromer in his book *Modern Egypt*.
28. *Al-Liwa'*, "The Banner," was the name of the newspaper established by Kamil.
29. *Diwan al-Khalil*, (Beirut: Dar al-Kitab al-'Arabi, 1967), 1: 308.
30. On Hafiz Ibrahim, see Badawi, *A Critical Introduction*, 42–47 and Jayyusi, *Trends and Movements*, 51–54.
31. *Diwan Hafiz Ibrahim*, ed. Ahmad Amin, Ahmad al-Zayn, and Ibrahim Ibyari (Cairo: al-Hay'a al-'Amma al-Misriya li al-Kitab, 1980), 2: 153.
32. See Ibn Rashiq, *al-'Umda*, 2: 76 for repetition in the classical Arabic elegy.
33. The verb *ba'ada*, "to become distant," is probably related etymologically to the verb *bada*, "to perish." See *Mute Immortals*, 168–171 for a discussion of the use of this formula in the pre-Islamic elegy.
34. *Misr al-fata*, "Young Egypt," a slogan of the time and later the name of an important political party. The word *fata* means "maiden" or "virgin."
35. See *Mute Immortals*, 18 ff.
36. Mustafa is the title of the Prophet, as mentioned above, and the term *sira* is used for the record of his life, which all Muslims must strive to imitate. The word *kamil* means "perfect."
37. Hafiz Ibrahim, *Diwan*, 2: 163.
38. See Suzanne P. Stetkevych, *Abu Tammam and the Poetics of the Abbasid Age* (Leiden: E.J. Brill, 1991), chap. 14, for a discussion of the relation between the *nasib* and the elegy in classical Arabic poetry.
39. Op. cit.
40. Sacks, *English Elegy*, 7.
41. *Diwan Hafiz*, 2: 162.

42. For an analysis of the cultural meanings of this theme, see *Mute Immortals*, 211–214, which discusses its appearance in pre-Islamic poetry.
43. *Diwan Abd al-Muttalib*, ed. Muhammad al-Hirawi (Cairo: Matba' al-I'timad, n.d.), 55.
44. The word *sa'd* is the name of a star of good fortune.
45. This is a reference to the *nasib* motif in which the beloved and the other women of her tribe depart in camel-borne litters.
46. This custom was practiced in nineteenth century Egypt; see Lane, *Manners*, 517.
47. See *Mute Immortals*, chapter 6, for a discussion of the importance of the rite of passage in pre-Islamic poetry.
48. *Diwan Abd al-Muttalib*, 41.
49. The mother of languages is classical Arabic.
50. Ahmad Shawqi, *Al-Shawqiyat*, (Beirut: Dar al-'Awda, 1988), 3: 29–30.

3 Order, Agency, and the Economy of Desire: Islamic Reformism and Arab Nationalism

1. "Governmentality," in *Power*, ed. James D. Faubion, trans. Robert Hurley and others (New York: The New Press, 2000), 201–222, 216–217.
2. Ibid., 217.
3. Foucault, *Security, Territory, Population*, ed. Michel Senellart, tr. Graham Burchell (New York: Palgrave Macmillan, 2007), 353.
4. Ibid., 341–349. "A new governmentality is born with the *économistes*," 348.
5. "Economic reason does not replace *raison d'Etat*, but gives it a new content and so gives new forms to state rationality." Ibid., 348.
6. See Pierre Sameul Du Pont de Nemours, *Physiocratie, ou, Constitution naturelle du gouvernement le plus avantageux au genre humain* (Yverdon: n.p., 1768–1769), vol. 1, chap. 2, 7; chap. 5, 24–25.
7. For al-Kawakibi's biography, see *Al-A'mal al-Kamila li al-Kawakibi*, ed. Muhammad Jamal Tahhan (Beirut: Markaz Dirasat al-Wahda al-'Arabiya, 1995), Introduction; EI[2], "al-Kawakibi," vol. 4. On his thought, see Elie Kedourie, *Arabic Political Memoirs and Other Studies* (London: Cass, 1974), chap. 5; Joseph G. Rahme, "Abd al-Rahman al-Kawakibi's Reformist Ideology, Arab Pan-Islamism, and the Internal other," *Journal of Islamic Studies* 10 (1999): 159–177.
8. See *A'mal*, 28; Youssef Choueiri, *Arab nationalism: Nation and State in the Arab World* (Oxford: Blackwell, 2000), 87.
9. EI[2], 776. See also her article, "Alfieri and al-Kawakibi," *Oriento Moderno* 34 (1954): 132–143. The book had been translated into Turkish. The organizing conception of describing the effects of tyranny on social institutions, customs, and values is common to both works. However, *Della Tirannide* contains more than twenty brief and unsystematically arranged chapters, while "The characteristics of despotism" contains only eight chapters, each one substantial and intensively argued. The Arabic work takes over many specific arguments and examples found in its Italian source, for example,

the argument that tyrannical rule leads to the breakdown of kinship ties due to the sexual violation of married women practiced by those in power, or the example of the Roman temple dedicated to fear as an embodiment of the tyrannical order. Also, al-Kawakibi takes over certain idiosyncratic views of Alfieri, such as the latter's aversion to the military and hatred of the institution of the standing army, regarded as a primary source of tyranny. There can be no doubt, therefore, that al-Kawakibi extensively plagiarized his Enlightenment predecessor.

10. *Della Tirannide*, 28.
11. Abd al-Rahman al-Kawakibi, *Tawabi' al-Istibdad wa Masari' al-Isti'bad*, in *Al-A'mal al-Kamila*, 430. Hereafter cited in the text.
12. On *namus* ee also *Umm al-Qura* in *A'mal*, 311.
13. Al-Kawakibi uses this term apparently to signify the understanding of society and program for ordering it implicit in authentic Islam (as al-Kawakibi sees it). Thus, it is the Islamic equivalent of Liberalism, Marxism, etc.
14. Sylvia Haim has pointed out the secular nature of al-Kawakibi's understanding of the nation. See "Islam and the Theory of Arab Nationalism," *Die Welt des Islams* 4, (2/3) (1955), 139.
15. This idea seems to come from Ibn Khaldun's theory that social order results from the action of religion upon group feeling. See chapter one above. Al-Kawakibi's statements about the Arabs in general show the influence of Ibn Khaldun.
16. The implication here is of course that God is identical to reason, but al-Kawakibi does not express this explicitly.
17. For al-Husri's biography and thought, see William L. Cleveland, *The Making of an Arab Nationalist: Ottomanism and Arabism in the Life and Thought of Sati' al-Husri*, (Princeton, NJ: Princeton University Press, 1971). On al-Husri's thought see Bassam Tibi, *Arab Nationalism: A Critical Inquiry*, tr. Marion Farouk-Sluglett and Peter Sluglett (London: Macmillan, 1981), 90–172.
18. These claims about the nation and its nature can be most conveniently accessed in *Ara' wa Ahadıth fi al-Wataniya wa al-Qawmiya*, 1985 (1944), 9–16, and *Ma hiya al-Qawmiya*, 1985 (1959), 29–41. All of al-Husri's works cited here have been republished by Markaz Dirasat al-Wahda al-Arabiya, Beirut. The date in parenthesis is the date of original publication. For discussion of al-Husri's theory of the nation, see Cleveland, chaps. 3–5; Choueiri, 101–124; Tibi, part III. For his views on language and the nation, see Yasir Suleiman, *The Arabic Language and National Identity* (Edinburgh: Edinburgh University Press, 2003), 126–146.
19. Cleveland, 69.
20. Ibid. e.g., 156–157.
21. *Ara' wa Ahadıth fi al-'Ilm wa al-Akhlaq wa al-Thaqafa*, 1985 (1951): 155–163.
22. These views on language are taken from *Ma Hiya al-Qawmiya?*, 1985 (1959): 45–63. For a full discussion of these views, see Suleiman, 134–140.
23. Ibid., 158.
24. *Safahat min al-Madi al-Qarib*, 1984 (1948), 39–40.
25. *Muhadarat fi Nushu' al-Fikra al-Qawmiya*, 1985 (1951), 181.
26. *Ara' wa Ahadıth fi al-Wataniya wa al-Qawmiya*, 45–57.

27. The views set forth here come from *Al-Iqlimiya: Judhuruha wa Budhuruha*, 1985 (1963), 12–16.
28. *Abhath Mukhtara fi al-Qawmiya al-'Arabiya*, 1985 (1964), 72–73.
29. *Safahat min al-Madi al-Qarib*, 42.
30. *Fi al-Lugha wa al-Adab wa 'Ilaqatihima bi al-Qawmiya*, 1985 (1958), 29.
31. *Ma hiya al-Qawmiya?* 207.
32. In his lecture, "Regimes of education in colonial politics: education without cultural content," in *Ahadith fi al-Tarbiya wa al-Ijtima'*, 1984 (1962), 83–91.
33. Ibid., 91.
34. *Fi al-Lugha wa al-Adab wa 'Ilaqatihima bi al-Qawmiya*, 29–32. For a discussion of al-Husri's views on linguistic reform, see Suleiman, 142–146.
35. *Fi al-Lugha wa al-Adab wa 'Ilaqatihima bi al-Qawmiya*, 29–30.
36. *Safahat min al-Madi al-Qarib*, 42.
37. Ibid., 74.
38. Ibid., 75.
39. *Hawl al-Qawmiya al-'Arabiya*, 1985 (1961), 87.
40. See his lecture, "Social education," in which he uses these expressions synonymously. *Ahadith fi al-Tarbiya wa al-Ijtima'*, 31.
41. *Ara' wa Ahadith fi al-'Ilm wa al-Akhlaq wa al-Thaqafa*, 32.
42. *Ahadith fi al-Tarbiya wa al-Ijtima'*, 26–36.
43. Al-Husri gives a slightly fuller description of the closed family unit in his article "East and West," in Ibid., 302. He does not mention the point about women in "Social education."
44. *Ahadith fi al-Tarbiya wa al-Ijtima'*, 35.
45. It is not clear to me whether al-Husri conceived of any link between the self-enclosed family structure of the East and colonialism, since elsewhere he ascribes the same moral defects to foreign rule. It may be that al-Husri changed his emphasis over time from the family to more general social conditions created by colonialism.
46. Ibid., 32–34.
47. Ibid., 37.
48. *Hawl al-Qawmiya al-'Arabiya*, 1985 (1961), 88.
49. See his article, "Active moral traits and positive virtues," *Ara' wa Ahadith fi al-'Ilm wa al-Akhlaq wa al-Thaqafa*, 167–172, at 171–172.
50. *Ahadith fi al-Tarbiya wa al-Ijtima'*, 36.
51. This comes from a speech entitled "Between material and spiritual powers," broadcast during World War II. *Safahat min al-Madi al-Qarib*, 44.
52. *Ara' wa Ahadith fi al-Wataniya wa al-Qawmiya*, 72.

4 The Moral Transformation of Femininity and the Rise of the Public–Private Distinction in Colonial Egypt

1. See especially Lila Abu-Lughod ed., *Remaking Women: Feminism and Modernity in the Middle East* (Princeton, PA: Princeton University Press, 1998); Beth Baron, *The Women's Awakening in Egypt: Culture, Society, and the Press* (New

Haven, CT: Yale University Press, 1994), and *Egypt as a Woman: Nationalism, Gender, and Politics* (Berkeley, CA: University of California Press, 2005); Marilyn Booth, *May Her Likes Be Multiplied: Biography and Gender Politics in Egypt* (Berkeley, CA: University of California Press, 2001); Lisa Pollard, *Nurturing the Nation: The Family Politics of Modernizing, Colonizing, and Liberating Egypt, 1805–1923* (Berkeley, CA: University of California Press, 2005); Mona L. Russell, *Creating the New Egyptian Woman: Consumerism, Education, and National Identity, 1863–1922* (New York: Palgrave Macmillan, 2004).
2. *Diwan*, 368.
3. Ibid., 168.
4. Ibid., 215.
5. Ibid., 216. The quotations and paraphrase are from lines 3 and 5–8 of the poem.
6. Ibid., 245.
7. Ibid., 211.
8. Ibid., 315, 396.
9. Ibid., 228.
10. Consider for example the poet's description of his grief over the death of his mother, which has the tenor of the following line: "She parted, and forbearance parted from me and I was visited time and again by a passion for her that emaciated my body and afflicted me with illness" (*Diwan*, 557).
11. I have made this argument regarding much earlier poetic representations of women in "Normative Notions of Public and Private in Early Islamic Culture" in *Harem Histories*, ed. Marilyn Booth, forthcoming.
12. See Jürgen Habermas, *The Structural Transformation of the Public Sphere: An Inquiry into a Category of Bourgeois Society*, tr. Thomas Burger (Cambridge, MA: MIT Press, 1998), 28, 49, 50.
13. As Foucault has argued, it is mistaken to interpret the exclusion of sexuality from public and private ideals as the repression of sexuality. See his refutation of "the repressive hypothesis" in *The History of Sexuality*, trans. Robert Hurley (New York: Vintage, 1980), vol. 1.
14. Abraham Marcus has provided a rich and suggestive study of pre-bourgeois norms and practices of privacy in "Privacy in Eighteenth-Century Aleppo: The Limits of Cultural Ideals," *International Journal of Middle Eastern Studies* 18 (1986): 165–183. He argues that the inhabitants of Aleppo had no explicit concept or "overarching ideal of privacy with a validity in its own right," but that norms connected with privacy "were actually derivates of more specific cultural preferences," values like "modesty, sexual morality, civility, respect, honor" (167). He distinguishes their attitudes from the modern notion of privacy. "In contrast with the obsessive harping on individualism, freedom, and personal autonomy in modern thought, the stress here was very much on the fulfillment of social obligations and mandatory practices necessary to guarantee the moral fabric of society as a whole" (168). Marcus's argument, however, that "what their ideals prescribed and recommended often collided with the demands and constraints of social circumstances" (178) shows a slippage between his concepts of "ideals" and "norms," which enables him to rely on,

though with many caveats, a false opposition or tension between norms and reality.
15. Ibn Hazm al-Andalusi, *Tawq al-Hamama fi-l-Ilfa wa-l-Ullaf*, ed. Ihsan Abbas (Tunis: Dar al-Ma'arif li-l-Tiba'a wa-l-Nashr, n.d.), 259.
16. Rifa'a al-Tahtawi, *Al-Murshid al-Amin li al-Banat wa al-Banin*, in *Al-A'mal al-Kamila li Rifa'a Rafi' al-Tahtawi*, ed. Muhammad Imara (Beirut: al-Mu'assasa al-'Arabiyya li al-Tiba'a wa al-Nashr, 1973), 2: 292–295, 393–395.
17. See especially pp. 639–645.
18. Ibid., 562. See also pp. 356, 391–392, 561, 635.
19. Ibid., 356. Emphasis added.
20. Ibid., 367–372.
21. Ibid., 373–375, 377–378.
22. Ibid., 375, 640–645.
23. *Al-Shawqiyat*, 1: 102–105. The date of the poem is given in Ahmad Shawqi, *al-Mawsu'a al-Shawqiya*, ed. Ibrahim al-Ibyari (Cairo: Anglo-Egyptian Press, 1982), part 1, vol.3, 33.
24. *Al-Shawqiyat*, 105.
25. This line (105) may be a reference to the women's demonstrations in the 1919 Revolution.
26. See pp. 46–48, 52. Habermas develops his view of the birth of humanity and freedom in the bourgeois home by contrast to the ancient Greek *oikos*. Whereas the former was conceived to be free of economic necessity and characterized by voluntary attachments, the latter was regarded as a domain of economic production, and thus necessity, and patriarchal domination (3–4, 28). For bourgeois individuals, the "intimate sphere of the conjugal family...and not the public sphere itself (as the Greek model would have it) was humanity's genuine site" (51–52).
27. Habermas recognizes the ideological dimension in what he calls the bourgeois family's "self-image," particularly in its suppression of the economic and social function of the family and in its reduction of patriarchal authority to voluntary relations of love. Nevertheless, he argues that there was necessarily some "subjective validity" to the familial ideals, else they could not have functioned. See pp. 46–48.
28. For a comprehensive account of the flood of articles and books published at the time in refutation and condemnation of Amin, see Mahir Hasan Fahmi, *Qasim Amin* (Cairo: al-Mu'asssasa al-Misriya al-'Amma li al-Ta'lif wa al-Nashr, n.d.), chap. 9.
29. Abduh's writings on issue's pertaining to women have been assembled and published in Muhammad Abduh, *al-Islam wa al-Mar'a fi Ra'y al-Imam Muhammad Abduh*, ed. Muhammad Imara (Cairo: al-Qahira li-al-Thaqafa al-'Arabiya, 1975).
30. Muhammad Imara, the editor of Qasim Amin's collected works, argues for Abduh's partial authorship of the book and recounts the history of the controversy. See Qasim Amin, *al-A'mal al-Kamila*, ed. Muhammad Imara (Cairo: Dar al-Shuruq, 1989), 124–133. A recent commentator, Zaynab al-Khudayri,

attempts to refute Imara's view in her introduction to an edition of Amin's *The New Woman*. See Zaynab Mahmud al-Khudayri, "Qira'a Jadida li-*al-Mar'a al-Jadida*" in Qasim Amin, *al-Mar'a al-Jadida* (Sina: Cairo, 1987), 31–36.

31. Abduh, *al-Islam wa al-Mar'a*, 74–76. Hereafter cited in the text.
32. Pollard, *Nurturing the Nation*, 154–161.
33. Marilyn Booth addresses this aspect of Amin's and others' writings on femininity in "Woman in Islam: Men and the 'Women's Press' in Turn-of-the-20th-Century Egypt," *International Journal of Middle Eastern Studies* 33 (2001), 171–201.
34. Qasim Amin, *al-Mar'a al-Jadida*, in Qasim Amin, *al-A'mal al-Kamila*, ed. Muhammad Imara (Cairo: Dar al-Shuruq, 1989), 417–517, 512. Hereafter cited in the text by page number.
35. *Tahrir al-Mar'a*, in *al-A'mal al-Kamila*, 247.
36. *Diwan*, 379.
37. Amin brings up the possible objection to his position that since women's function in the home is so critical, they should devote their full attention to it. He counters this by arguing that women who participate in the public sphere do not compromise their domestic duties, citing accounts of the American states in which women legislators had been elected.
38. See for example, Lisa Pollard, *Nurturing the Nation*, 161.
39. See Nabawiya Musa, *al-Mar'a wa al-'Amal* (Alexandria: al-Matba'a al-Wataniya, 1920), p.16. Aflatun quotes long passages from *The New Woman* in support of her feminist demands. See *Nahnu... al-Nisa' al-Misriyat* (Cairo: Matba'at al-Sa'ada, 1950), 90–98.
40. Abdullah Fikri, *al-Athar al-Fikriya*, ed. Amin Fikri (Cairo: al-Matba'a al-Kubra al-Amiriya, 1897), 36.
41. On Nasif's life, thought, and influence, see the articles published in *Min Ra'idat al-Qarn al-'Ishrin*, ed. Huda al-Sadda (Cairo: Multaqa al-Mar'a wa al-Dhakira, 2001), 23–90.
42. A collection of Nasif's speeches and articles was published in 1911 under the title *Nisa'iyat*, and was republished after her death in 1920. A more comprehensive collection was later made by her brother, *Athar Bahithat al-Badiya*, ed. Majd al-Din Hifni Nasif (Cairo: al-Mu'assasa al-Misriya al-'Amma li-l-ta'lif wa-l-tarjama wa-l-tiba'a wa-l-nashr, 1962).
43. *Athar Bahithat al-Badiya*, 281. See also pp. 102–103. Subsequent references are cited by page number in the text.
44. Nasif was on occasion pressed on her position, for example by Nabawiya Musa (280). In one of her poems, she defends herself against those who misinterpret her views, addressing an imagined female interlocutor (300–301):
    As for non-concealment (*sufur*), its status in law is not difficult.
    Of the authorities, some have prohibited it and others sanctioned it.
    It is permissible by consensus among them in the seeking of marriage.
    The veil (*niqab*) is not *hijab*, so lengthen it or shorten it...
    After the rulings of authorities there is no room for prattlers,
    So why have you heaped blame on me and joined my critics?...

You say, "The veil, you speak not of it." Yes, I made but a start, so you finish.
And why, I wonder, have you no interest in the matters I speak of?
45. Libya was invaded by Italy in 1911. Support of the Libyan resistance was a *cause célèbre* in Egypt, in which Nasif took an active role. See, for instance, her speech urging her female audience to aid the Libyan wounded (121).
46. Allowing women to attend public prayers is the first of a list of suggestions for the advancement of women made by Nasif at a national conference in 1910. See *Athar*, 124–129, 159–165.
47. See especially pp. 80–84, 91–94, 99–100, 106–110, 112–113, 170–180, 217–231.
48. See especially pp. 82, 84, 95–97, 102, 109.
49. See her article, "To the Fathers of Girls and the Religious Scholars," 293–296.

5 Fiction, Hegemony, and Aesthetic Citizenship

1. On the development of moral philosophy in eighteenth century Europe, see J.B. Schneewind, *The Invention of Autonomy: A History of Modern Moral Philosophy* (Cambridge: Cambridge University Press, 1998). On the change in psychological categories, see Amélie Oksenberg Rorty, "From Passions to Emotions and Sentiments," *Philosophy* 57(220) (1982): 159–172; Annette Baier, "What Emotions Are About", *Philosophical Perspectives* 4 (1990): 1–29; Susan James, *Passion and Action: The Emotions in Seventeenth-Century Philosophy* (Oxford: Clarendon, 1997); James Dixon, *From Passions to Emotions: The Creation of a Secular Psychological Category* (Cambridge: Cambridge University Press, 2003).
2. Jonathan Culler, "Anderson and the Novel," *Diacritics* 29.4 (Winter 1999): 23.
3. Ibid., 37.
4. Ibid., 37.
5. For Schmitt's distinction see Carl Schmitt, *The Concept of the Political*, trans. George Schwab (Chicago, IL: University of Chicago Press, 1996 [1932]), especially 27–49. For a fuller exposition of the ultimately moral nature of Schmitt's argument, see "Notes on *The Concept of the Political*" by Leo Strauss, appended to the same volume, 81–107 and also, Noorani, "The Rhetoric of Security," *Centennial Review* 5.1 (Spring 2005): 13–41.
6. Fredric Jameson, "Third World Literature in the Age of Multi-National Capitalism," *Social Text*, 15 (Autumn 1986): 69.
7. Ibid., 71.
8. Ibid., 72.
9. Ibid., 76.
10. Ibid., 69, original emphasis removed.
11. Ibid., 73.
12. See Chapter 4.

13. Friedrich Schiller, *On the Aesthetic Education of Man*, trans. Reginald Snell (New York: Dover, 2004).
14. For the discussion of the deficit of modern society, see pp. 36–43.
15. For the discussion of how beauty unites and liberates these faculties, see especially pp. 96–109.
16. Ahmad Amin, *Kitab al-Akhlaq* (Cairo: Maktabat al-Nahda al-Misriya, 1967), 10.
17. Ibid., 15.
18. Ibid., 49.
19. Muhammad Husayn Haykal, *Thawrat al-Adab* (Cairo: Maktabat al-Nahda al-Misriyya, 1965). On Haykal's thought and political activity, see Charles Smith, *Islam and the Search for Social Order in Modern Egypt: A Biography of Muhammad Husayn Haykal* (Albany, NY: State University of New York Press, 1983).
20. Salama Musa, *Fann al-Hubb wa al-Haya* (Beirut: Maktabat al-Ma'arif, n.d.). This book consists primarily of articles published in the 1940s and perhaps earlier.
21. "We don't cooperate in sexual pleasure; rather, we steal it in mad ecstasy and in a momentary seizure that we quickly lose and return to what is nearly despair, stasis and repugnance." 86.
22. Musa gives contradictory and unreconciled accounts of the origin of love and rationality. In one section, Musa argues that love and art are the product of "confined" and sublimated sexuality (51). Elsewhere, he opposes sexual instinct, which is "blind" and "violent," to the instinct of maternal love, which he argues is the true origin of human love and rationality (76). This duality of instinct is left unresolved.
23. Sayyid Qutb, *Al-adala al-ijtima'iya fi al-islam* (Cairo: Isa al-Babi al-Halabi, 1964), 4–19. This book, *Social Justice in Islam*, was first published in 1949.
24. Qutb calls this principle *"al-hakimiya,"* divine rulership. Ibid., 94.
25. M.M. Bakhtin, "The *Bildungsroman* and its Significance in the History of Realism (Toward a Historical Typology of the Novel)," in M.M. Bakhtin, *Speech Genres & Other Late Essays*, trans. Vern W. McGee (Austin. TX: University of Texas, 1986), 22–23.
26. On the *Bildungsroman*, see also Franco Moretti, *The Way of the World: The Bildungsroman in European Culture*, trans. Albert Sbragia (London: Verso, 2000). On this form in Arabic, see Muhammad Siddiq, *Arab Culture and the Novel: Genre, Identity and Agency in Egyptian Fiction* (London: Routledge, 2007).
27. On this novel, see Jeff Shalan, "Writing the Nation: The Emergence of Egypt in the Modern Arabic Novel," *Journal of Arabic Literature* 33(3) (2002): 211–247; Paul Starkey, *From the Ivory Tower: A Critical Study of Tawfiq al-Hakim* (London: Ithaca Press, 1987), 84–92, 118–129; Mahmud Amin al-Alim, *Tawfiq al-Hakim Mufakkiran wa Fannanan* (Dar Shuhdi li-al-Nashr: Cairo, 1985), 41–51; Abd al-Muhsin Taha Badr, *Tatawwur al-Riwaya al-'Arabiya al-Haditha fi Misr 1880–1938* (Cairo: Dar al-Ma'arif, 1963). On

al-Hakim's thought, see Jurj Tarabishi, *Lu'bat al-Hulm wa al-Waqi'* (Beirut: Dar al-Tali'a, 1972).

28. Tawfiq al-Hakim, *'Awdat al-Ruh* (Cairo: Maktabat al-Adab, n.d.), 2 vols., 2: 246. All further references to this work will be made in the text by volume and page number.

29. Shalan, in "Writing the Nation" (244–246), argues that social communion requires the "displacement" or "sacrifice" of Saniya. His view is that Saniya's character plays two contradictory roles in the novel—a mythic role, as Isis, and the disembodied "worshipped one," which unifies the community, and the role of a desirable female, which attracts males as individuals and causes antagonism. The novel attempts to resolve this, unsuccessfully, by replacing Saniya with Muhsin. The problem with this view is that the nature of Saniya's mythical meaning and how it induces unity is unclear. It cannot be simply that she resembles the picture of Isis in Muhsin's textbook. In fact, Muhsin does not worship her because of any perceived mythical meaning, but because of her beauty, which stimulates authentic desire. Moreover, although Saniya is excluded from social integration at the spiritual level, she remains necessary for inducing it. This is more apparent in her relationship with Mustafa, which Shalan does not discuss.

30. On the moral superiority of the Egyptian peasants in respect to Arab bedouins, 2: 24–28. For the tyranny and cruelty of the Turkish element of the ruling class, 2: 16–23.

31. The novel has been widely criticized for its manner of depicting the 1919 Revolution and incorporating it into the narrative, as well as for its general lack of historicity. See for instance al-Alim, *Tawfiq al-Hakim* 41–51; Badr, *Tatawwur al-Riwaya*, 386; Shalan, "Writing the Nation," 245.

32. On the class-hierarchical function of aesthetic taste, see Pierre Bourdieu, *Distinction: A Social Critique of the Judgment of Taste* (Cambridge, MA: Harvard University Press, 1984).

6 Excess, Rebellion, and Revolution: Egyptian Modernity in the *Trilogy*

1. On the *Trilogy* see Rasheed El-Enany, *Naguib Mahfouz: The Pursuit of Meaning* (London: Routledge, 1993), 68–88; Muhammad Siddiq, *Arab Culture and the Novel*, 120–147; Ghali Shukri, *al-Muntami: dirasa fi adab Nagib Mahfuz* (Beirut: Dar al-Afaq al-Jadida, 1982); Mahmud Amin al-Alim, *Ta'ammulat fi 'Alam Najib Mahfuz* (Cairo: al-Hay'a al-Misriya al-'Amma li al-Ta'lif wa al-Nashr, 1970), chap. 3.

2. The influence of the vitalist philosopher Henri Bergson ("*élan vital*") on Mahfuz is well-known, and Bergson is mentioned in the *Trilogy* (911, 934). See El-Enany, *Naguib Mahfouz*, pp.14–16. Bergson had a general popularity among Egyptian thinkers in the 1930s and thereafter. See for example, David Semah, *Four Egyptian Literary Critics* (Leiden: Brill, 1974), 99, 100, 163.

3. The failure of the main characters in the *Trilogy* to achieve maturity and integration has been pointed out by Christian Szyska. See "Liminality, Structure, and Anti-Structure in Najib Mahfuz's Cairo *Trilogy*," in *Understanding Near Eastern Literatures*, eds. Verena Klemm and Beatrice Gruendler (Wiesbaden: Reichert Verlag, 2000), 215–229. Szyska connects this failure with the social-historical factor of "cultural transitions in which traditional patterns of ritual passages lose their power to relate the subject to existence" (227). I will argue that this failure is a fundamental representational strategy of the *Trilogy*.
4. The eminent writer al-Aqqad, for example, held that artistic genius derives from psychic illness, and that therefore psychoanalysis provides the only scientific basis for literary criticism. Aqqad and a number of other critics wrote psychoanalytic studies of classical authors. He also authored a novel, *Sara*, which relies on psychoanalytic elements.
5. Mahfuz began his career in letters publishing short philosophical articles for Musa's journal *al-Majalla al-Jadida* throughout the 1930s. In the *Trilogy*, the Marxist activist Ahmad Shawkat joins the staff of the journal "al-Insan al-Jadid," whose editor is 'Adli Karim, the character based on Musa.
6. Salama Musa, *Fann al-Hubb wa al-Haya*, 17.
7. Ibid., 86.
8. I have in mind here Mahjub Abd al-Da'im, in *al-Qahira al-Jadida* ("The new Cairo," 1946); Hamida in *Zuqaq al-Midaqq* (Midaqq Alley, 1947); and less explicitly, Hasanayn in *Bidaya wa Nihaya* ("A beginning and an end," 1949).
9. Mahjub is sexually attracted to his wealthy relative's daughter because of her aristocratic status and carriage rather than her looks alone. Although Hamida happily becomes a prostitute, "her deviance was not in the strength of her lust...she craved with her soul and body after appearances, power and battle..." (1: 756). Hasanayn desires the aristocratic daughter of his family's wealthy patron instead of his fiancée to whom he is more attracted for the same reasons as Mahjub. "How beautiful it would be to own this mansion and lie on this girl...To mount her would be to mount an entire class!" he thinks. And the narrator comments, "it was not lust alone but power and domination" (1: 265; see also 1: 282). In the *Trilogy*, numerous characters employ their sexuality to further their social ambitions.
10. The most extreme example of this type is Nafisa, in *Bidaya wa Nihaya*. "She was nothing but a captive of the body and of poverty, not knowing how to deliver herself from them." *Mu'allafat*, 2: 267.
11. Examples in the *Trilogy* are the Shawkat brothers who marry Aisha and Khadija, and the mature Isma'il Latif, Kamal's formerly wealthy and dissolute friend.
12. Christian Szyska refers to this division as one between "structure" and "anti-structure," which he seems to regard, however, as characterizing the world of the novel as a whole rather than just the traditional order of Sayyid Ahmad. See his article "Liminality, Structure, and Anti-Structure in Najib Mahfuz's Cairo *Trilogy*," especially 221.
13. *Bayn al-Qasrayn* in *al-Mu'allafat al-Kamila* (Beirut: Maktabat Lubnan, 1991), 2: 347–348. All references to the *Trilogy* hereafter will be made in the text by page number of this volume.

14. The narrator comments to this effect on a number of occasions. Take, for example, Sayyid Ahmad's desire to marry Khadija before her younger sister Aisha, despite countervailing pressures, in order to avoid injuring Khadija's feelings. The narrator tells us that this is because of his "delicate heart, more delicate than most would guess, indeed, more delicate than it should be...how happy it made him to sacrifice anything of value for the sake of the happiness of his daughters..." (441).
15. *Khan al-Khalili*, in *al-Mu'allafat al-Kamila*, 1: 536.
16. The description of this syndrome belongs to the early development of Freud's oedipal theory; it is unclear how it fits into the theory as it later developed. See "On the Universal Tendency to Debasement in Love," in *The Complete Psychological Works of Sigmund Freud*, ed. James Strachey (London: The Hogarth Press, 1957), 11: 177–190. This article is cited by Muhammad Siddiq in his analysis of Kamal in the *Trilogy* (*Arab Culture and the Novel*, 222, n.44). Siddiq however does not mention Kamil of *al-Sarab*, for whom this "syndrome" is much more apparent. Kamal in the *Trilogy* is not shown to have attraction for women he finds ugly, and it is made clear that the prostitute he frequents in the third book differs from Aida in that she is voluptuous, but in no way portrayed as repulsive.
17. *Al-Sarab*, in *Mu'allafat*, 2: 37.
18. The opposition between renunciation of the world and gratification in it, as the two poles of human desire, is characterized in the *Trilogy* and elsewhere as the opposition between the ascetic poet Abu al-Ala' al-Ma'arri and the wine poet Omar Khayyam. See, for example, the biographical précis of the socialist character Ali Taha in *al-Qahira al-Jadida* (*The New Cairo*) in *al-Mu'allafat al-Kamila*, 1: 438–439.
19. Muhammad Siddiq argues from a psychoanalytic perspective, in *Arab Culture and the Novel*, that Kamal's infatuation with his sister is the central feature of his character (see pp. 137–139). In my reading, she is but one of a series of objects of desire culminating in Aida.
20. 350. Women do not generally smoke in public in Egypt, even to the present day. In the *Trilogy*, Amina is horrified when she finds out that Aisha has taken up smoking at home with her husband. Later, after Aisha loses her husband and two sons, she is allowed to smoke in her father's house, and this habit serves as a mark of her devastation.
21. The association of blond hair with love and moral/political betrayal recurs in Mahfuz's fiction. For example, in the story "God's world," a married, middle-aged, down-trodden office servant falls in love with a street girl known as "the English girl" for her blond hair. He absconds with his bureau's payroll and elopes with her, only to catch her one night trying to steal the money from him. See "Dunya Allah" in *Dunya Allah* (Cairo: Maktabat Misr, 1963).
22. Emphasis added. Kamal's predecessor Kamil had the same realization. "I now realize the secret of the ecstasy of wine. It is love. Love and the ecstasy of wine are from the same sap that drips from the essence of the spirit. Is happy love anything other than extended drunkenness?" (2: 52). This connection between love, intoxication, and the life force seems to come from an extended

passage on the topic by Abbas Mahmud al-Aqqad in his article "The Origin of Beauty in the View of Science," in *Mutala'at fi al-Kutub wa al-Haya* (Beirut: Dar al-Kitab al-'Arabi, 1966), 69.

23. He is clearly named after the legendary Yemeni king, Shaddad ibn Ad, who built the fabulous city of Iram to outdo God's paradise, only for God to strike him down by turning everyone in it to stone. Thus, Shaddad Bey's glorious mansion is lost and eventually demolished.

24. Nearly twenty years after last seeing Aida, Kamal still feels that if he were to learn that Aida had sometime returned his love, "it would console him of all the pain he felt in the past and present and he would consider himself happy among beings and that his life had not passed in vain..." (927). Later, when he falls in love with Aida's younger sister, it is still Aida that he looks for in her but fails to find (932, 943). Nevertheless, letting her slip away allows him to relive the loss of Aida once more (948).

25. When Sayyid Ahmad signs the petition declaring Sa'd Zaghlul to be the representative of the Egyptian people, he tells the friend who has brought it to him, "I am so happy with this patriotic petition that it is if I were drunk on my eighth glass between the thighs of Zubayda!" (491). The narrator discusses Sayyid Ahmad's patriotic feelings and limits on 491–492.

26. The lack of political and social content in Fahmi's patriotism and its personal nature is pointed out by Sami Khashaba in "Fahmi 'Abd al-Jawad," *Najib Mahfuz: Ibda' Nisf Qarn*, ed. Ghali Shukri (Beirut: Dar al-Shuruq, 1989), 77–90.

27. Two other women, the *'alima* Zubayda, and her niece Zannuba, are not exceptions to the novel's punishment of beauty/sexuality. This is because they conform to the rules of their "legitimate" position within the traditional order, which is to provide pleasure to its patriarchs. When Zannuba gets married, she conforms to her new rules as a respectable middle-class wife, and gives up the manipulation of her beauty and sexuality. It is interesting the extent to which the novel treats the traditional order as fully legitimate and punishes all transgressions of it. Miriam Cooke discusses the "fallen" female characters in Mahfuz in "Men Constructed in the Mirror of Prostitution," in *Naguib Mahfouz: From Regional Fame to Global Recognition*, ed. Michael Beard and Adnan Haydar, (Syracuse: Syracuse University Press, 1993), 106–125.

28. *Atahaddathu Ilaykum*, 45.

29. 883, 936, 954. The sagely editor of Ahmad's journal, modeled on Salama Musa, says the following of the Muslim Brotherhood: "Don't you see that they address people's minds with our language, speaking of the socialism of Islam?... If their revolution precedes ours they will realize some of our principles at least partially, but they cannot stop the advancing movement of time toward its necessary goal." (954).

30. *al-Muntami* (Cairo: Dar al-Ma'arif bi-Misr, 1969), 62.

31. Kamal himself recognizes this. "He envied [Ahmad] his courage and strength of will aside from other qualities that were denied him, above all [Ahmad's] faith, work and marrying, as though [Ahmad] had been sent to the family in order to redeem his own passivity and negativity" (941). Reflecting on both

brothers: "The new generation cuts its difficult path toward a clear goal without doubt or perplexity; what is the secret of his own pernicious illness?" (872).
32. Mahfuz on numerous occasions identified himself with Kamal, and claimed that many others did as well. For example, "the intellectual crisis of Kamal was the crisis of our entire generation; I regarded it as particular to myself until friends and critics also laid claim to it." *Atahaddathu Ilaykum*, 48.
33. Kamal's close friend happens to be a Copt and brings the issue of minority oppression into the novel (881–882). Ahmad must overcome his "bourgeois" expectations regarding femininity, with the help of his future wife, before she agrees to their marriage (911–912, 936, 938).
34. It is significant that as the novel closes, Kamal, having learned of Aida's death and facing the imminent death of his mother, repudiates his "childish romanticism" (968).

Bibliography

Abd al-Muttalib, Muhammad. *Diwan Abd al-Muttalib*. Ed. Muhammad al-Hirawi. Cairo: Matba' al-I'timad, n.d.

Abduh, Muhammad. *al-Islam wa al-Mar'a fi Ra'y al-Imam Muhammad 'Abduh*. Ed. Muhammad 'Imara. Cairo: al-Qahira li-al-Thaqafa al-'Arabiya, 1975.

Al-Azmeh, Aziz. *Ibn Khaldun, an Essay in Reinterpretation*. London: Cass, 1982.

——— *Muslim Kingship: Power and the Sacred in Muslim, Christian and Pagan Polities*. London: I.B. Tauris, 1997.

al-Afghani, Jamal al-Din and Muhammad Abduh. *al-'Urwa al-Wuthqa*. Ed. Salah al-Din al-Bustani. Cairo: Dar al-'Arab, 1993.

Aflatun, Inji. *Nahnu... al-Nisa' al-Misriyat*. Cairo: Matba'at al-Sa'ada, 1950.

al-Alim, Mahmud Amin. *Ta'ammulat fi 'alam Najib Mahfuz*. Cairo: al-Hay'a al-Misriya al-'Amma li al-Ta'lif wa al-Nashr, 1970.

Allen, Roger M. A., Hilary Kilpatrick, and Ed de Moor. *Love and Sexuality in Modern Arabic Literature*. London: Saqi Books, 1995.

Amin, Ahmad. *Kitab al-Akhlaq*. Cairo: Maktabat al-Nahda al-Misriya, 1967.

Amin, Qasim. *al-A'mal al-Kamila*. Ed. Muhammad 'Imara. Cairo: Dar al-Shuruq, 1989.

——— *al-Mar'a al-Jadida*. In *al-A'mal al-Kamila*.

——— *Tahrir al-Mar'a*. In *al-A'mal al-Kamila*.

Anderson, Benedict R. *Imagined Communities: Reflections on the Origin and Spread of Nationalism*. London: Verso, 1991.

Antonius, George. *The Arab Awakening: The Story of the Arab National Movement*. London: H. Hamilton, 1938.

al-Aqqad, Abbas Mahmud. *Mutala'at fi al-kutub wa al-haya*. Beirut: Dar al-Kitab al-'Arabi, 1966.

Bakhtin, M. M. *Speech Genres & Other Late Essays*. Trans. Vern W. McGee. Austin, TX: University of Texas, 1986.

Badr, Abd al-Muhsin Taha. *Najib Mahfuz al-Ru'ya wa al-Ada*. Cairo: Dar al-Thaqafa, 1978.

——— *Tatawwur al-Riwaya al-'Arabiya al-Haditha fi Misr 1880–1938*. Cairo: Dar al-Ma'arif, 1963.

Baron, Beth. *The Women's Awakening in Egypt: Culture, Society, and the Press*. New Haven, CT: Yale University Press, 1994.

——— *Egypt as a Woman: Nationalism, Gender, and Politics*. Berkeley, CA: University of California Press, 2005.

al-Barudi, Mahmud Sami. *Diwan al-Barudi*. Eds. Ali Jarim and Muhammad Shafiq Ma'ruf. Cairo: Dar al-Ma'arif, 1971.
Bayly, C. A. *Origins of Nationality in South Asia: Patriotism and Ethical Government in the Making of Modern India*. Delhi: Oxford University Press, 2001.
Berque, Jacques *Egypt: Imperialism and Revolution*. Trans. Jean Stewart. London: Faber & Faber, 1972.
Booth, Marilyn. *May Her Likes Be Multiplied: Biography and Gender Politics in Egypt*. Berkeley, CA: University of California Press, 2001.
——— "*Woman in Islam*: Men and the 'Women's Press' in Turn-of-the-20th-Century Egypt," *International Journal of Middle Eastern Studies* 33 (2001): 171–201.
Bourdieu, Pierre. *Distinction: A Social Critique of the Judgement of Taste*. Cambridge, MA: Harvard University Press, 1984.
Breuilly, John. *Nationalism and the State*. Manchester: Manchester University Press, 1993.
al-Buhturi, al-Walid b. Ubayd. *Diwan al-Buhturi*. Ed. Hasan Kamil Sayrafi. Cairo: Dar al-Ma'arif, 1963.
Chakrabarty, Dipesh. *Provincializing Europe: Postcolonial Thought and Historical Difference*. Princeton, NJ: Princeton University Press, 2000.
Chatterjee, Partha. *Nationalist Thought and the Colonial World: A Derivative Discourse?* Third World books. London: Zed Books, 1986.
Cole, Juan Ricardo. *Colonialism and Revolution in the Middle East: Social and Cultural Origins of Egypt's 'Urabi Movement*. Princeton, NJ: Princeton University Press, 1993.
Cooke, Miriam. "Men Constructed in the Mirror of Prostitution." In *Naguib Mahfouz: From Regional Fame to Global Recognition*. Eds. Michael Beard and Adnan Haydar (pp. 106–125). Syracuse: Syracuse University Press, 1993.
Crone, Patricia. *God's Rule: Government and Islam*. New York: Columbia University Press, 2004.
Culler, Jonathan, "Anderson and the Novel", *Diacritics* 29.4 (Winter 1999): 20–39, 23.
al-Dasuqi, Umar. *Fi al-adab al-hadith*. Cairo: Dar al-fikr al-'Arabi, 1964.
Dayf, Shawqi. *al-Ritha'*. Cairo: Dar al-Ma'arif, 1968.
Dawn, C. Ernest. *From Ottomanism to Arabism; Essays on the Origins of Arab Nationalism*. Urbana, IL: University of Illinois Press, 1973.
Dixon, Thomas. *From Passions to Emotions: The Creation of a Secular Psychological Category*. Cambridge: Cambridge University Press, 2003.
Du Pont de Nemours, Pierre Samuel, and François Quesnay. *Physiocratie, ou, Constitution naturelle du gouvernement le plus avantageux au genre humain*. Yverdon: [s.n.], 1768.
El-Enany, Rasheed. *Naguib Mahfouz: The Pursuit of Meaning*. London: Routledge, 1993.
Eppel, Michael. "The Elite, the Effendiyya, and the Growth of Nationalism and Pan-Arabism in Hashemite Iraq, 1921–1958," *International Journal of Middle East Studies* 30(2) (1998): 227–250.

Fahmi, Mahir Hasan. *Qasim Amin* Cairo: al-Mu'asssasa al-Misriya al-'Amma li al-Ta'lif wa al-Nashr, n.d.
Fakhry, Majid. *Ethical Theories in Islam.* Leiden: E.J. Brill, 1991.
al-Farazdaq. *Diwan al-Farazdaq.* Beirut: Dar Sadir, 1966.
Fikri, Abdullah. *al-Athar al-fikriya.* Ed. Amin Fikri. Cairo: al-Matba'a al-Kubra al-Amiriya, 1897.
Foucault, Michel. *The History of Sexuality.* New York: Pantheon Books, 1978.
——— *Power.* Ed. James D. Faubion. New York: New Press, 2000.
——— *Security, Territory, Population: Lectures at the Collège de France.* Ed. Michel Senellart. Trans. Graham Burchell. Basingstoke: Palgrave Macmillan, 2007.
Freud, Sigmund. *The Standard Edition of the Complete Psychological Works of Sigmund Freud.* Ed. James Strachey, 23 vols., London, 1957.
——— "On the Universal Tendency to Debasement in Love," in *The Standard Edition*, vol. 11, 177–190.
——— "On Narcissism: An Introduction," in *The Standard Edition*, vol. 14.
——— "The Ego and the Id," in *The Standard Edition*, vol. 19.
Gellner, Ernest. *Nations and Nationalism.* Ithaca, NY: Cornell University Press, 1983.
Gershoni, I., and James P. Jankowski. *Redefining the Egyptian Nation, 1930–1945.* Cambridge: Cambridge University Press, 1995.
——— *Commemorating the Nation: Collective Memory, Public Commemoration, and National Identity in Twentieth-Century Egypt.* Chicago: Middle East Documentation Center, 2004.
al-Ghazali, Abu Hamid Muhammad. *Ihya' 'ulum al-din.* 5 vols. Halab: Dar al-Wa'y, 1998.
——— *Mizan al-'amal.* Ed. Sulayman Dunya. Cairo: Dar al-Ma'arif, 1964.
Gibb, H. A. R. *The Encyclopaedia of Islam.* Leiden: Brill, 1960.
Gramsci, Antonio. *Selections from the Prison Notebooks of Antonio Gramsci.* Trans. Quintin Hoare and Geoffrey Nowell-Smith. New York: International Publishers, 1972.
Guha, Ranajit. *Dominance Without Hegemony: History and Power in Colonial India.* Delhi: Oxford University Press, 1998.
Habermas, Jürgen. *The Structural Transformation of the Public Sphere: An Inquiry into a Category of Bourgeois Society.* Trans. Thomas Burger. Cambridge, MA: MIT Press, 1998.
al-Hadidi, Ali Muhammad. *Mahmud Sami al-Barudi, sha'ir al-nahda.* Cairo: al-Maktaba al-Anglu-Misriya, 1969.
al-Hadidy, Alaa al-Din. "Mustafa al-Nahhas and Political Leadership." In *Contemporary Egypt through Egyptian Eyes: Essays in Honour of P.J. Vatikiotis.* Ed. Charles Tripp (pp. 72–88). London: Routledge, 1993.
Haim, Sylvia. "Alfieri and al-Kawakibi," *Oriento Moderno* 34 (1954): 132–143.
——— "Islam and the Theory of Arab Nationalism," *Die Welt des Islams* 4(2/3) (1955): 124–149.
al-Hakim, Tawfiq. *'Awdat al-ruh.* Cairo: Maktabat al-Adab, n.d.
Haqqi, Yayhya. "Marathi Shawqi," in *al-Majalla* 144 (1968): 62–63.

Haykal, Muhammad Husayn. *Thawrat al-adab.* Cairo: Maktabat al-Nahda al-Misriya, 1965.
Hirschman, Albert O. *The Passions and the Interests: Political Arguments for Capitalism Before Its Triumph.* Princeton, NJ: Princeton University Press, 1997.
Hourani, Albert. *Arabic Thought in the Liberal Age 1798–1939.* London: Oxford University Press, 1962.
Horkheimer, Max, and Theodor W. Adorno. *Dialectic of Enlightenment.* New York: Continuum, 1982.
al-Husri, Sati'. *Abhath mukhtara fi al-qawmiya al-'arabiya.* Beirut: Markaz al-Dirasat al-Wahda al-'Arabiya, 1985.
—— *Ahadith fi al-tarbiya wa al-ijtima'.* Beirut: Markaz al-Dirasat al-Wahda al-'Arabiya, 1984.
—— *Ara' wa ahadıth fi al-wataniya wa al-qawmiya.* Beirut: Markaz al-Dirasat al-Wahda al-'Arabiya, 1985.
—— *Fi al-lugha wa al-adab wa 'ilaqatihima bi al-qawmiya.* Beirut: Markaz al-Dirasat al-Wahda al-'Arabiya, 1985.
—— *Hawl al-qawmiya al-'Arabiya.* Beirut: Markaz al-Dirasat al-Wahda al-'Arabiya, 1985.
—— *al-Iqlimiya: judhuruha wa budhuruha.* Beirut: Markaz al-Dirasat al-Wahda al-'Arabiya, 1985.
—— *Ma hiya al-qawmiya.* Beirut: Markaz al-Dirasat al-Wahda al-'Arabiya, 1985.
—— *Muhadarat fi nushu' al-fikra al-qawmiya.* Beirut: Markaz al-Dirasat al-Wahda al-'Arabiya, 1985.
—— *Safahat min al-madi al-qarib.* Beirut: Markaz al-Dirasat al-Wahda al-'Arabiya, 1984.
Ibn al-Mu'tazz, Abdullah. *Diwan ash'ar al-amir Abi al-Abbas Ibn al-Mu'tazz.* Ed. Muhammad Badi' Sharif. Cairo: Dar al-Ma'arif, 1977.
Ibn Hazm al-Andalusi, *Tawq al-hamama fi-l-ilfa wa-l-ullaf*. Ed. Ihsan Abbas. Tunis: Dar al-Ma'arif li-l-Tiba'a wa-l-Nashr, n.d.
Ibn Khaldun, Abd al-Rahman b. Muhammad, *Tarikh Ibn Khaldun.* Beirut: Dar al-Kutub al-'Ilmiyah, 1992.
Ibn Rashiq al-Qayrawani. *Kitab al-'umda fi mahasin al-shi'r wa adabihi wa naqdihi.* Beirut: Dar al-Jil, 1981.
Ibn Taymiya, Ahmad b. Abd al-Halim. *al-Siyasa al-shar'iya fi islah al-ra'i wa al-ra'iya.* Giza: Dar al-Furuq, 2008.
Ibrahim, Hafiz. *Diwan Hafiz Ibrahim.* Ed. Ahmad Amin, Ahmad al-Zayn, and Ibrahim Ibyari. Cairo: al-Hay'a al-'Amma al-Misriya li al-Kitab, 1980.
Ishaq, Adib. *Muntakhabat dimn arba'at ajza'.* Alexandria: Matba'at al-Adab, 1885?
al-Jahiz, Amr b. Bahr. *Rasa'il al-Jahiz.* Ed. Abd al-Salam Harun. Cairo: Maktabat al-Khanji, 1964.
Fredric Jameson. "Third World Literature in the Age of Multi-National Capitalism," *Social Text* 15 (1986): 65–88.
Jankowski, James P., and I. Gershoni. *Rethinking Nationalism in the Arab Middle East.* New York: Columbia University Press, 1997.

Keddie, Nikki R. *Sayyid Jamal Ad-Din "Al-Afghani"; A Political Biography.* Berkeley, CA: University of California Press, 1972.
Kedourie, Elie. *Nationalism.* New York: Praeger, 1961.
——— *Arab Political Memoirs and Other Studies.* London: Cass, 1974.
Khalidi, Rashid. *The Origins of Arab Nationalism.* New York: Columbia University Press, 1991.
Khashaba, Sami. "Fahmi 'Abd al-Jawad." In *Najib Mahfuz: Ibda' nisf qarn.* Ed. Ghali Shukri (pp. 77–90). Beirut: Dar al-Shuruq, 1989.
Khatib, Bushra. *al-Ritha' fi al-shi'r al-jahili wa sadr al-Islam.* Baghdad: Mudiriyat Matba'at al-Idara Mahalliya, 1977.
Khouri, Mounah Abdallah. *Poetry and the Making of Modern Egypt (1882–1922).* Leiden: E.J. Brill, 1971.
al-Khudayri, Zaynab Mahmud. "Qira'a Jadida li-*al-Mar'a al-Jadida*." In Qasim Amin, *al-Mar'a al-jadida.* Sina: Cairo, 1987.
Laclau, Ernesto, and Chantal Mouffe. *Hegemony and Socialist Strategy: Towards a Radical Democratic Politics.* London: Verso, 1985.
Lane, E.W. *An Account of the Manners and Customs of the Modern Egyptians.* London: Ward, Lock and Co., 1890.
Lockman, Zachary. "Imagining the Working Class: Culture, Nationalism, and Class Formation in Egypt, 1899–1914," *Poetics Today* 15(2) (1994): 157–190.
Loraux, Nicole. *The Invention of Athens.* Translated by Alan Sheridan. Cambridge, MA: Harvard University Press, 1986.
Mahdi, Muhsin. *Ibn Khaldun's Philosophy of History: A Study in the Philosophic Foundation of the Science of Culture.* Chicago, IL: University of Chicago Press, 1964.
Mahfuz, Nagib. *al-Mu'allafat al-kamila.* Beirut: Maktabat Lubnan, 1994.
——— *al-Qahira al-jadida.* In *al-Mu'allafat al-kamila,* vol. 1.
——— *Khan al-Khalili.* In *al-Mu'allafat al-kamila,* vol. 1.
——— *Zuqaq al-Midaqq.* In *al-Mu'allafat al-kamila,* vol. 1.
——— *Al-sarab.* In *al-Mu'allafat al-kamila,* vol. 2.
——— *Bidaya wa nihaya.* In *al-Mu'allafat al-kamila,* vol. 2.
——— *Bayn al-Qasrayn.* In *al-Mu'allafat al-kamila,* vol. 2.
——— *Qasr al-Shawq.* In *al-Mu'allafat al-kamila,* vol. 2.
——— *Al-Sukkariya.* In *al-Mu'allafat al-kamila,* vol. 2.
——— *Dunya Allah.* Cairo: Maktabat Misr, 1963.
——— *Atahaddathu ilaykum.* Beirut: Dar al-'Awda, 1977.
al-Marsafi, Husayn. *al-Wasila al-adabiya li-l-'ulum al-'Arabiya.* Cairo: al-Matba'a al-Malikiya, 1289–1292 A.H.
Marcus, Abraham. "Privacy in Eighteenth-Century Aleppo: The Limits of Cultural Ideals," *International Journal of Middle Eastern Studies* 18 (1986): 165–183.
al-Mawardi, Ali b. Muhammad. *Adab al-dunya wa-al-din.* Ed. Abd Allah Ahmad Abu Zina. Cairo: Dar al-Sha'b, 1979.
——— *al-Ahkam al-sultaniya wa al-wilayat al-diniya.* Ed. Muhammad Fahmi Adil Sirjani. Cairo: al-Maktaba al-Tawfiqiya, 1978.
Miskawayh, Abu Ali Ahmad b. Muhammad al-Razi. *Tahdhib al-akhlaq wa ta'thir al-a'raq.* Beirut: Dar Maktabat al-Haya, 1980.

Mitchell, Timothy. *Colonising Egypt.* Cambridge: Cambridge University Press, 1988.
Moreh, Shmuel. *Studies in Modern Arabic Prose and Poetry.* Leiden: E.J. Brill, 1988.
Moretti, Franco. *The Way of the World: The Bildungsroman in European Culture.* Trans. Albert Sbragia. London: Verso, 2000.
Musa, Nabawiya. *al-Mar'a wa al-'amal.* Alexandria: al-Matba'a al-Wataniya, 1920.
Musa, Salama. *Fann al-hubb wa al-haya.* Beirut: Maktabat al-Ma'arif, n.d.
Mutran, Khalil. *Diwan al-Khalil.* Beirut: Dar al-Kitab al-'Arabi, 1967.
Nasif, Malak Hifni. *Athar Bahithat al-Badiya.* Ed. Majd al-Din Hifni Nasif. Cairo: al-Mu'assasa al-Misriya al-'Amma li-l-ta'lif wa al-tarjama wa al-tiba'a wa al-nashr, 1962.
Noorani, Yaseen. "Heterotopia and the Wine Poem in Early Islamic Culture." *International Journal of Middle East Studies* 36 (August 2004): 345–366.
——— "The Rhetoric of Security." *Centennial Review* 5.1 (Spring 2005): 13–41.
Pollard, Lisa. *Nurturing the Nation: The Family Politics of Modernizing, Colonizing and Liberating Egypt (1805/1923).* Berkeley, CA: University of California Press, 2005.
Qutb, Sayyid. *al-'Adala al-ijtima'iya fi al-islam.* Cairo: Isa al-Babi al-Halabi, 1964.
Rabi', Muhammad Mahmud. *al-Nazariya al-siyasiya li-Ibn Khaldun.* Cairo: Dar al-Hana, 1981.
al-Rafi'i, Abd al-Rahman. *Mustafa Kamil ba'ith al-haraka al-wataniya.* Cairo: Dar al-Nahda al-Misriya, 1962.
Rahme, Joseph G. "Abd al-Rahman al-Kawakibi's Reformist Ideology, Arab Pan-Islamism, and the Internal other," *Journal of Islamic Studies* 10 (1999):159–177.
Russell, Mona L. *Creating the New Egyptian Woman: Consumerism, Education, and National Identity, 1863–1922.* New York: Palgrave Macmillan, 2004.
Ryzova, Lucie. "Egyptianizing Modernity through the 'New *Effendiya*' : Social and Cultural Constructions of the Middle Class in Egypt under the Monarchy." In *Re-Envisioning Egypt 1919–1952.* Eds. Arthur Goldschmidt, Amy J. Johnson, Barak A. Salmoni (pp. 124–163). New York: American University in Cairo Press, 2005.
Sabri, Isma'il. *Diwan Isma'il Sabri Basha.* Ed. Ahmad al-Zayn. Cairo: Lajnat al-ta'lif wa al-tarjama wa al-nashr, 1938.
Sabri, Muhammad. *al-Shawqiyat al-Majhula.* Cairo: Dar al-Kutub, 1961.
Sacks, Peter M. *The English Elegy: Studies in the Genre from Spenser to Yeats.* Baltimore, MD: Johns Hopkins Press, 1985.
al-Sadda, Huda, ed. *Min Ra'idat al-Qarn al-'Ishrin,* Ed. Huda al-Sadda. Cairo: Multaqa al-Mar'a wa al-Dhakira, 2001.
Sa'di. *Kulliyat-i Sa'di.* Ed. Muhammad Ali Furughi. Tehran: Sazman-i Intisharat-i Javidan, 1963.
Schiller, Friedrich. Translated by Reginald Snell. *On the Aesthetic Education of Man.* Mineola, NY: Dover Publications, 2004.

Schmitt, Carl. *The Concept of the Political*. Translated by Charles Schwab. Chicago, IL: University of Chicago Press, 1996.
Schneewind, J. B. *The Invention of Autonomy: A History of Modern Moral Philosophy*. Cambridge: Cambridge University Press, 1998.
Schölch, Alexander. *Egypt for the Egyptians!: The Socio-Political Crisis in Egypt, 1878–1882*. London: Published for the Middle East Centre, St. Antony's College, Oxford [by] Ithaca Press, 1981.
Selim, Samah. *The Novel and the Rural Imaginary in Egypt, 1880–1985*. New York: RoutledgeCurzon, 2004.
——— "The Narrative Craft: realism and fiction in the Arabic canon," *Edebiyat* 14 (1–2) (2003): 109–128.
Semah, David. *Four Egyptian Literary Critics*. Leiden: Brill, 1974.
Shakry, Omnia "Schooled Mothers and Structured Play: Child Rearing in Turn-of-the-Century Egypt." In *Remaking Women: Feminism and Modernity in the Middle East*. Ed. Lila Abu-Lughod (pp. 126–170). Princeton, NJ: Princeton University Press, 1998.
Shalan, Jeff. "Writing the Nation: The Emergence of Egypt in the Modern Arabic Novel." *Journal of Arabic Literature* 33(3) (2002): 211–247.
Sharabi, Hisham. *Arab Intellectuals and the West: The Formative Years, 1875–1914*. Baltimore, MD: Johns Hopkins Press, 1970.
——— *Neopatriarchy: A Theory of Distorted Change in Arab Society*. New York: Oxford University Press, 1992.
Shawqi, Ahmad. *al-Shawqiyat*, 2nd ed. Cairo: Matba'at al-Islah, 1911.
——— *al-Shawqiyat*. Beirut. Dar al-'Awda, 1988.
——— *al-Mawsu'a al-Shawqiya*. Ed, Ibrahim Ibyari. Cairo: al-Maktaba al-Anglu-Misriya, 1982.
Shukri, Ghali. *al-Muntami: dirasa fi adab Nagib Mahfuz*. Beirut: Dar al-Afaq al-Jadida, 1982.
Shuri, Mustafa. *Shi'r al-Ritha' fi Sadr al-Islam*. Cairo: Dar al-Ma'arif, 1986.
Siddiq, Muhammad. *Arab Culture and the Novel: Genre, Identity and Agency in Egyptian Fiction*. London: Routledge, 2007.
Smith, Anthony D. *National Identity. Ethnonationalism in Comparative Perspective*. Reno: University of Nevada Press, 1991.
Smith, Charles D. *Islam and the Search for Social Order in Modern Egypt: A Biography of Muhammad Husayn Haykal*. Albany, NY: State University of New York Press, 1983.
Somekh, S. "The Neo-classical Arabic Poets." In *The Cambridge History of Arabic Literature: Modern Arabic Literature*. Cambridge: Cambridge University Press, 1992.
Sperl, Stefan. *Mannerism in Arabic Poetry*. Cambridge: Cambridge University Press, 1989.
Starkey, Paul. *From the Ivory Tower: A Critical Study of Tawfiq Al-Hakim*. London: Ithaca for the Middle East Centre, St. Antony's College, Oxford, 1987.
Stetkevych, Jaroslav. *The Zephyrs of Najd*. Chicago, IL: University of Chicago Press, 1993.

Stetkevych, Suzanne. *Abu Tammam and the Poetics of the Abbasid Age.* Leiden: E.J. Brill, 1991.
——— *The Mute Immortals Speak.* Ithaca, NY: Cornell University Press, 1993.
——— *The Poetics of Islamic Legitimacy.* Bloomington, IN: Indiana University Press, 2002.
Strauss, Leo. "Notes on The Concept of the Political." Ed. Carl Schmitt, *The Concept of the Political*, 81–107.
al-Tahtawi, Rifa'a Rafi'. *Al-Murshid al-amin li al-banat wa al-banin*. In *al-A'mal al-kamila li Rifa'a Rafi' al-Tahtawi*. Ed. Muhammad Imara. Beirut: al-Mu'assasa al-'Arabiya li-al-Tiba'a wa al-Nashr, 1973.
Tarabishi, Jurj. *Lu'bat al-hulm wa al-waqi':dirasa fi adab Tawfiq al-Hakim*. Beirut: Dar al-Tali'a, 1972.
Tibi, Bassam. *Arab Nationalism: Between Islam and the Nation-State.* New York: St. Martin's Press, 1997.
Weintraub, Jeff. "The Theory and Politics of the Public/Private Distinction." *Public and Private in Thought and Practice: Perspectives on a Grand Dichotomy.* Ed. Jeff Weintraub and Krishan Kumar (pp. 1–42). Chicago, IL: University of Chicago Press, 1997.
al-Yaziji, Ibrahim. *al-'Iqd: diwan.* Beirut: Dar Marun Abbud, 1983.

Index

Abbas Hilmi (Khedive), 53, 54, 55, 56
Abd al-Hamid II, 76
Abd al-Muttalib, Muhammad, 66–69
Abduh, Muhammad, 36, 37, 75, 126–127, 129, 139, 221 n. 25
Adib Ishaq, 217 n. 24
Adorno, Theodor, 18
aesthetics, 10, 22, 134, 146, 150–152, 155–163, 169–170
Afghani, Jalal al-Din, 36, 75
Aflatun, Inji, 136
Alfieri, Vittorio, 77, 81
Amin, Ahmad, 157
Amin, Qasim, 11, 21, 75, 111, 120, 125–126, 127–139, 144, 145, 146, 157, 210
Anderson, Benedict, 95
  on nationality, 6–7
  on the novel, 151–152
al-Aqqad, Abbas Mahmud, 231 n. 4, 233 n. 22
Auerbach, Erich, 172

Bahithat al-Badiya, *see* Nasif, Malak Hifni
Bakhtin, M. M., 161–162
al-Barudi, Mahmud Sami, 21, 24, 36–48, 52, 73, 75, 79, 111–119, 128, 131, 138, 141, 146
beauty (and moral order), 30, 141, 151, 156–170, 172, 184–190, 196–199, 203, 207
Bergson, Henri, 230 n. 2

Bildungsroman, 162–163, 173, 202
bourgeois class status, 14, 21, 49–70, 120–122, 124–125, 141, 143, 147, 201, 206
Breuilly, John, 5

citizenship, 1–4, 7, 9–11, 20–22, 73, 78, 83, 88, 90, 104, 110, 117, 122, 210, 211
  aesthetic dimension, 21, 149–170, 171, 208
  in funeral elegy, 49, 50, 65–66, 69–70
  and gender, 108–110, 120–147

Derrida, Jacques, 18, 19, 215 n. 38
Dinshaway incident, 55–56

efendiya, 21, 49–52, 56, 69, 169, 179
Enlightenment, 4, 5, 17–18, 123, 130
ethnicity, 3–4, 77, 88, 105, 137, 152, 163

family feeling (in nationalism), 5
Feuerbach, Ludwig Andreas, 161
Fichte, Johann Gottlieb, 95, 97
Fikri, Abdullah, 37, 138–139
Foucault, Michel, 72–73, 104, 225 n. 13
Freud, Sigmund, 57–58, 65, 232 n. 16
funeral elegy, 21, 51–53, 56–57

Gellner, Ernest, 4
al-Ghazali, Abu Hamid Muhammad, 21, 26–30

244 INDEX

governmentality, 72–73
Gramsci, Antonio, 12–14, 16, 17, 19, 212

Habermas, Jürgen, 109, 116, 122–123
al-Hakim, Tawfiq, 152, 210
  'Awdat al-Ruh (*Return of the Spirit*), 22, 136, 163–172, 174, 183, 185, 186, 187, 194, 205
Haykal, Muhammad Husayn, 156–158
hegemony, 12–20, 74
  bourgeois, 122–124
  in fiction, 150–152, 155, 161–163, 169–170, 171, 174, 204–207
  gender, 108, 111, 123–125, 128, 135–137
  Gramsci, 12–14, 16
  Laclau and Mouffe, 14–15
  Subaltern Studies, 14, 16–18
Herder, Johann Gottfried von, 95
hijab (and virtue), 138–139
Horkheimer, Max, 18
Hume, David, 4, 149
al-Husri, Sati', 3, 11, 21, 74, 91–106, 210

Ibn Hazm, Abu Muhammad Ali b. Ahmad, 118
Ibn Khaldun, Abd al-Rahman, 21, 30–34
Ibn Taymiya, Taqi al-Din Ahmad, 26
Ibrahim, Hafiz, 52, 61–62, 63–64, 66
imagined communities, 6, 95, 153
Isma'il (Khedive), 37, 38, 50, 53

al-Jabarti, Abd al-Rahman, 35
Jahiz, Abu Uthman Amr b. Bahr, 25
Jameson, Fredric, 152, 154–155

Kamil, Mustafa, 53, 54, 55, 59, 60–66, 127–128, 129
Kant, Emmanuel, 4, 150

al-Kawakibi, Abd al-Rahman, 11, 21, 74–91, 102, 105–106
Kedourie, Elie, 4

Lutfi al-Sayyid, Ahmad, 129

Mahfuz, Nagib, 201, 212
  Bidaya wa Nihaya, 231
  Khan al-Khalili, 184
  al-Qahira al-Jadida, 231, 232 n. 18
  al-Sarab, 184–186, 232 n. 22
  Trilogy, 171–208
  Zuqaq al-Midaqq, 231
al-Marsafi, Husayn, 37
marthiya, *see* funeral elegy
al-Mawardi, 25–26
Muhammad Ali (Khedive), 37, 50
Musa, Nabawiya, 136, 227–228 n. 44
Musa, Salama, 159, 177, 212, 233 n. 29
Mutran, Khalil, 52, 60–64

nahda, 68, 87, 131–132, 141
Nasif, Hifni, 139
Nasif, Malak Hifni, 21, 111, 139–146
national allegory, 154–155
national selfhood, 7–15, 23–24, 36, 42–48, 51, 56–58, 64–66, 69–70, 73–75, 79, 81–84, 86–89, 90–92, 95–105, 108–110, 120–122, 125, 128, 131–132, 134, 136–137, 141–143, 146–147, 149–150, 156–159, 161–171, 173–174, 199–200, 202–208, 210–212
nationalism
  aesthetic (romantic), 152, 163–171, 183
  Arab, 21, 46, 74, 91–106
  contrasted to reformism, 74, 105
  distinct from nationality, 1, 3, 106, 203
  Egyptian, 59, 163–169
  theories of, 2, 4–7, 17, 18

nationality, *see* national selfhood
  distinction from nationalism, 1, 3, 106, 203

panegyric poetry, 34, 37, 38, 52, 53–57, 58, 65, 68
public-private order, 10, 20, 21, 159, 161
  and bourgeois class status, 49–70
  and fiction, 150–151, 152, 155, 162–163, 164, 168, 173, 179, 194, 199, 200, 207, 211
  and gender, 71–147
  and premodern norms, 116–117

qasida, *see* panegyric poetry
Qutb, Sayyid, 159–161, 210

realist novel, 146, 149, 150–152, 155, 161–163, 171, 172, 173, 176–178, 182, 184, 206
repressive hypothesis, 158, 159, 207
Romanticism, 5, 152, 163, 186, 189, 234 n. 34

Sabri, Isma'il, 55–56
al-Sayyadi, Abu al-Huda, 76
Schiller, Friedrich, 149, 156–157, 163
Schmitt, Carl, 152
self-negation (of desire), 8–9, 30, 39–42, 46–47, 57–58, 108–109, 113–114, 134, 138, 161, 172–173, 179–181, 183–184, 199–200, 203
Shawqi, Ahmad, 52, 54, 69, 120–121, 124–125
Shelley, Percy Bysshe, 149
Smith, Anthony, 4–5, 213 n. 14
sovereignty (lordship, *siyada*, *sultan*), 2, 5, 9, 20, 24–27, 30–34, 37–38, 42, 47–48, 50–51, 54–56, 68–70, 111–114, 118, 133, 141

al-Tahtawi, Rifa'a Rafi', 119
Tawfiq (Khedive), 37, 38, 53

Urabi Revolt, 37, 38, 120, 126

virtue (classical), 1, 2, 7–9, 11, 23–48, 51–52, 54, 56, 57, 60, 63, 68, 73, 74–75, 90–91, 109, 111–119, 121–122, 131–132, 138–139

wijdan (moral sensibility), 157
  in Qasim Amin, 129, 134
  in Sayyid Qutb, 160

al-Yaziji, Ibrahim, 21, 24, 46–48, 73, 75

Zaghlul, Sa'd, 59, 63, 67, 129, 164, 175, 187, 190, 195, 196
Ziyada, Mayy, 144